Politics and Drama

Change, Challenge and Transition in
Bernard Shaw and Orhan Asena

Önder ÇAKIRTAŞ

WIPF & STOCK · Eugene, Oregon

Wipf and Stock Publishers
199 W 8th Ave, Suite 3
Eugene, OR 97401

Politics and Drama
Change, Challenge, and Transition in Bernard Shaw
and Orhan Asena
By Cakirtas, Onder
Copyright©2016 Apostolos
ISBN 13: 978-1-5326-6907-1
Publication date 9/16/2018
Previously published by Apostolos, 2016

To my family.

ACKNOWLEDGEMENTS

I would like to express my gratitude to the many people who saw me through this book; to all those who provided support, talked things over, read, wrote, offered comments, allowed me to quote their remarks and assisted in the editing, proofreading, and design.

I would like to thank my supervisor Assoc. Prof. Dr. Ömer Şekerci for enabling me to publish this book. Above all I want to thank all my family, who supported and encouraged me in spite of all the time it took me away from them. It was a long and difficult journey for them.

Thanks to Distinguished Prof. Christopher Innes for enabling me to have his name on the back cover of my book with his encouraging remarks.

I would like to thank Ömer Aytaç Aykaç, Muhammed İkbal Candan and İlker Özçelik for helping me in the process of the selection of front cover and book design. Thanks to Mathew Bartlett my Commissioning Editor who encouraged me.

Thanks to Apostolos Publishing staff—without you this book would never find its way to the Web and to so many people.

Last and not least: I beg forgiveness of all those who have been with me over the course of the years and whose names I have failed to mention.

FOREWORD

This study underpins an improved revision of attitudes towards "change, challenge and transition of politics and political ideologies" in British and Turkish Drama in the 1900s and 1950s with regard, on the one hand, to George Bernard Shaw's social and political moves, his metaphorical and mythological standpoints, his "literal pen" as a weapon against the retrogressive policies of the "individual" and community, and against the traditional "well-made play"; and on the other hand, to the work of Orhan Asena, who seems to be a transmitter of the transition from the Ottoman Empire to the Republic of Turkey—a socialist who is keen on the social situation of the transition period—and the metamorphoses within some of his significant historic-politic and socio-politic plays in terms of a logical periodization of them.

The study is based upon two vital names of British and Turkish theatre and the political overtones observed in their works. In addition, the evolution in political philosophy from ancient Greece to the present, together with other ideologies that influenced political thought are dealt with, and the political themes in British and Turkish theatre are tackled on a comparative basis. Detailed studies are made of Bernard Shaw's and Orhan Asena's political considerations and the implications of these thoughts on their plays.

Accordingly, within the following five chapters, I shall explore how the playwrights portray the time period of 1900s/1950s in terms of the sub-themes of politics and inter/national identity in Britain and Turkey, contrasting and paralleling the views of Shaw and Asena and their political references—namely, Victorianism in Britain and Republicanism in Turkey. I shall thus attempt to compare and contrast a modern British and a Turkish playwright, each representing different strands of nationalities and legacies of history, culture, and politics. It is my aim by so doing to frame a logical periodization of politics in Modern Turkish and British Drama from its inception to the present day by focusing on leading playwrights of the periods.

Önder ÇAKIRTAŞ, May, 2016

CONTENTS

INTRODUCTION 7

CHAPTER 1: POLITICS AND IDEOLOGY 18

    Politics: Evolution in the Act of Governance 18

    Ideology and Political Ideologies... 37

        Political Ideologies 48

        Socialism and Communism 49

        Republicanism, Laicism and Nationalism 52

        Kemalism.. 57

CHAPTER 2: POLITICS IN DRAMA.. 60

    Politics in British Drama 61

    Politics in Turkish Drama 89

CHAPTER 3: BERNARD SHAW AND ORHAN ASENA 110

    Political Evolution in Bernard Shaw... 112

    Political Evolution in Orhan Asena 126

CHAPTER 4: POLITICAL LANGUAGES OF SHAW AND ASENA.. 138

    Political Language of Bernard Shaw.. 139

    Political Language of Orhan Asena 157

CHAPTER 5: SHAW VERSUS ASENA... 176

APPENDIX 186

    SYNOPSIS OF ORHAN ASENA'S PLAYS 186

BIBLIOGRAPHY 191

INTRODUCTION

Politics and the differing thoughts related to the interrelation and interpretation of power, governance and authority, have been a common topic touched by various scholars, intellectuals, authors, and philosophers since antiquity—as a basis in the history of political thought.[1] The Medieval Period and the Renaissance provide the backbone of the political history of the world, and thus the history of political philosophy.[2] Political thinking was further developed in the Age of Enlightenment, with political science—and thus politics itself—evolving from rudimentary organisms of self-rule and monarchy into the multifaceted democratic and communist systems that prevailed the Modern Era.[3] In the same way, the political ideologies which underpinned these developments in political systems have themselves evolved over a long period, from nebulously demarcated margins, to the more rigid ideas of Socialism, Anarchism, Marxism, Nationalism, Liberalism, Feminism, Libertarianism, Fascism, Conservatism, etc. which endure to the present day.[4] Taking Aristotle's dictum that "Man is by nature an animal fit for state"[5] into consideration, it would be thoroughly in order to engage with the politics of any playwright's *magnum opus* regarding their anthropogenic, geologic, politic, and philosophic convictions. Here, it is obligatory to mention George Bernard Shaw and Orhan Asena regarding their politics-based literary works, especially since both playwrights are somewhat unconventional in terms of what they attempt to deal with.

George Bernard Shaw re-evaluates the crack between the consciousness of his own characters and the political realities found within Britain and the world—and indeed, this is possibly the crucial strain of his drama. He desires to reconnoiter both worlds and through pen and paper

---

[1] Andrew Heywood, *Political Theory*, Palgrave Macmillan, New York, 2004, 2–14.
[2] Gabriel A. Almond, *Ventures in Political Science: Narratives and Reflections*, Lynne Rienner Publishers, London, 2002, 30–37.
[3] Ibid., 32–35.
[4] Heywood, 2004, 51–88.
[5] Aristotle, *Politics*, trans. by Trevor J. Saunders, Oxford University Press, New York, 2002, 3.

record what he observes. As a Western thinker, Shaw attempts to reveal forgotten and overlooked aspects of Victorian society.

In parallel with Shaw, Orhan Asena targets issues that nurture subtle inquiries about where one must draw the line between the lenience of politics and the nuisance of politics in terms of public autonomy. He attempts to centre on these concerns not from the point of view of a politician but from the point of view of a citizen who recognizes the discomfort and distress of others in the new Republican Turkey, where, as Orhan Pamuk observes, "secular nationalists and theocrats compete to impose what seem to be equally dubious ideas of how to force people to be free."[6]

Considering the periods in which the two playwrights lived, it is evident that in England, the *Victorian* epoch was the basic indicative factor that ruled both literature and drama, whilst in Turkey it was the *Republican* epoch—based on the grounds of *Tanzimat* (The Rescript of Gülhane)—which established a ground for a new phase of revival in literature and drama.

In England, as Allardyce Nicollin highlights, theatre flourished throughout Queen Victoria's reign. With major improvements in the quality of public life, theatres became very widely frequented with large audiences comprised of all classes of society; the changing atmosphere of that era—specifically in the dramatic arts—resulted in an evolution not only in literature, but also in the other major subjects of politics, public affairs, women's rights, and even religion.[7] As interpreted by Una Ellis-Fermor in her review article, this evolution was of a kind which was "working simultaneously in the architecture and ancillary arts of the theatre, in the capacity and tastes of the audience, in the actor's and the dramatic critic's conception of his function and—part

---

[6] Alexander Star, "Orhan Pamuk: 'I Was Not a Political Person' (An Interview)", http://www.nytimes.com/2004/08/15/books/review/STAR15.html., Accessed: 12. 02. 2015
[7] Allardyce Nicollin, *History of Late Nineteenth Century Drama*, Cambridge University Press, Cambridge, 1946, 27–29.

result, part cause of these—in the drama itself".[8] These tastes of the audience were commonly echoed by many Victorian playwrights including Fabian socialist George Bernard Shaw, whose primary concerns were the social problems of education, religion, marriage, and class privilege.[9]

As a leading and prolific author, Shaw, "frequently spoke and debated at meetings for social and political causes ... for several years he was a municipal officeholder ... an early and active member of the Fabian Society ... co-founder of the Labour Party."[10] Upon his encounter with Henry George during a lecture on *Progress and Poverty,* and after his close reading of *Progress and Poverty* (1879), Shaw announced that "I immediately became a Socialist, and from that hour I was a man with some business in the world."[11] His socialist leanings and his rise as a political activist encompassed all his life and were echoed in nearly all of his plays.[12] He mirrored the very basic uneasiness of society using his pen as a "political weapon," endeavouring to influence public opinion against "scrofula, cowardice, cruelty, hypocrisy, political imbecility, and all other fruits of oppression and malnutrition."[13]

Shaw saw that meaning in life was to be found by "being used for a purpose recognized by yourself [oneself] as a mighty one."[14] Taking Nietzsche's *Ubermensch* (Superman) as his ideal, his Socialism sought to specify that the universal human objective could only be accomplished when man overpowers his natural appetites and pledges himself to scholarly ingenuity.[15] All the same, Shaw saw that this ideal

---

[8] Una Ellis-Fermor, "The Review of History of Late Nineteenth Century Drama" in *The Review of English Studies* Vol. 23, No. 90 (Apr 1947), 183 (italics mine).
[9] Arthur Ganz, *George Bernard Shaw*, Macmillan, Hong Kong, 1983, 5–25.
[10] Stanley Kauffmann, "George Bernard Shaw: Twentieth Century Victorian Author" in *Performing Arts Journal*, Vol. 10, No. 2 (1986), 54–55
[11] Jack Schwartzman, quoted in "Henry George and George Bernard Shaw: Comparison and Contrast: The Two 19th Century Intellectual Leaders Stood for Ethical Democracy vs. Socialist Statism" in *The American Journal of Economics and Sociology* Vol. 49, No. 1 (1990), 118.
[12] Gilbert C. Chesterton, *George Bernard Shaw*, Plimpton Press, New York, 1909, 7–11.
[13] George Bernard Shaw, *Preface to Major Barbara*, E-book, The University of Adelaide, 2014, 6.
[14] George Bernard Shaw, *Preface to Man and Superman*, E-book, The University of Adelaide, 2014, 14.
[15] Azhar Suleiman, *George Bernard Shaw*, Mena Printing, 2010, Baghdad, 15–16.

was still a long way off from being implemented in practice.[16] Yet for his part, Shaw practised all his beliefs through his political activities and as a pioneer of Fabian Society—"which advocated the evolutionary rather than the revolutionary approach to Socialism"[17]—and as a supporter of moderate politics, he tried to get some knowledge of the democratic process. In one of his letters to Kingsley Martin, he claimed to be a Communist[18] with the words: "There is no public man in England more completely committed to Communism, and in particular to the support of the Russian system, than I."[19] As a thinker and philosopher, he was not only influenced by Nietzsche but also by Bergson[20] and though, as a socialist, he supported the equality of all people, and loathed discrimination based on gender and social class, Shaw "was convinced that only an all-powerful State was capable of controlling the means of production"[21] and therefore, surprisingly, he "espoused dictatorship,"[22] "his admiration for dictators was almost unbounded. Hitler, Mussolini ... and Stalin—all these absolute rulers received his admiration."[23]

Shaw's political personality, reuniting Socialism, Fabianism, Communism, anti-democracy, Philosophy, and Dictatorship, was strengthened through a rejection of the "totalitarianism of idealism"[24]—an idealism contradicting realism within the perspective of a realist "daring more and more to face facts and tell himself the truth."[25] Telling the truth was the basic evidence of his ideal morality and this is

---

[16] Schwartzman, quoted in, 1990, 123.
[17] Kauffmann, 1986, 123.
[18] George Bernard Shaw, *Collected Letters*, ed. D. H. Laurence, Max Reinhardt, London, 1988, 629.
[19] Ibid., 629.
[20] Schwartzman, 1990, 124.
[21] Schwartzman, quoted in, 1990, 123.
[22] Ibid., 123.
[23] St. John G. Ervine, *Bernard Shaw: His Life, Work and Friends*, William Morrow & Co, 1972, 460.
[24] Paul Lewton, "George Bernard Shaw: Theory, Language, and Drama in the Nineties" in *The Yearbook of English Studies*, Vol. 9, Theatrical Literature Special Number (1979), 157.
[25] George Bernard Shaw, *The Quintessence of Ibsenism*, The University Press, Cambridge, 1913, 22.

emphasized in *Arms and the Man* (1894), where he contends that the problem is with the ideals, not with the man. His illustration of the conflict between idealism and realism was reevaluated in *A Doll's House* (1879) reflecting his proclamation in *The Quintessence of Ibsenism* (1891):

> the policy of forcing individuals to act on the assumption that all ideals are real, and to recognize and accept such action as standard moral conduct, absolutely valid under all circumstances, contrary conduct or any advocacy of it being discountenanced and punished as immoral, may therefore be described as the policy of Idealism.[26]

As an accomplished socialist, he was the "author of some five dozen plays, his mountain of writings includes five completed novels, a number of short stories, lengthy treatises on politics and economics, four volumes of theatre criticism, three volumes of music criticism, and a volume of art criticism."[27] Reflecting his political views, specifically his Socialist philosophy, through his *Fabian Essays* (1892), Shaw indirectly revealed the transition of a few distinctive political thoughts and philosophies through his literary works. These political evolutions underpinned not only Fabianism and Socialism, but also Communism, Anti-Democracy, Stalinism, Egalitarianism, and Liberalism. His protest against inequality brought Feminism onto the Victorian stage and—mostly affected by his mother's "assertion of female power and her defiance of assigned female roles concerning sexuality, respectability, and career fulfillment"[28]—Shaw rebelled against gender defined roles of women in a way that may be seen in his *Pygmalion* (1912–13), *Saint Joan* (1923), and *Mrs Warren's Profession* (1893).

In a similar way, reflecting on the comparable problems of a new country, Orhan Asena was among those who headed for the political stage of Turkey's theatre. After the proclamation of the Republic in

---

[26] Ibid., 41.
[27] Sally Peters, *Bernard Shaw: The Ascent of the Superman,* Yale University Press, 1998, 3.
[28] Ibid., 6.

Turkey, the new government utilized the state-backed theatre as part of its drive towards a socialist culture, seeing it as a priceless opportunity to canvass the public for support for the new regime. Hence, this theatrical movement in Turkey was not shaped by a kind of "liquid modernity" (as Zygmund Bauman calls it) but rather by the deliberate attempt of its patrons to find a way out of the dilemma of being backed by a ruling regime who sought to control theatre content. In Turkey, as was the case in England, whole communities were affected by these histrionic programmes and activities. During the 1950s and upon the foundation of Republican Turkey, many playwrights produced new plays that embraced the turbulent formation of the new regime.

The playwrights of the early years of the Republican era, turning their attention more specifically to Turkish-Ottomanic history and to social issues, tried to portray the judicial, political, and spiritual changes in the new Turkey. The transformation period included some noticeable conflicts with the government, and the establishment of a literary company of semiprofessional authors who introduced the first phases of Western theatre to Turkish Literature. Establishing its base under the *Tanzimat*, drama prospered and "in 1839, there were four theatre buildings in the capital—two of which hosted foreign circus shows."[29] Subsequently, local theatres flourished all through the empire. The translations of European plays were fashioned as early examples of modern theatre. The first original play in Turkish was introduced by İbrahim Şinasi with his criticism of the match-making practice via *Şair Evlenmesi* (The Marriage of the Poet) (1859).[30]

The blossoming of the theatrical movement in Turkey fostered serious debates; authors and critics alike began to revise the ideological trends of the time.[31] Orhan Asena, titled by some the Shakespeare of Turkish

---

[29] M. Şükrü Hanioğlu, *A Brief History of the Late Ottoman Empire*, Princeton University Press, Princeton and London, 2008, 100.
[30] Aslıhan Ünlü, *Türk Tiyatrosunun Antropolojisi*, Aşina Kitaplar, Ankara, 2006, 116.
[31] Ibid., 116–124.

drama,[32] produced historical plays which touched on questions of power, politics, and autonomy—things which had played a major role in the formation of Turkey's Ottomanic past—and became the foremost of the Republican playwrights. In Turkey during that period, discussions on the tone of drama centred around national and internal questions emphasizing the Ottomanic past as a medium of expression.

The common point here between Asena and Shaw is that political language opened new pathways for theatre between the two clashing identities: the new and the old. Asena, just like Shaw, aspired to reflect the social problems of the period, and through his plays he underlined a protest against what Tahsin Saraç describes as "the old order", which—referring to Asena's *Gılgameş (Tanrılar ve İnsanlar—Gods and Men)* (1959)—he describes as: "*an order which embraced* ... quarrels, fights on social values, various bigotries setting individuals against and dividing persons border by border, numerous tyrannies appealed for the sake of one dogma or another, customs, traditions, differing regimes."[33]

Being a strict humanist and an intellectual, Orhan Asena shared similar views to Shaw, and both yearned to use language as an instrument to transmit their views, dealing with real-life issues as the true subjects of their drama. Here, as intellectuals of late 19th/early 20th centuries of two different countries, Shaw and Asena both exemplify what Gilles Deleuze refers to as: "the indignity of speaking for others."[34] This is true for Asena as much as it is for Bernard Shaw; as speakers of concrete truth, Asena projects the realism of the Turkish Republic, while the latter inclines to the realism of Victorian England. As a speaker speaking for others, Asena exemplifies human-centered (non-gendered) plays. A Polish Turcologist, Teresa Cicierska Chtapowa, in

---

[32] Hami Çağdaş, "Türk Tiyatrosunun Shakespeare'i Öldü" in Hürriyet Daily News, http://hurarsiv.hurriyet.com.tr/goster/ShowNew.aspx?id=-226855, 2001, Accessed 12.10.2014.
[33] Orhan Asena, *Tanrılar ve İnsanlar*, Mitos Boyut Yayınları, İstanbul, 2010, 127–28. (Italics mine).
[34] Michel Foucault, "Intellectuals and Power: A Conversation Between Michel Foucault and Gilles Deleuze" in *Language, Counter-Memory, Practice,* ed. Donald F. Bouchard, Cornell University Press, New York, 1977, 209.

her study on *The Idea of Revolution in Orhan Asena's Early Plays*[35] (1979), elaborates the idea of humanism as "The common point or the common denominator in all his drama is his deep humanism. To Asena, the starting point is always man. A man with inexhaustible wealth of possibilities."[36]

Asena's Humanist and Socialist leanings shaping his political stance in direct contrast with his Kemalist and Republican vision. He strongly addressed the relationship between rulers and those whom they ruled, dealing with rebellion and action-reaction phenomena.[37] He detested the reactionists of Ottoman heritage, and to him, the new Turkish Republic—seizing the West—"was the world of freedom, comfort, individual dignity, of reason, of decency, and of beauty and art."[38] Through some of his plays, specifically in *Korku* (Fear) (1956), *Gılgameş* (Gods and Men), *Ya Devlet Başa Ya Kuzgun Leşe* (Either Victory or Death) (1983), Asena revealed his diagnosis of Western idealization, which according to Berkes is as follows: "there was absolutely nothing in the old dissipated, rotten home environment and past to be liked, from which to derive inspiration, to love, with which to identify."[39] Asena thus attached his views to Turkish Nationalism and developed a drama that envisioned the paradoxes of the policies of two distinctive groups: on the one hand conservatives and Islamists (Adnan Menderes and others); and on the other hand Republicans, Laicists, and Kemalists (Mustafa Kemal Atatürk and others).

This book is concerned with comparing and contrasting the political views of George Bernard Shaw and Orhan Asena. With this in mind, it seems reasonable to provide the reader with an outline of the

---

[35] The original text was written in Polish, and it was translated to Turkish by Tahsin Saraç. The quotes were translated by the writer of this thesis into English from the Turkish script.
[36] Teresa Cicierska Chtapowa, *The Idea of Revolution in Orhan Asena's Early Plays*, quoted in Hülya Nutku, Folia Orientalia, Poland, 1979, 23.
[37] Oğuz Budak, *Türkiye'nin Sosyal/Kültürel Değişim Sürecinde Orhan Asena Tiyatrosu*, Ankara, 2008, 53–99.
[38] Niyazi Berkes, *The Development of Secularism in Turkey*, Hurstand Company, London, 1998, 292.
[39] Ibid., 292.

arguments at an early stage, so here goes. We shall first of all deal with the preliminary data about politics, its evolution from the beginning of classical antiquity to modern era with reference to some well-known politicians, philosophers, and statesmen. We shall then focus more specifically on the politics in English and Turkish Dramas, before more narrowly contrasting Shaw's and Asena's place in such literature. The main body involves an examination Shaw's and Asena's evolutionary views of politics, and their points of view about the corruption of politics, the usage of political power, and political abuse within their selected plays. In conclusion, I shall endeavour to provide comparative and contrastive links between the political language of Bernard Shaw and Orhan Asena in close context with their plays.

I hope that this book will go some way towards encouraging further comparative studies in drama in Turkey. This study on Bernard Shaw and Orhan Asena—and exclusively on politics within their dramatic plays—is an essential contribution to such comparative and contrastive studies, for I believe their works to have a relevance far broader than the limited scope of what they had observed in their respective societies. Their theatre was regarded by the public as *avant garde* and it gave them a vital means of broadcasting their ideology to the public. In addition, both dramatists fit in to the same generation—the early 20th century generation that countersigned the disintegration of a multinational empire (the Ottoman) and the liberation of individual states and "individual" persons.[40] Moreover, the early 20th century proved to be a prosperous period for drama and theatre in both Britain[41] and Turkey[42] in that drama and theatre *avant gardists*—as a reaction against or *vis à vis* classical drama—started to tackle politics, customs, traditions, manners, public affairs, and governmental policies

---

[40] Dina Rizk Khoury, "The Ottoman Centre Versus Provincial Power-Holders: An Analysis of the Historiography" in *The Cambridge History of Turkey,* Vol 3, Cambridge University Press, Cambridge, 2006, 136.
[41] Christopher Innes, *Modern British Drama*, Cambridge University Press, Cambridge, 1990, 4–11.
[42] Metin And, *50 Yılın Türk Tiyatrosu*, İş Bankası Kültür Yayınları, İstanbul, 1973, 1–26.

to promote a liberation of personal experience.[43] Dramatists were enthused both by the world-shattering sense of change dominant at the time and by the unending critical drifts of political thoughts in the world, specifically in Europe. In these respects, this book also contributes to the literature in two ways; first, by projecting how socio-political norms or thoughts affect dramatic literature and dramatic performances, revealing dissimilar ideological uniqueness that is applicable to political drama comparatively and contrastively. Second, this study contributes to the analysis of the discrepancies between the differing arrangements of comparative literary research method. This is a pretty novel point of view, and one that may possibly inspire further practical approaches in the future.

Taking the theories of comparative literature as a starting-point, the current study sets out to discover the theatrical linkage between the two playwrights and, secondly, to catch the affiliation between their dramatic works and other such majors as politics, history, philosophy, allegory and religion. This study aims to contribute more to the understanding of the evolution in politics and poetics of the dramatic works of George Bernard Shaw and Orhan Asena through the study of the conjoint influences on these works, and by applying textual analysis to those selected works of two playwrights.

In literature reviews, it may be readily observed that whilst there have been many theoretical studies which have scrutinized the works of each playwright, there has been until now no up-to-date study that unites both. For conciseness, the present study will be limited to Bernard Shaw's six selected politics-contented works: *Arms and the Man* (1894), *Mrs. Warren's Profession* (1893), *Major Barbara* (1905), *Pygmalion* (1912–13), *Widowers' Houses* (1892), *Candida* (1894), and Orhan Asena's six selected politics-contented works *Hürrem Sultan* (1960), *Ya Devlet Başa Ya Kuzgun Leşe* (1983), *Tanrılar ve İnsanlar* (1959), *Şili*

---

[43] Innes, 1990, 4–11. Sevda Şener, *Gelişim Sürecinde Türk Tiyatrosu*, Mitos-Boyut Yayınları, İstanbul, 2011, 5–14.

Üçlemesi (1975–78), *Tohum ve Toprak* (1964), and *Korku* (1956). In the appendix, I have given a synopsis of the plays of Orhan Asena; but I should think that there is no need to give the synopsis of Bernard Shaw's plays, as they are easily accessible through a variety of sources.

CHAPTER 1: POLITICS AND IDEOLOGY

It is a known fact that many writers, scholars, philosophers, and paradigms have contributed to the design and maturity of politics and political thought throughout the ages. In this chapter we shall identify these scholars, what milieus would be practical in accepting their thoughts, and how those thoughts have fashioned the dissertation of politics and political philosophies.

Politics: Evolution in the Act of Governance

In a broad sense, politics is "the activity through which people make, preserve and amend the general rules under which they live."[44] More narrowly, politics, as a science, is the skeleton of the all the rules related to justice, law, state, public autonomy, governmental control, etc.[45] The dictionary definition of the term is "the activities associated with the governance of a country or area, especially the debate between parties having power,"[46] "activities that relate to influencing the actions and policies of a government or getting and keeping power in a government."[47] To be clear, the term has been used with a variety of definitions, some of which are conciliatory, while some seem to be conflicting. Andrew Heywood, in *Political Theory* (2004), characterizes politics as a "social activity",[48] while Martin Needler, in *Identity, Interest and Ideology* (1996), goes to the heart of the individual and identifies "the concept of *interest*" as fundamental to the study of politics.[49]

---

[44] Heywood, 2004, 4.
[45] David Robertson, *The Routledge Dictionary of Politics*, Routledge, London and New York, 2004, 388–89.
[46] *Politics*, Online Oxford Dictionary, http://www.oxforddictionaries.com/definition/english/politics, Accessed: 09.02.2015.
[47] *Politics*, Online Merriam-Webster Dictionary, http://www.merriam-webster.com/dictionary/politics, Accessed: 09.02.2015.
[48] Heywood, 2004, 2.
[49] Martin Needler, *Identity, Interest and Ideology*, Praeger Publishers, Westport, 1996, 5.

From the Ancient Greeks to the present day, deliberated as a universal truth in the world tradition in terms of authority, power, and public affairs, politics has been described by differing statesmen, politicians, scholars, and philosophers at various times.[50] Known as a conservative Prussian statesman, Otto von Bismarck describes politics as "the art of the possible",[51] while Isaac D'Israeli, a British writer and scholar, defines it as "the art of governing mankind through deceiving them."[52] Being a decorated person of World War I, German politician and the leader of the Nazi Party, Adolf Hitler pronounced politics as "the art of carrying out the life struggle of a nation for its earthly existence."[53] Harold Laswell attunes the existence of politics to the "authority" and he explains that "politics determines the process of who gets what, when, and how,"[54] an idea which denotes that politics regulates the strategies and aims which the governing system will follow. Rog Hague et al., in *Comparative Government and Politics* (2004), address politics as "a collective activity, involving people who accept a common membership or at least acknowledge a shared fate"[55] which embraces the process of collective decision-making, and—though meanderingly—represents the combination of political ideologies, thoughts, philosophies, and parties. T. A. Van Dijk defines politics as "one of the social domains whose practices are virtually exclusively discursive."[56]

The history of political thinking has been based upon the link between the State and individuals; the idea of "interest" has been a major phenomenon for the individual even when it is in the presence of the

---

[50] Heywood, 2004, 5–21.
[51] Roger Scruton, quoted in *The Palgrave Macmillan Dictionary of Political Thought*, Palgrave Macmillan, New York, 2007, 534.
[52] Ibid., 535.
[53] Moyra Grant, quoted in *Key Ideas in Politics*, Nelson Thornes Ltd, Cheltenham, 2003, 140.
[54] Harold D. Laswell, *Politics: Who Gets What, When, How*, Whittlesey House, New York, 1936, 13–21.
[55] Rog Hague et al., *Comparative Government and Politics*, Palgrave Macmillan, New York, 2004, 3.
[56] Teun A. Van Dijk, *Politics, Ideology, and Discourse*, Elsevier Ltd, Madrid, 2006, 728.

State.[57] The differing and heterogeneous regimes and polities have, for the most part, given birth to avant-garde political thoughts and ideologies throughout the history of humanity.[58] The changes, alterations, and metamorphoses have unfolded an evolution in political thinking, and these shifts have produced a multiplicity of variances and diversifications among thinkers, philosophers, intellectuals, and scholars.[59]

The history of politics and political thought is, in the main, attributed to Classical antiquity, especially Ancient Greece and Ancient Rome;[60] indeed the very idea of "conflict and cooperation" has kept people (starting from the various heterogeneous/homogenous groups of the classical antiquity till the globalized/homogenized postmodern communities) quite busy.[61] Throughout the history of humanity, politics—as a major image of *persona* and *polis*—has established itself as an imperative, thought-provoking, and stimulating form of nature. *Polis*, whose business was described as the "care of the soul"[62] by Plato, was also the name of a political model in Ancient Greece. The citizens who were under this model were claimed to be in accord with the rules of the city, and those who were not were believed to be "indifferent". The *poleis* were governed by political units consisting of bodies of citizens, and the politics of Ancient Greece was not pluralistic like the present day; the lack of democracy (the fact that not all the people were grouped in political matters) had produced a system which allowed a minor group of citizens to have policy making concessions.[63]

Discoursing on the questions of "just and unjust", Plato—as "the father of idealism in philosophy, in politics, in literature"[64]—in *The Republic*

---

[57] Heywood, 2004, 4.
[58] Ellen Grigsby, *Analyzing Politics*, Wadsworth, Belmont, 2009, 12–17.
[59] Ibid., 12–17.
[60] Ibid., 12.
[61] Heywood, 2004, 4.
[62] Scruton, quoted in, 2007, 513.
[63] Ibid., 513.
[64] Benjamin Jowett, *The Works of Plato: Analysis of Plato and the Republic*, Cosimo Inc, New York, 2010, 4.

(around 380 BCE), reveals for the most part the early base of politics—the concord of the individual and the State.[65] Taking Plato's *The Republic* into account, it is vital to see that in world politics, many affinities may be outlined within Platonic ideas; these perspectives are not only visible in the works of the early writers, but in great modern writers as well.[66] Conceptualizing the *Ideal State,* Plato separates the *ideal* from the *phenomenon*; he believes that the two are strictly conflicting in that the former comprises eternal and unchanging principles, whilst the latter includes temporariness and various reflections of ideas.[67] Thus, Plato is certain of that "Such a State is hardly to be realized in this world and would quickly degenerate."[68] His political stance is rooted in the idea that a State is ideal only when "philosophers are kings, or the kings and princes of this world have the spirit and power of philosophy, and political greatness and wisdom meet in one, and those commoner natures who pursue either to the exclusion of the other are compelled to stand aside."[69]

Influenced and inspired significantly by Socrates's views, Plato greatly influenced Western political thought in countless ways.[70] *The Republic* had a substantial impact on the political writings of Milton and Locke, Rousseau, Jean Paul, and Goethe, on the writings of Berkeley and Coleridge, and writings of many modern thinkers.[71] Several of the latest notions of modern theorists and politicians, such as justice, knowledge, law, and equality, were projected by him in *The Republic.*[72]

Aristotle, on the other hand, was obliged to Plato in terms of his political point of view; however, Aristotle rejected Plato's view that "politics is the eternal and unchanging principle, whilst the

---

[65] Brian Redhead, *Political Thought From Plato to NATO*, British Broadcasting Corporation, London, 1984, 9–12.
[66] Ibid., 9–18.
[67] Christopher Rowe, "Plato: The Search for an Ideal Form of State" in *Political Thought from Plato to NATO*, British Broadcasting Corporation, London, 1984, 18–24.
[68] Jowett, , 2010, 6.
[69] Plato, *The Republic* (trans. by Benjamin Jowett), Cosimo Inc, New York, 2010, 212.
[70] Rowe, 1984, 20.
[71] Jowett, 2010, 5.
[72] Ibid., xxiv–lxi.

phenomenon includes temporariness and various reflections of ideas."[73] Instead, Aristotle stressed the view that the reality is within the present world and that in order to do politics, a person should be aware of the real life situations which would direct him to the real answers behind the changes, improvements, developments, and disproval of ideas. Emphasizing the direct relation of the above mentioned phenomena to the idea of *the personal is political*, with his famous dictum "man is by nature a political animal", Aristotle addressed the impact of politics on human evolution in regard with a well-oriented state/community or society.[74] He deemed that it is only within a political civic system that men can live the good life; from this vantage point, now, politics consists of principled actions associated with generating a fair social order.[75] This is what Aristotle called "the highest master science"[76] in *Nicomachean Ethics* (BCE 350). Interrelating ethics to the core of politics, Aristotle conveys that a good politician is the one who knows ethical virtues very well, "since he wants to make citizens good and obedient to the laws."[77]

In the very first chapter of book one in *Politics* (BCE 350), Aristotle suggests that "mankind always act in order to obtain that which they think good,"[78] an idea which shows every indication of continuing to develop into the new political thoughts stemming from the desire to obtain "the good". Subdividing *Politics* into 8 chapters,[79] in the first part of the book, Aristotle focuses more on the political functions and the nature of politics. He argues that the State restructuring in the form of *polis* is natural, and that slavery is natural and normal. In *Politics*

---

[73] Peter Nicholson, "Aristotle: Ideals and Realities" in *Political Thought From Plato to NATO*, British Broadcasting Corporation, London, 1984, 34.
[74] Ibid., 34–36.
[75] Ibid., 38–43.
[76] Aristotle, *Nicomachean Ethics,* trans. and ed. Roger Crisp, Cambridge University Press, Cambridge, 2000, 4.
[77] Ibid., 20.
[78] Aristotle, *Politics,* trans. Benjamin Jowett, Clarendon Press, 1885, 1.
[79] See Aristotle, *Politics*, trans. Trevor J. Saunders, Oxford University Press, New York, 2002, vii–194.

Aristotle affirms that "for that which can use its intellect to look ahead is by nature ruler and by nature master, while that which has the bodily strength to labour is ruled, and is by nature a slave. Hence master and slave benefit from the same thing."[80] He tries to detail the principles of such components as *polis*, family, and class on which political systems prevail. Underpinning politics on the basis of human interests, Aristotle reveals the common directions of political arena not only in terms of Antiquity but also those of our modern day.[81]

As an advocate of Aristotelian philosophy, aiming to make people accept Aristotle's view that Man is by nature a political being,[82] Sir Thomas Aquinas (1225–1274)—a leading thinker and theologian of the Medieval Era—considerably influenced Western thought, and much of recent thinking has developed from an expansion or disapproval of his philosophies, predominantly in the spheres of integrity and political philosophy.[83] Being a pioneering philosopher of scholasticism, and a man of moral principles, Aquinas dealt chiefly with ethics and aesthetics which took Aristotelian ethics as their base. Many scholars, writers, and philosophers believe that Aquinas's virtue ethics were a way of escaping utilitarianism.[84]

Aquinas, just like Aristotle, believes that the family is the basic unit of political communities.[85] However, he challenges the notion that the family is the best model for the "good" of the members of the unit. In *Commentary on Politics* (1271–1272), he evaluates the naturalness of politics and ethics,[86] and the comparison of the naturalness of politics

---

[80] Ibid., 2.
[81] Nicholson, 1984, 43.
[82] Antony Black, "St Thomas Aquinas: The State and Morality" in *Political Thought from Plato to NATO*, British Broadcasting Corporation, London, 1984, 61.
[83] Janet Coleman, "St Augustine: At The End Of The Roman Empire Christian Political Thought" in *Political Thought From Plato to NATO*, British Broadcasting Corporation, London, 1984, 45-46.
[84] Black, 1984, 61-62.
[85] Ibid., 56.
[86] Thomas Aquinas, *Commentary On Aristotle's Politics,* trans. Richard J. Regan, Hackett Publishing Company, Inc., Indianapolis and Cambridge, 2007, 16.

to the naturalness of moral virtue is revealed to be more apt.[87] Exemplifying the structure of political institutions by analyzing a stereotypical village and its usefulness and effectiveness, he urges the idea that a gathering of a number of villages serves better for the common interests of the villagers, and thus the objective of the political public becomes the good of the whole, or the public good (the good of all the members—a kind of democracy), which Aquinas asserts is "superior to, and more god-like than, the good of an individual."[88]

Taking a deterministic standpoint, Niccolo Machiavelli (1469–1527) challenged the views which preceded him.[89] As a Renaissance writer, diplomat, philosopher, and politician, Machiavelli takes humanity to the centre in his studies and believes that "human nature is an unstable amalgam of stupidity, cupidity and malice."[90] He is an idealist of republicanism[91] and he is reputed to be an originator of modern political science, and more explicitly political ethics.[92] Setting out his political, ethical, and republican visions in his major distinctive books titled *The Prince* (written about 1513) and the less famous *Discourses* (written between 1513 and 1519)[93] Machiavelli assesses the prevailing power of fate and human virtue, leading to the crucial conclusion that each human being is the victim of his own destiny.[94] Concentrating on the "hereditary" regime in *The Prince* (1513)—a short political treatise—Machiavelli explains the interchanges of the new and the old princes: to hold authority, the hereditary prince must judiciously stabilize the interests of a range of sociopolitical bodies with which the public is familiarized.[95] Perhaps his inclination towards the notion that

---

[87] Ibid., 68–76.
[88] Ibid., 7–8.
[89] Sydney Anglo, "Niccolo Machiavelli: The Anatomy of Political and Military Decadence" in *Political Thought from Plato to NATO*, British Broadcasting Corporation, London, 1984, 73.
[90] Ibid., 78.
[91] Ibid., 78.
[92] Ibid., 82.
[93] Leo Strauss, *Thoughts On Machiavelli*, The Free Press, Qzencoe, Illinois, 1958, x.
[94] Anglo, 1984, 78–79
[95] Niccolo Machiavelli, *The Prince,* trans. Harvey C. Mansfield, University of Chicago Press, Chicago and London, 1998, 6–16.

man is a malicious being is what led to his reputation as a "teacher of evil", as Leo Strauss strongly emphasizes in *Thoughts on Machiavelli*,[96] "The theme of the *Discourses* is the possibility and desirability of reviving ancient virtue."[97] Machiavelli stresses the notion that states and empires rise and collapse; the reason behind the rise is virtue while it is moral corruption that leads to the collapse.[98] His philosophy maintains that a politician, statesmen, leader of any country may murder any of his rivals when it is for the sake of the common good.[99]

> Machiavelli ... contends that a founder who is concerned with the common good, as distinguished from a tyrant, cannot be blamed if he commits murder in order to achieve his good end; the discussion is based on the fundamental and traditional distinction between the prince and the tyrant, between the common good and the private good, between virtue and ambition.[100]

Contrary to Plato and Aristotle, Machiavelli contends that a prince cannot stabilize himself with an unreal ideal society as his goal.[101] Thus, Machiavelli—through these amendments—levels political idealism and mirrors political realism which is an ultimate breakthrough in terms of the political thought.[102]

The scope of politics has changed over time, advancing the style and characteristics of political movements.[103] The relationship between religion (specifically the power of Christianity and its advocates, the churches) and politics has been the concern of many philosophers and

---

[96] Strauss, 1958, 9–10.
[97] Ibid., 20.
[98] Anglo, 1984, 78–79
[99] Ibid., 77.
[100] Strauss, 1958, 44.
[101] Anglo, 1984, 81–82.
[102] Isaiah Berlin, *Against the Current: Essays in the History of Ideas,* ed. Henry Hardy, Princeton University Press, Princeton, 2013, 34.
[103] Henk E. S. Woldring, "On the Purpose of the State: Continuity and Change in Political Theories" in *The Failure of Modernism: The Cartesian Legacy and Contemporary Pluralism,* ed. Brendan Sweetman, American Maritain Association, 1999, 155–170.

thinkers.[104] John Calvin is among those who challenged the association between political performance and political theology.[105] He was one of the main figures in the growth of the organism of Christian theology that is much later named after him: Calvinism.[106] "His treatment of politics, like that of Thomas Aquinas and of other Scholastics, makes that topic a province of theology."[107]

Being a strict Reformer, Calvin, through his writings and sermons, provided a basis for the division of theology and the wheels of government that undergird the secular administration commanded by God; he establishes that the secular regime is of great significance not just for the worldly people but for the Christians, and that the secular (the word laic is more suitable) government facilitates the separate execution of the jurisdiction of government and religion.[108]

In his *Institutes of Christian Religion* (1536), which serves "a reviving impulse to thinking in the areas of Christian doctrine and social duty,"[109] Calvin declines "to offer, at least in outline, a model of the order of a Christian commonwealth".[110] He portrays the laic management as a utility which must embrace both justice and other worldly phenomena and the implementation of religion and the prohibition of contrary thoughts. Mostly assessing political powers in the context of religion and God, Calvin accepts the Lutheran emphasis on the protection of religion.[111] He believes the fact that religion and politics are two pillars that cannot be completely abstracted from each other.[112]

---

[104] Redhead, 1984, 9–18.
[105] Harro Hopl, "Jean Calvin: The Disciplined Commonwealth" in *Political Thought from Plato to NATO*, British Broadcasting Corporation, London, 1984, 85.
[106] Scruton, 2007, 74.
[107] John T. Mcneill, ed., *The Institutes of Christian Religion*, Westminster John Knox Press, Louisville and London, 1960, lxvi.
[108] Hopl, 1984, 86–96.
[109] Mcneill, ed., 1960, xxix.
[110] Hopl, 1984, 90.
[111] Ibid., 92.
[112] Ibid., 92.

Calvin did not believe that political and religious matters are ultimately separable, any more than other Reformers did. Again, he could not possibly be thought to have regarded civil laws and institutions as matters remote from theology, given his view of the content of Scripture and the quite unqualified dominance of the moral element in his conception of law.[113]

John Calvin is at pains to stress, in *Institutes of Christian Religion*, that political regimes are necessary in order to stifle the irregularities, disorders, turbulences, and panics that are the principal catalyzers of tyranny and tyrants.[114] He articulates what Andrew Heywood underlines in *Politics* as the close link between "the phenomena of conflict and cooperation"[115] which has perpetuated its existence within the humanities in an increasingly interdisciplinary and discussed realm.[116] He reflects the idea of cooperation through the overall participation of citizens to the civil administration, and the idea of conflict through some popular rulers and protestors against tyrants. The idea of civil administration reveals his protest against absolute monarchy. His antagonism against absolute monarchy and autocracy is supported by his advocates, who go beyond his ideas of liberalism.[117]

The idea of conflict is also echoed by Thomas Hobbes through his well-known *Leviathan* (1651). However, Hobbes's position is something different from that of Calvin; for Hobbes expresses what Harold Laswell reveals in *Politics: Who Gets What, When, How* (1936), saying that "the study of politics is the study of influence and influential"[118] which takes us necessarily to the notion that politics is human-centred, and that Hobbes reveals the tie between the State and individuals corresponding with the "influence" and "influential". *Leviathan* discloses how the State overcomes the deep-rooted conflicts among the

---

[113] Harro Höpfl, *The Christian Polity of John Calvin*, Cambridge University Press, Cambridge, 1982, 149.
[114] Mcneill, ed., 1960, lxvi.
[115] Heywood, 2004, 4.
[116] Ibid., 4.
[117] Dirk J. Smit, *Essays on Being Reformed,* ed. Robert Vosloo, Sun Media, Stellenbosch, 2009, 99.
[118] Laswell, 1936, 295.

people. Hobbes refers to the wars among the people and articulates (in *Leviathan*) that there have been power struggles among conflicting statesmen and kings throughout history, and the rule of succession and authority has been a matter of power.[119]

> To this war of every man against every man, this also is consequent: that nothing can be unjust. The notions of right and wrong, justice and injustice have there no place. Where there is no common power, there is no law: where no law, no injustice. Force and fraud are in war the two cardinal virtues.[120]

As Hobbes notes, men naturally search for their own self-interested satisfaction; nevertheless such eccentricity inevitably results in war, as "every man is enemy to every man"[121] and "their eyes fixed on one another."[122] The State is the single "common power"[123] that creates a single authority to regulate true justice and law enforcement between individuals who are in power struggles.[124] This depiction is not far away from Aristotelian politics revealed through justice which "is the bond of men in states, for the administration of justice, which is the determination of what is just, is the principle of order in political society."[125] Taking Hobbes's views into consideration, what is stressed is the self-centeredness and self-defense of individuals who are gathered under a single roof—the State [this is what Aristotle articulates as "order"]—by which they contract to give in piece of their innate autonomy to an unconditional power in order to maintain law and justice.[126] To Hobbes, the State establishes the "notions of right

---

[119] Richard Tuck, "Thomas Hobbes: The Sceptical State" in *Political Thought from Plato to NATO*, British Broadcasting Corporation, London, 1984, 96–102.
[120] Thomas Hobbes, *Leviathan,* ed. J. C. A. Gaskin, Oxford University Press, 1998, 85.
[121] Ibid., 84.
[122] Ibid., 85.
[123] Ibid., 85.
[124] Tuck, 1984, 106–107.
[125] Aristotle, 1885, 3.
[126] Tuck, 1984, 104–105.

and wrong, justice and injustice"¹²⁷ and law comprises all the mannerisms, rules, and orders in the society.

The conclusion of Stephen J. Finn that "Hobbes's political philosophy, in other words, is more about theory than practice"¹²⁸ is connected with Hobbes's depiction of the train of thoughts which, he believes, are "being *regulated* by some desire, and design."¹²⁹ Making an assertion that politics and civil philosophy are "of consequences from the *institution* of commonwealths, to the *rights,* and *duties* of the *body politic* or *sovereign*"¹³⁰ he provides a basis for individual self-protection and the sovereignty of the State. He, thus, considers a "coercive solution ... [for] humans [who] are naturally at war with each other unless there is a power to keep them in check."¹³¹

Being a contemporary of Hobbes, John Locke also focuses on these special issues and exclusively dedicates himself to these topics, reflecting quite a lot of prominent and tentatively knowledgeable scholastic ideas.¹³² Primarily "remembered as a defender of empiricism in epistemology and of individualist liberalism in political theory",¹³³ John Locke showed a great amount of interest in political philosophy. Believed to be "written as a justification for the Revolution"¹³⁴ that erupted in England in 1688, Locke's *Two Treatises of Government* (1689) touches on political philosophy; the book is separated into the *First Treatise* and the *Second Treatise*. The *First Treatise* refutes the view of Robert Filmer's *Patriarcha* (1680) and attacks patriarchalism, whilst the *Second Treatise,* taking natural rights as

---

[127] Hobbes, 1998, 85.
[128] Stephen J. Finn, *Thomas Hobbes and the Politics of Natural Philosophy*, Continuum, London, 2004, 5.
[129] Hobbes, 1998, 16.
[130] Ibid., 56.
[131] Finn, 2004, 67.
[132] Eric Mack et al., *John Locke*, Continuum International Publishing Group, London, 2009, 3.
[133] Ibid., 3.
[134] Ian Shapiro, ed., *Two Treatises of Government and A Letter Concerning Toleration*, Yale University Press, New Haven and London, 2003, x.

standpoint, expresses Locke's thoughts for a more sophisticated civilization.[135]

Locke, just like Thomas Hobbes, stresses the significance of the State or Government in respect to the trustworthiness of the individuals in a society based on the complexity of the regional division of labour.[136] Where he differs from the views of Hobbes, however, is that Locke finds resistance and revolution quite necessary in case of an inexcusable injustice. What he takes as the principal continuum of political order lies in what Thomas Aquinas called "the public good".

> Political power, then, I take to be a right of making laws with penalties of death, and consequently all less penalties, for the regulating and preserving of property, and of employing the force of the community, in the execution of such laws, and in the defense of the commonwealth from foreign injury; and all this only for the public good.[137]

John Dunn, a professor specializing on John Locke, attributes Locke's political philosophy to the concept of trust. In his *The Concept Of "Trust" in The Politics Of John Locke* (1984), Dunn sets the reasonable doings of the individuals as a fundamental basis for politics, "because what they have good reason to do depends directly and profoundly on how far they can and should trust and rely upon one another."[138] This is the exact depiction of what is responsible for the conflict of the individuals; to trust one another (the political philosophy of Locke) is a way to make individuals free from conflicts or war against each other (the political philosophy of John Calvin and Thomas Hobbes). Greg Forster observes the concept of trust within Locke's political philosophy regarding Locke's approach to freedom for religion, and he

---

[135] John Dunn (a), "John Locke: The Politics of Trust" in *Political Thought from Plato to NATO*, British Broadcasting Corporation, London, 1984, 109–119.
[136] Ibid., 113.
[137] John Lock, *Two Treatises of Government and A Letter Concerning Toleration,* ed. Ian Shapiro, Yale University Press, New Haven and London, 2003, 101.
[138] John Dunn (b), "The Concept of 'Trust' in The Politics of John Locke" in *Philosophy in History*, Cambridge University Press, Cambridge, 1984, 279.

tackles with Locke's approach to moral compromise; he believes that "Locke's theory of limited government arises from this portrayal of political power as a trust given under God's law",[139] thus, the authority comes through the trust which is bestowed by God to the rulers.

On the other hand, Eric Mack and John Meadowcroft, in *John Locke* (2009), address Locke's theories on natural freedom, natural rights, and natural law.[140] The fact that it is a natural reality that man is free, has some natural rights, and there is a natural divine law for him is explained in *Two Treatises of Government* where Locke explains the idea of perfect freedom as follows:

> To understand political power right, and derive it from its original, we must consider what state all men are naturally in, and that is, a state of perfect freedom to order their actions and dispose of their possessions and persons, as they think fit, within the bounds of the law of nature; without asking leave, or depending upon the will of any other man.[141]

The perfect freedom is only based on loyalties and trustworthiness of people towards each other and towards the State[142] which "is both the constitutive virtue of, and the key causal precondition for the existence of, any society."[143] Thus, John Locke portrays a basic politics which corresponds with liberalism. The modern scholars regarding Locke's political philosophy consider him "as a libertarian defender of absolute individual rights"[144] who bases the roots of political power and its origin within human nature; as "a secularist who sought to remove religion from politics"[145] and "a rationalist who sought to found natural law doctrine on pure reason, unassisted by revelation."[146]

---

[139] Greg Forster, *John Locke's Politics of Moral Consensus*, Cambridge University Press, Cambridge, 2005, 251.
[140] Eric Mack et al., 2009, 1–179.
[141] Lock, 2003, 101.
[142] Dunn, 1984, 112.
[143] Dunn (b), 1984, 287.
[144] Forster, 2005, 3.
[145] Ibid., 3.
[146] Ibid., 3.

Another successful political philosopher, and one of the leading thinkers of the 18th century, Jean Jacques Rousseau is also among those who contributed to the formation of political thoughts and ethics.[147] Aggrandizing democracy and outlining totalitarianism, Rousseau's *The Social Contract* (1762) proposes instituting a political society which deals with the monetary problems of the general public.[148] Rousseau, just like Thomas Hobbes, takes men to the centre of his political studies, and as he puts across in his *Emile, or On Education* (1762) "Society must be studied by means of men, and men by means of society. Those who want to treat politics and morals separately will never understand anything of either of the two."[149] As stated by Susan Dunn in the introduction to *The Social Contract*:

> In order to fathom the different causes of inequality and analyze the successive stages in its development, Rousseau decided to play the role of theoretical anthropologist, hypothesizing about the lives that people might have led in the "state of nature," before social relations and organized society molded and corrupted human behavior.[150]

Rousseau, in his *Discourse on Inequality* (1754), argues that the goal of the *Social Contract* is to create a consensus for the creation of an agreed political system,[151] because he believed that "human nature is basically good, [and] ... rejected the idea of original sin"[152] which is the reason behind his view that it is maladministration that makes citizens wrong or wicked and "if modern individuals appeared corrupt, unequal, and enslaved, it is society—not human nature—that is to blame."[153]

---

[147] Robert Wokler, "Jean: Jacques Rousseau: Moral Decadence and The Pursuit of Liberty" in *Political Thought from Plato to NATO*, British Broadcasting Corporation, London, 1984, 120.
[148] Ibid., 126–30.
[149] Jean Jacques Rousseau, *Emile, or On Education,* trans. Allan Bloom, Basic Books, USA, 1979, 285.
[150] Susan Dunn, ed., *The Social Contract and The First and Second Discourses*, Yale University Press, New Haven and London, 2002, 5.
[151] Wokler, 1984, 127.
[152] Robert N. Bellah, *The Robert Bellah Reader*, Duke University Press, Durham and London, 182.
[153] Dunn, ed., 2002, 6.

The Social Contract contracts a desired list of rules by which every individual will be liberated since they all forfeit the same amount of rights and impose the same duties on all.[154] The basic emphasis of Rousseau is to settle the notion that it is inconsistent for a human being to capitulate his liberty for servitude, and that man is the single authority that must have a right to decide on the bylaws under which he survives.[155] Rousseau's insistence on the statement that "man was born free, and everywhere he is in chains"[156] explicitly posits the sovereignty of man, though he believes there are some laws which impose burdens on him. Rousseau's contract enacts new commandments for the sake of human goodness and social order[157] which "is a sacred right, and provides a foundation for all other rights."[158] Rousseau also reveals that one of the other factors of social order lies in "the common good", for it is shared interests that make people a group and "the social bond is formed by what these interests have in common; if there were no point at which every interest met, no society could exist."[159] According to Rousseau's *The Social Contract*, the political facets of the social order are to be alienated into two:

(a) a sovereign comprising of the total populace that epitomizes the general will which serves as a unity of statutory authority within the state,[160]

> that sovereignty, being only the exercise of the general will, can never be transferred, and that the sovereign, which cannot be other than a collective entity, cannot be represented except by itself; power can be delegated, but the will cannot.[161]

---

[154] Wokler, 1984, 127–128.
[155] Ibid., 128.
[156] Jean Jacques Rousseau, *The Social Contract and The First and Second Discourses,* ed. Susan Dunn, Yale University Press, New Haven and London, 2002, 156.
[157] Wokler, 1984, 129.
[158] Rousseau, 2002, 156.
[159] Ibid., 170.
[160] Dunn, ed., 2002, 9–10.
[161] Rousseau, 2002, 170.

(b) the government, being essential in terms of dealing with specific issues[162] like "an application of the law, a particular act which determines the case of the law, as will be clearly seen when the idea attached to the word *law* is defined,"[163] and edicts or rules; Rousseau defines a social order composed of general will for the sake of "common good" in which government must take its role as an isolated figure from the sovereign body. Thus, "the ideal society he proposes in *The Social Contract* is, more than anything else, a communitarian society in which the responsibilities and duties of citizenship outweigh individual rights and freedoms."[164]

Adam Smith, an efficacious moral philosopher and a forerunner of political economy, is also concerned with that kind of communitarian society in which he goes deep inside the social philosophy.[165] His philosophy, more basically, touches on ethics and human life.[166] In *The Theory of Moral Sentiments* (1759), Adam Smith develops the idea of moral philosophy and he urges the readers to concentrate upon the "certain practical and political applications of moral theory, and especially with the virtues of prudence, benevolence, and self-command, and the vices of pride and vanity."[167] He strongly stresses the significance of law and legislatures, and he reveals that "they make part of the great system of government, and the wheels of the political machine seem to move with more harmony and ease by means of them."[168] He, for the utilities of communitarian society, underscores the fact that social interactions are the pillars of the conscience.[169] So, he suggests a theory of sympathy: that it is "a very ingenious attempt to

---

[162] Dunn, ed., 2002, 9–10.
[163] Rousseau, 2002, 171.
[164] Dunn, ed., 2002, 9.
[165] John Robertson, "Adam Smith: The Enlightenment and the Philosophy of Society" in *Political Thought from Plato to NATO*, British Broadcasting Corporation, London, 1984, 135.
[166] Ibid., 135.
[167] D. D. Raphael et al., eds., *The Theory of Moral Sentiments*, Liberty Fund, Inc., Indianapolis, 1984, 44
[168] Adam Smith, *The Theory of Moral Sentiments,* ed. D.D. Raphael et al., Liberty Fund, Inc., Indianapolis, 1984, 185.
[169] Robertson, 1984, 136.

account for the principal phenomena in the moral world from this one general principle."¹⁷⁰ This theory suggests the deed of witnessing others that makes public conscious of themselves and the ethics of their own manners.

> Upon some occasions sympathy may seem to arise merely from the view of a certain emotion in another person. The passions, upon some occasions, may seem to be transfused from one man to another, instantaneously and antecedent to any knowledge of what excited them in the person principally concerned.¹⁷¹

Thus, Smith perceives the natural social order as an elementary deduction of diverse facets of human nature that is governed by sympathy and moral growth which generate the character of political or ideological identity.¹⁷² In parallel with these comments, Donald Winch underlines the hint of "sympathy" and upholds that "it represents a major flaw in commercial or civilized society, undermining many of those virtues and mechanisms of 'sympathy' which Smith had maintained in the *Theory of Moral Sentiments* were essential to social harmony and beneficence."¹⁷³

Conversely, John Stuart Mill, famous for his concept of liberty and liberalism, categorized the Victorian norms of ethics and morality into the "contenders" of liberalism.¹⁷⁴ A well-known 19th century political philosopher and thinker, Mill focused on the banalities of Victorian moral disciplines and moral pressures.¹⁷⁵ In *On Liberty* (1859), Mill articulates his visions on liberty by elucidating individualistic phenomena, revealing the reciprocal relationships of humans.¹⁷⁶ His understanding of the concept of freedom made him a well-known

---

[170] Raphael et al., eds., 1984, 3
[171] Ibid., 11.
[172] Ibid., 1–46.
[173] Donald Winch, *Adam Smith's Politics*, Cambridge University Press, Cambridge, 1978, 83.
[174] John Gray, "John Stuart Mill: The Crisis of Liberalism" in *Political Thought from Plato to NATO*, British Broadcasting Corporation, London, 1984, 148.
[175] Ibid., 148.
[176] John Stuart Mill, *On Liberty,* eds. David Bromwich and George Kateb, Yale University Press, New Haven and London, 2003, 219.

figure in feminism.¹⁷⁷ He was a great devotee of education as humankind's rudimentary right, and he believed that "since all differences between individuals and classes of men result from differences of education, education is the sovereign remedy for individual or class inferiority, and the means for raising the whole human race to the level of its noblest individuals."¹⁷⁸ Thus, Mill attempts to establish the base of the "individual freedoms of thought, association and life-style on the ground that only in a context of liberty in which many competing 'experiments of living' may be tried can each of us hope to seek and find his own distinctive happiness."¹⁷⁹

Mill's political ideas, for the most part, take their origin from his father James Mill's political actions. Like his father, Stuart Mill was an enthusiast of free speech, free thinking, equality, voting rights for women, and reformism; his leanings towards feminism gave rise to his specific protests against the inequalities specifically within the legislatures of 19th century Victorian Britain.¹⁸⁰ His insistence on replacing "the word 'man' with the word 'person'"¹⁸¹ signifies his political posture among his contemporaries. So, in *On Liberty*, Mill pays attention to "Civil, or Social Liberty: the nature and limits of the power which can be legitimately exercised by society over the individual."¹⁸² As a consequence, he addresses a communitarian regime which holds the power not as a weapon against but for the sake of humanity.¹⁸³ "The limitation, therefore, of the power of government over individuals loses none of its importance when the holders of power are regularly accountable to the community; that is, to the

---

¹⁷⁷ Gray, 1984, 155.
¹⁷⁸ Edward Alexander, *Matthew Artnold and John Stuart Mill*, Routledge, London and New York, 101.
¹⁷⁹ Gray, 1984, 152.
¹⁸⁰ David Bromwich, "A Note On the Life and Thought of John Stuart Mill" in *On Liberty*, eds. David Bromwich and George Kateb, Yale University Press, New Haven and London, 2003, 2–18.
¹⁸¹ John Cunningham Wood, ed., *John Stuart Mill*, Routledge, London and New York, 1991, 289.
¹⁸² Mill, 2003, 73.
¹⁸³ Gray, 1984, 153.

strongest part therein."[184] In parallel with these notions, Mill conveys that only when a regime is able to accomplish such an advantageous norm of politics may it acquire a sophisticated capability of self-esteem; that is the only way that factual liberty overcomes. His philosophies, his political perspectives, and his doctrines are all dictums for his successors, particularly for those of 20th century.[185]

Many modern political thinkers and philosophers such as Bernard Russell, R. H. Tawney, John Rawls, Herbert Marcuse and Hannah Arendt have tackled what their predecessors had established.[186]

Ideology and Political Ideologies

Emmet Kennedy, in *The History of Ideology* (1979), starts with the words "Historians of ideas,"[187] proposing the dominant definition of the concept of ideology related to "a set of ideas". Ideology, in the most basic sense, is a system of ideas and ideals, especially one which forms the basis of economic or political theory and policy"; it is "the set of beliefs characteristic of a social group or individual", and "the science of ideas; the study of their origin and nature."[188]

A variety of definitions are employed in ideology, which include: "a universal system of thought explaining the human condition; a theory of the historical process in which there was the certainty of a better future"[189] endorsing one's individual outlook among people, or groups; "a *text,* woven of a whole tissue of different conceptual strands; it is traced through by divergent histories, and it is probably more

---

[184] Mill, 2003, 76.
[185] Gray, 1984, 148–158.
[186] Alan Ryan, "The Moderns: Liberalism Revived" in *Political Thought from Plato to NATO*, British Broadcasting Corporation, London, 1984, 171–75.
[187] Emmet Kennedy, "Ideology" from Destutt De Tracy to Marx" in *Journal of the History of Ideas*, Vol. 40, No. 3 (Jul–Sep, 1979), 353.
[188] Ideology, *Oxford Online Dictionary*, http://www.oxforddictionaries.com/definition/english/ideology Accessed: 10.01.2015
[189] Frank Bealey et al., *The Blackwell Dictionary of Political Science*, Blackwell Publishing Ltd., 1999, 156.

important to assess what is valuable,"[190] which reveals compromise with other supporting questions; and "an 'idea-science' (ideology), which means that it resembled more what could be described as a critical dissection of ideas and their derivation from sensory perceptions"[191] making edicts and implementing brainstorming, together with critical idea exchange.[192]

As reflected by Jan Rehmann, in *Theories of Ideology* (2013), "one of the basic findings in theories of ideology and discourse is that the meaning of a term, [as it is in ideology], is not fixed once and for all, but subject to change."[193] The same view is suggested by Terry Eagleton in *Ideology* (1991) in which Eagleton states "Nobody has yet come up with a single adequate definition of ideology."[194] As George Lichtheim observes "the history of the concept serving as a guide to the actual interplay of 'real' and 'ideal' factors whose dialectic is obscurely intended in the formulation of the concept itself."[195] Thus, the scholars, philosophers or academics go in search of the history of the concept to reveal the methodologies and theories for the 'real' and 'ideal' metamorphoses in its shaping. In his article titled *History of the Ideology* (1979), Emmet Kennedy expressed that the root of the concept goes back to Antoine Destutt de Tracy in 1796, who brought together the words *idea*, and *-logy*, assigning "science of ideas"[196] as a meaning for the concept. Considering ideology "as a natural science of ideas,"[197] Jan Rahmann tries to explain "the pre-Marxian history of the concept, that is, from Destutt de Tracy, who had introduced the neologism 'ideology' in order to conceptualize an exact *science* of ideas."[198]

---

[190] Terry Eagleton, *Ideology*, Verso Publishing, New York and London, 1991, 1.
[191] Jan Rehmann, *Theories of Ideology*, Brill, Leiden and Boston, 2013, 15.
[192] Ibid., 15.
[193] Ibid., 15.
[194] Eagleton, 1991, 1.
[195] George Lichtheim, "The Concept of Ideology" in *History and Theory*, Vol. 4, No. 2 (1965), 164.
[196] Kennedy, 1979, 353.
[197] Rehmann, 2013, 15.
[198] Ibid., 8.

Searching for the history of the concept, Kennedy attributes the base of 'ideology' to the exceedingly notorious idealistic and opinionated disputes and clashes of the French Revolution and he continues with the subsequent words: "What happened to 'ideology' illustrates very well what happened to the Enlightenment after the French Revolution."[199] While within its modern usage, the term is customarily used to denote a position which resists a thorough and systematic notion of humanity, it was—as emphasized above—initially used to label an explicit *science*.[200] However, in parallel with the other theories, models, and notions, 'ideology' has gone through a "semantic shift from the systematic knowledge of an object to the object itself, from the critical analysis of ideas to the ideas themselves"[201] and this removal has led to the shape of "the ideology of ideology"[202] within the modern milieu. It has even been considered to have "no history, which does not at all mean that it has no history (quite the opposite, since it is but a pale reflection, empty and inverted, of real history), but, rather, that it has no history of its own"[203] which takes its backbone from Louis Althusser's theory that "ideology has no history". Terry Eagleton, Jan Rehmann and Louis Althusser et al. have the common thought in that they all regard Napoleon's usage of ideology as "pejorative", and Louis Althusser expresses:

> When Napoleon uttered his famous phrase: "the Ideologues are no use", he had them and only them in mind—not, obviously, himself, the number-one ideologue (ideologue in the Marxist sense) of the bourgeois social formation that had been "saved" from the Terror, who knew (or did not know: no matter, because

---

[199] Kennedy, 1979, 354.
[200] Ibid., 353–54.
[201] Rehmann, 2013, 15.
[202] Lucio Colletti et al., *From Rousseau to Lenin*, Monthly Review Press, New York and London, 1972, 44.
[203] Louis Althusser, *On The Reproduction of Capitalism*, trans. G. M. Goshgarian, Verso, London and New York, 2014, 175.

he practiced it) that one cannot do without ideology and ideologues. This held first and foremost for him.[204]

Whilst the concept of ideology is interchangeable in respect with the swiftly changing world order, world policies and human needs in terms of "the evolution in ideas", the concept has been reevaluated among different scholars from the 19th century onwards.[205] According to Karl Mannheim, "the final and most important step in the creation of the total conception of ideology likewise arose out of the historical-social process,"[206] by which the creation of ideology is attuned specifically to the Napoleonic Wars regarding its historical-social base. Mannheim continues:

> When "class" took the place of "folk" or nation as the bearer of the historically evolving consciousness, the same theoretical tradition, to which we have already referred, absorbed the realization which meanwhile had grown up through the social process, namely that the structure of the society and its corresponding intellectual forms vary with the relations between social classes.[207]

Emphasizing the "unity of consciousness" in his *Ideology and Utopia*, Mannheim underlines most powerfully the ideological alterations as "dynamic" and "in constant process of becoming"—a state at once ironic in terms of his idea of "the totally distorted mind which falsifies everything"[208] and reference to the "false consciousness … which lends to the total conception of ideology a special significance and relevance for the understanding of our social life."[209] He thus intertwines historical and social supremacy over the rationalization of ideology. The idea of "false consciousness" goes back to several philosophers and

---

[204] Althusser, 2014, 171.
[205] Eagleton, 1991, 71 and 89.
[206] Karl Mannheim, *Ideology and Utopia*, Routledge, New York, 1936, 60.
[207] Ibid., 60.
[208] Ibid., 62.
[209] Ibid., 62.

intellectuals interpreting the concept of ideology by attaching the meaning to numerous paradigms.[210] The evolutionary shift in its meaning has something to do with Karl Marx, and Friedrich Engels "for whom ideologies were a form of 'false consciousness'; thus, the working class may have misguided ideas about the conditions of its existence as a result of their indoctrination by those who control the means of production."[211] As stated by Eagleton, "one central lineage, from Hegel and Marx to Georg Lukacs and some later Marxist thinkers, has been much preoccupied with ideas of true and false cognition, with ideology as illusion, distortion and mystification"[212] which necessarily denotes what Karl Marx emphasizes through '"false consciousness".

Karl Marx, in the introduction of *A Contribution to the Critique of Political Economy* (1859), expresses "the mode of production in the material life determines the general character of the social, political and spiritual processes of life",[213] and he continues, "it is not the consciousness of men that determines their existence, but, on the contrary, their social existence determines their consciousness."[214] For that statement, Georg Lukacs uncovers "only when the core of existence stands revealed as a social process can existence be seen as the product, albeit the hitherto unconscious product, of human activity."[215] Thus, in the Marxist view—taking the products and productions to the centre—the ruled and the rulers are economically intertwined in a human society composed of a mode of consciousness which routes their existence. As revealed by Louis Althusser in *Ideology and Ideological State Apparatuses* (1970):

> Marx conceived the structure of every society as constituted by "levels" or "instances" articulated by a specific determination: the

---

[210] Eagleton, 1991, 10–15.
[211] Dijk, 2006, 728.
[212] Eagleton, 1991, 3.
[213] Karl Marx, *A Contribution to the Critique of Political Economy*, Charles H. Kerr Comp., Chicago, 1904, 11.
[214] Ibid., 11–12.
[215] Georg Lukacs, *History and Class Consciousness: Studies in Marxist Dialectics*, trans. Rodney Livingstone, The Mit Press, Cambridge, 1968, 19.

infrastructure, or economic base (the "unity" of the productive forces and the relations of production) and the *superstructure*, which itself contains two "levels" or "instances": the politico-legal (law and the state) and ideology (the different ideologies, religious, ethical, legal, political, etc.).[216]

The production is shown to be the main means that divides the human society into two parts: the base and superstructure symbolizing the economic, political, and ideological affair in which *base* signifies the associations of production and methods of production, and *superstructure* indicates the overriding ideology (authorized, governmental organisms).[217] Marx suggests in his theory that the economic base which embraces the services of production, working conditions, distribution of work, and procedural divisions, regulates the political superstructure of a society.[218] He attunes this to "the period of social revolution"[219] in which the requirements and conveniences of human life are shaped "with the change of the economic foundation"[220] and "the entire immense superstructure is more or less rapidly transformed."[221] The Marxist ideology puts forward that the affairs of the base group of the superstructure are rooted in the productions by which the interests of governmental authorities or ruling class regulate the superstructure and the mode of the moderating ideology.[222] This moderation of ideology is deliberated through:

> the material transformation of the economic conditions of the production which can be determined with the precision of natural science, and the legal, political, religious, aesthetic, or

---

[216] Louis Althusser, *Ideology and Ideological State Apparatuses*, trans. Ben Brewser, Verso, London and New York, 2014, 237.
[217] Tom Bottomore, ed., *A Dictionary of Marxist Thought*, Blackwell Publishers, Oxford, 1991, 45-48.
[218] Ibid., 45-48.
[219] Marx, 1904, 12.
[220] Ibid., 12.
[221] Ibid., 12.
[222] Bottomore, ed., 1991, 45-48.

> philosophic—in short ideological forms in which men become conscious of this conflict and fight it out.[223]

On the other hand, Eagleton, in *Ideology*, attributes these economic conditions of the production to an operation which works "all by itself"[224] for the late capitalist society, and he emphasizes that "it is not 'consciousness' or 'ideology' which welds it together, but its own complex systemic operations"[225] which denotes the end of ideology, or it may be regarded in terms of Eagletonic perspective combining 'meaning and ideology' together with 'non-meaning and capitalism'[226]. This point of view may also be correlated to what Emmet Kennedy signifies in his article that "it has not yet been fully explained how 'ideology'"—the synonym Destutt de Tracy (1754–1836) proposed in 1796 for "science of ideas" (understood in the sensationalist tradition of Condillac)—could come to mean "false class consciousness."[227] However, it is clear that Karl Marx does not synthesize a totally variable "ideology" paradigm that shows varieties from society to society, and this point of view is expressed in *German Ideology* (1846) as follows:

> There is no specific difference between German idealism and the ideology of all the other nations. The latter too regards the world as dominated by ideas, ideas and concepts as the determining principles, and certain notions as the mystery of the material world accessible to the philosophers.[228]

The idea of consciousness—or class consciousness—is also touched upon and backed by György Lukács who was one of the forefathers of Western Marxism.[229] Emphasizing the *new methods* within Orthodox Marxism, Lukacs tries to re-formulate the Marxist ideology through the forms of theory and practice[230] which "would be a form that enables the

---

[223] Marx, 1904, 12.
[224] Eagleton, 1991, 37.
[225] Ibid., 37.
[226] Ibid., 37.
[227] Kennedy, 1979, 353.
[228] Karl Max and Frederick Engels, *German Ideology*, Premetheus Books, New York, 1998, 30.
[229] Eagleton, 1991, 94.
[230] Ibid., 94–95.

masses to become conscious of their socially necessary or fortuitous actions, without ensuring a genuine and necessary bond between consciousness and action."[231] This is something connected to ideology-theory which "was coined in the 1970s in order to designate a refoundation of Marxist research into ideology stimulated by Louis Althusser."[232]

Georg Lukacs, in *History and Class Consciousness* (1923), explains what Marx means by "change through transformation" in the following words: "Every substantial change that is of concern to knowledge manifests itself as a change in relation to the whole and through this as a change in the form of objectivity itself,"[233] which denotes his urge for a methodological shift in terms of Marxist ideology. "This is why only the dialectical conception of totality can enable us to understand *reality as a social process.*"[234] Critiquing Marxist revisionism by taking dialectical materialism as his goal, Lukacs proclaims the predominance of societal affairs, and he believes that through "reality" and "thought", the consciousness is shaped.[235] He states:

> Marx urged us to understand "the sensuous world", the object, reality, as human sensuous activity. This means that man must become conscious of himself as a social being, as simultaneously the subject and object of the socio-historical process.[236]

The awareness of consciousness is also reproduced by the Italian Marxist Antonio Gramsci.[237] He expresses this awareness through Lenin's "hegemony"; however, he produces a novel phenomenon called "cultural hegemony" as a method of conserving and justifying the

---

[231] Lukacs, 1968, 2.
[232] Rehmann, 2013, 4.
[233] Lukacs, 1968, 13.
[234] Ibid., 13.
[235] Setphen A. Resnick et al., eds., *New Departures in Marxian Theory*, Routledge, New York, 2006, 35.
[236] Lukacs, 1968, 19.
[237] Eagleton, 1991, 36, 50.

capitalist state,[238] and again, he introduces a modern style of governance titled "civil society"[239] that was for the most part influenced by Machiavelli's *Prince*.[240] Yet Gramsci's philosophy is not limited to the theoretical readings of those preceding him; he, for the most part, goes in search of the ideological and political realities of his period and through these facts he reproduces an avant-garde awareness of consciousness.[241] As Antonio Santucci et al. suggest, "Gramsci did not set out to explain historical reality armed with some full-fledged concept, such as hegemony;"[242] because he, "repeatedly stressed the importance of paying attention to phenomena in all their particularity and specificity."[243] They continue, "rather, he examined the minutiae of concrete social, economic, cultural and political relations as they are lived by individuals in their specific historical circumstances,"[244] and thus, "he acquired an increasingly complex understanding of how hegemony operates in many diverse ways and under many aspects within the capillaries of society."[245]

Believing intellectual and moral power to be key for "hegemony", Gramsci connects the principal of hegemony to consent, "even before the material conquest of power"[246] by which he improves a critical exploration of how the ruling class can launch and sustain its rule over the other societal classes. Gramsci also links the notion of public awareness to the function of hegemony, thus, stressing the role of civil society, "which Gramsci placed between economic structure and the state that must be radically transformed in a concrete way and not only on legal paper or scientists' books."[247]

---

[238] T. J. Jakson Lears, "The Concept of Cultural Hegemony: Problems and Possibilities" in *The American Historical Review*, Vol. 90, Issue 3 (June 1985), 568.
[239] Ibid., 570.
[240] Carlos Nelson Coutinho, *Gramsci's Political Thought*, Koninklijke Brill NV, Leiden, 2012, 110.
[241] Lears, 1985, 567–593.
[242] Antonio A. Santucci et al., *Antonio Gramsci*, Monthly Review Press, New York, 2010, 17.
[243] Ibid., 17.
[244] Ibid., 17.
[245] Ibid., 17.
[246] Santucci et al., 2010, 154.
[247] Ibid., 156.

Just like Georg Lukacs, Louis Althusser—highly affected by Gramsci—is also among Orthodox Marxists who suggests a money-oriented idea of ideology.[248] As expressed by Etienne Balibar in the foreword of *On the Reproduction of Capitalism* (1968), Althusser gives "great importance to developing the 'Marxist' theory of ideology or even producing a theory from scratch, with a view to refounding or reconstructing historical materialism."[249] However, Althusser volunteered the use of the theory of the *Ideological State Apparatus* to illuminate his philosophy of ideology in which, as stated by Jacques Bidet in *On the Reproduction of Capitalism,* he "explains, in systematic fashion, his conception of historical materialism, the conditions for the reproduction of capitalist society, and the revolutionary struggle that seeks to put an end to it."[250] Emphasizing the distinction between "state" and "private", Althusser reveals *Ideological State Apparatus* as a reaction against what he calls "(repressive) state apparatus."[251]

In order to advance the theory of the state it is necessary to take into account not only the distinction between state power and state apparatus, but also another reality which is clearly on the side of the (repressive) state apparatus—but which must not be confused with it. I shall call this reality by its concept: the Ideological State Apparatuses.[252]

"Althusser expressly places himself in the line of what he calls the 'classics of Marxism'."[253] Nevertheless, he goes into a deep analysis of Marxist ideology and he draws the attention to the theoretical basis of such existing authorized organisms as "the government, the administration, the army, the police, the courts, the prisons, etc., which

---

[248] Daniel Jakopovich, *The Concept of Class*, Cambridge Studies in Social Research SSRG Publications, Cambridge, 2014, 5.
[249] Etienne Balibar, *Foreword to On The Reproduction Of Capitalism*, trans. G. M. Goshgarian, Verso, London and New York, 2014, x.
[250] Jacques Bidet, *Introduction to On The Reproduction Of Capitalism*, trans. G. M. Goshgarian, Verso, London and New York, 2014, xx.
[251] Althusser, 2014, 243.
[252] Ibid., 242.
[253] Bidet, 2014, xx.

constitute ... the Repressive State Apparatus"²⁵⁴ that Althusser believes to be the material institutions of Marxist theory—"functioning by violence."²⁵⁵ Instead, he produces *Ideological State Apparatuses—vis a vis* the Repressive—which "function 'by ideology'".²⁵⁶

---

²⁵⁴ Althusser, 2014, 243.
²⁵⁵ Ibid., 243.
²⁵⁶ Ibid., 244.

Political Ideologies

Our emphasis, within this subtitle, will be on a few political ideologies which will have a noteworthy impact on the core of our study—encompassing both George Bernard Shaw's and Orhan Asena's literary career and literary works. Therefore, the main basics of such major ideologies as Socialism, Communism, Republicanism, Laicism, Nationalism and Kemalism will be the focus of this part of the study. The core of the above mentioned ideologies will be illuminated within the analysis of the plays in chapters three and four.

Taking Althusser's contentious statement that: "Ideology is sheer illusion; sheer dream, in other words, nothingness. All its reality lies outside it. Ideology is thus conceived of as an imaginary construct,"[257] into consideration, we should get rid of the "cluster of conscious and/or unconscious ideas" in the current world we live in. Yet it seems very few would wish to attempt this. Here, Althusser unveils the significance of the external factors which are basis for the "reality" of ideology.[258] This transformation from imaginary to reality is portrayed by Slavoj Zizek in the *Sublime Object of Ideology* (1989) as follows:

> ideology is not simply a "false consciousness", an illusory representation of reality, it is rather this reality itself which is already to be conceived as "ideological" – "ideological" is a social reality whose very existence implies the non-knowledge of its participants as to its essence—that is, the social effectivity, the very reproduction of which implies that the individuals 'do not know what they are doing.'[259]

The emphasis of the two writers above signifies the role of a "common sense" through the depiction of reality within the establishment of ideology in society. The political ideologies are, thus, conceived to take

---

[257] Althusser, 2014, 174–75.
[258] Ibid., 175.
[259] Slavoj Zizek, *The Sublime Object of Ideology*, Verso, London and New York, 1989, 15–16.

their shape through the reproduction of "social effectivity" and "social reality".[260]

In general readings, a political ideology is a definite principled mixture of ethics, philosophies, policies, mythologies or ciphers of a communal affectivity, communal reality and communal movement, association, group, or assembly that elucidate how labours are dealt with, and in which procedures some political and cultural designs for a positive societal order are suggested.[261] As a consequence, the political ideology is concerned with "the structure of ideology, that is, the manner and extent to which political attitudes are cognitively organized"[262] in a real society. Preserving the traditional outburst of ideology, a single left-right dimension also embraces the political mannerisms of ideological thoughts.

As expressed by John T. Jost et al., the political opponents "associated the right with such terms as 'conservative', 'system maintenance', 'order', 'individualism', 'capitalism', 'nationalism', and 'fascism'", while "they associated the left with 'progressive', 'system change', 'equality', 'solidarity', 'protest', 'opposition', 'radical', 'socialism' and 'communism'". Thus, political ideologies are composed of every unique hint of thought which provokes man to be either supporter of the "left" or "right" wing of the communal standing.

Socialism and Communism

Concentrating, for the most part, on the left-side of ideology, George Bernard Shaw was among the pioneers of Socialism. According to Sidney Webb et al. "Socialism ... is not a Utopia which they have invented, but a principle of social organization which they assert to have been discovered by the patient investigators into sociology."[263]

---

[260] Ibid., 15–16.
[261] John T. Jost et al., "Political Ideology: Its Structure, Functions, and Elective Affinities" in *The Annual Review of Psychology*, Issue 60 (2009), 309.
[262] Ibid., 310.
[263] Sidney Webb et al., *Socialism and Individualism*, John Lane Company, New York, 1911, 6.

Here, Shaw underpins the significance of the social and economic system as a unit of organization. Erzsebet Szalai, in *Socialism-An Analysis of its Past and Future* (2005), hints at the same views as Shaw, and she goes on to categorize Socialism in two ways: (a) "existing socialism" which "constituted an autonomous social and economic system"[264]—the same idea proposed by Shaw—and (b) "the social formation called state socialism [that] was in reality a social system located between state socialism and state capitalism—a transitory society which it would be more legitimate and exact to call semi-peripheral socialism."[265]

Shaw and his colleagues believe that "Socialism is, indeed, nothing but the extension of democratic self-government from the political to the industrial world"[266] which accentuates the indispensable significance of democracy. They continue, "and it is hard to resist the conclusion that it is an inevitable outcome of the joint effects of the economic and political revolutions of the past century,"[267] a statement which emphasizes the significance of economic revolutions. The fact that Socialist leanings of some thinkers have risen against "complete industrial individualism, in which, however, unrestrained private ownership of land and capital was accompanied by subjection to a political oligarchy"[268] does reveal the basic tenets of socialism in which social and economic systems are typified by social rights of the methods of production and mutual decision-making of the financial system.[269] Shaw and his followers established the foundation of the characteristics of Socialism through their well-known group named Fabian Society which:

---

[264] Erzsébet Szalai, *Socialism: An Analysis of Its Past and Future*, Central European University Press, Budapest and New York, 2005, 3.
[265] Ibid., 3.
[266] Webb et al., 1911, 22.
[267] Ibid., 22.
[268] G. Bernard Shaw, *Fabian Essays in Socialism*, ed. H.G. Wilshire, Homboldt Publishing Co., New York, 1891, 10.
[269] Bealey et al., 1999, 304.

consists of men and women who are Socialists, that is to say, in the words of its "Basis" of those who aim at the reorganization of society by the emancipation of Land and Industrial Capital from individual and class ownership, and the vesting of them in the community for the general benefit.[270]

Webb et al. consider that the main reason behind the pressure for social reform is "immediately connected with the administration of industry and the distribution of wealth"[271] which are the backbones of the "inequality of income."[272] However, this is not the case in Capitalism. According to Erzsebet Szalai, "while in capitalist societies it is the ownership of capital that legitimizes disposal over surplus production, in state socialism, the 'modern system of redistribution,' it is the redistributors' or intellectuals' knowledge that has the same function of according legitimacy."[273] What Shaw, in his own way, addressed through his Socialist views was the idea of an economy-based social order which held democracy with great respect. Thus, Shaw, in *Fabian Essays*, has the last word: "The economic side of the democratic idea is, in fact, Socialism itself."[274]

Alternatively, Chris M. Hann, in *Socialism: Ideals, Ideologies and Local Practice* (1993), correlates Socialism with Communism using "primitive communism"[275] as a reference to Socialism. Hann states "as far as the difference between 'socialism' and 'communism' is concerned, the former has generally been taken to refer to a more or less protracted transitional stage in progress towards the latter, the classless, ultimate destination of human societies."[276] Here, Hann uncovers the democratic phase of Socialism in which class bias is moderated—which is the basic

---

[270] Sidney Webb et al., *Introduction to Socialism and Individualism*, John Lane Company, New York, 1911, not aligned.
[271] Ibid., 10.
[272] Ibid., 11.
[273] Szalai, 2005, 4.
[274] Shaw, 1891, 12.
[275] C. M. Hann, ed., *Socialism Ideals, Ideologies, and Local Practice*, Routledge, London and New York, 1993, 3.
[276] Ibid., 23-24.

portrayal of democratic social order.²⁷⁷ However, Harold Wydra contradicts Hann, saying instead that in order to "understand the emergence of democracy, therefore, we need to engage with the experiential basis of communism by examining the potential for the emergence of something new, whose authority in the newly constituted order may be legitimate and durable."²⁷⁸ Wydra echoes this sentiment: "any mirrored opposition between communism and democracy is flawed".²⁷⁹ And he continues, "Rather, the emergence of democracy—despite numerous influences from 'outside'—has been, to an important extent, a quest for meaning and self-grounding in response to traumatic experiences 'within' communism."²⁸⁰

But if there are to be independent centres of economic power as a precondition of civil society—and that is the widespread and urgent intuition of most of those who actually had to endure communism—it follows that the ideal of complete social control over material resources must not be implemented.²⁸¹

The connection between communism and socialism, therefore, lies in the idea that it must be a principle to generate a social and economic egalitarianism, irrespective of such concerns as social divisions or hereditary capital.

Republicanism, Laicism and Nationalism

Cécile Laborde and John Maynor in *Republicanism and Political Theory* (2008) assert "To be free, on the republican view, is to be free from arbitrary power: thus the republican concept of freedom offers a parsimonious conceptual basis for the defense of a normative ideal of

---

[277] Ibid., 23–24.
[278] Harold Wydra, *Communism and the Emergence of Democracy*, Cambridge University Press, New York, 2006, 4.
[279] Ibid., 24.
[280] Ibid., 26.
[281] C. M. Hann, ed., 1993, xi.

political citizenship as non-subjection to arbitrary rule."[282] Here, it is requisite to explore the concept of freedom within the implementation of republican ideals. Republican ideology is rooted in the idea that the state as a republic is governed by the leader of state who is a spokesperson for the public that is in power, rather than being subject matter of the leader of state.[283] However, the core of this philosophy lies in the thought of freedom specifically for those who are ruled; this idea is mirrored by Per Mouritsen as "Republicans were indeed centrally concerned with liberty, and its meaning did not change much over the centuries."[284] Roger Scruton, in *Dictionary of Political Thought* (2007), defines republicanism as "usually used to denote a particular tradition in political thought, which defends government of offices, representation of the people and the rule of law, as the pre-conditions of a free citizenry",[285] whilst Frank Bealey, in *Dictionary of Political Science* (1999), reveals that its origin comes from the Latin word "*res publica*, which originally meant public affairs",[286] and he continues:

> From this it came to mean the realm of politics and then the state. Today to say that a country is a republic means that it is not a monarchy: its head of state is a president and not a hereditary monarch. Those in monarchies who wish to make their countries republics are known as "republicans".[287]

This well-accepted meaning hints at the absence of monarchy; it may possibly specify a regime comprised of rule by many people and by law.[288] Roger Scruton attributes the concept of republicanism to such philosophers as "Machiavelli, Montesquieu and Kant, among others,"[289]

---

[282] Cécile Laborde and John Maynor, eds., *Republicanism and Political Theory*, Blackwell Publishing, Malden, 2008, 2.
[283] Scruton 2007, 594.
[284] Per Mouritsen, "Four Models of Republican Liberty and Self-Government" in *Republicanism in Theory and Practice,* eds. Iseult Honohan and Jeremy Jennings, Routledge, London and New York, 2006, 13–14.
[285] Scruton 2007, 594.
[286] Bealey et al., 1999, 286.
[287] Ibid., 286.
[288] Robertson, 2004, 425.
[289] Scruton 2007, 594.

and he suggests that "republicanism is not necessarily opposed to monarchy, being concerned with the way in which the power of the state is deployed and limited, and in the fundamental accountability of the state towards the citizens that compose it."[290] Nevertheless, Per Mouritsen informs us that Machiavelli is the creator of Classical Republicanism in which he "treats civic involvement as merely the condition for retaining our liberty."[291]

As it is changeable from state to state depending on their cultural and historical agenda, the implementation of republicanism may show some differing connotations within the regimes of countries. In the United Kingdom, maturing in the nineteenth century, republicanism was "eclipsed by utilitarianism and thus that an understanding of liberty as non-domination was replaced in British political thought by the conception of freedom as the absence of interference and coercion."[292] In Turkey, on the other hand, an imperative stimulus of Republicanism fashioned a modern republican identity in 1923 after the downfall of the Ottoman Empire.[293] Till the republican revolt of Mustafa Kemal Atatürk in the 1920s, the Ottoman Empire imposed a hereditary aristocracy and sultanate-curbing pro-republic philosophies.[294]

Atatürk reports six rudimentary principles of the modern Turkish Republic by which he defines the new nation; Atatürk's principles are Republicanism, Populism, Laicism, Reformism, Nationalism, and Statism among which Laicism is "regarded by Kemalism as an essential part of the process whereby modern political institutions could be constructed, hence it remains one of the 'six principles' of the Turkish Republican People's Party".[295] In its basic sense, Laicism is "the belief

---

[290] Ibid., 594.
[291] Quote in Mouritsen, 2006, 18.
[292] Iseult Honohan and Jeremy Jennings, eds., *Republicanism in Theory and Practice*, Routledge, London and New York, 2006, 4.
[293] Feroz Ahmad, *The Making of Modern Turkey*, Routledge, London and New York, 1993, 3.
[294] Gábor Ágoston and Bruce Masters, *Encyclopedia of the Ottoman Empire*, Infobase Publishing, New York, 2009, 56–59.
[295] Scruton 2007, 376.

that civil functions performed erstwhile by priesthood ought to be transferred to the laity especially functions of a judicial and educational kind."[296] In Turkish scripts, the term is expressed to be the segregation of religion and state; the meaning is exclusively related to the independence of state affairs, administrative structure of community and the law, these being taken completely out of religious hands, being grounded on reason and science instead.[297]

Özer Ozankaya, in *Türkiye'de Laiklik* (1990), defines Laicism as "the separation of religion and state affairs," a situation which he regards as very "superficial, ambiguous and therefore inadequate."[298] He believes that Laicism in Turkey is the base of both science and democracy, and he strongly rejects the view that Laicism is against Islamic governance.[299] Ozankaya, labelling Turkish Revolution as "Turkish Enlightenment", maintains that in the 20th century it was Atatürk who had a permanent effect on the functions of the new Republic, and he accomplished this revolution only because "the essence of the revolution was in laic nature."[300] Ozankaya holds the view that the significance of Laicism, as the fundamental to other five principles rests in the fact that it is both "the indispensable element of Turkish Revolution"[301] and "the overall essence of the effort of a contemporary, national, and democratic society."[302] Furthermore, he echoes that "a laic social order and laic worldview are basic indispensable requirements for realization of national identity and national independence..., in a satisfied and advanced degree."[303] Thus, he correlates Laicism with Nationalism and the other principles.

---

[296] Ibid., 376.
[297] İhsan Tayhani, "Türkiye Cumhuriyeti'nin Temeli: Laiklik" in Ankara Üniversitesi Türk İnkılâp Tarihi Enstitüsü Atatürk Yolu Dergisi, Vol. 43 (2009), 519-20.
[298] Özer Ozankaya, Türkiye'de Laiklik, Cem Yayınevi, İstanbul, 1990, 5. Translated by the author from Turkish.
[299] Ibid., 5.
[300] Ibid., 10.
[301] Ibid., 15.
[302] Ibid., 15.
[303] Ibid., 15.

Roger Scruton defines nationalism as "(a) the sentiment and ideology of attachment to a nation and to its interest",[304] and "(b) the theory that a state (perhaps every state) should be founded in a nation, and that a nation should be constituted as a state,"[305] the latter definition being more applicable within the study of social sciences. In world politics, the term "nationalism" embraced the 19th and 20th centuries, and specifically the two World Wars. As expressed by I. Honohan and J. Jennings:

> The nineteenth and much of the twentieth century have been understood as a period in which republicanism virtually vanished from the political scene, in which socialism and nationalism were the dominant ideologies and liberalism and utilitarianism were the prevailing political philosophies.[306]

In Turkey, Turkish nationalism originated with the fall of the Ottoman Empire and with the modern state under the rule of Atatürk.[307] Ziya Gökalp, one of the forerunners of Turkish nationalism, advocates ironically the idea of the nation-state, and attempts to portray the detachments between the idea of nation and state as follows: "the state is a nation already established (*nation de fait*), whereas the ideal of nationalism meant the nucleus of a nationality based on will (*nation de volonte*)".[308] Soner Cagaptay, though inversely, goes deep into the racism-related phenomenon of Turkishness and he suggests leaning on Turkish nationalism "beginning with a study of the birth and entrenchment of the notion of Turkishness in the first half of the twentieth century, when modern Turkey emerged as a nation-state."[309]

---

[304] Scruton 2007, 465.
[305] Ibid., 465.
[306] Honohan et al., eds., 2006, 4.
[307] Stanford J. Shaw and Ezel Kural Shaw, *History of The Ottoman Empire and Modern Turkey*, Vol. II, Cambridge University Press, Cambridge, 1977, 130, 289–90.
[308] Niyazi Berkes, ed., *Turkish Nationalism and Western Civilization*, Columbia University Press, New York, 1959, 72.
[309] Soner Cagaptay, *Islam, Secularism, and Nationalism in Modern Turkey*, Routledge, London and New York, 2006, 2.

Taner Akcam, on the other hand, relates the newly built nation to a "hybrid" identity and conveys that "Turkish nationalism, as a political movement, arrived only in the 20th century. This late arrival of the national identity created chronic self-doubt and constant vacillation between exaggerated praise of one's value on the one hand, and suffering from an inferiority complex on the other."[310] The notion of hybridity prevails in the major works of many writers during the transition period, and the idea of nationalism is, for the most part, advocated by nationalist writers. The core of their writings, most commonly, nourishes what Roger Scruton describes as "national identity"[311] which "involves, not only the territorial integrity, common language, custom and culture noted above as essential to the idea of a nation, but also consciousness of these, as determining distinct rights and duties"[312].

Kemalism

Sena Karasipahi defines Kemalism as "the attempt by Mustafa Kemal and other modernist elites to establish a secular and progressive nation state after the model of the civilized and modernized West."[313] Roger Scruton defines it as "advocacy of the doctrines and policies of Kemal Atatürk (1880–1938), Turkish military leader and statesman, who abolished the sultanate, and founded the modern Turkish republic in a spirit of Turkish nationalism."[314] The idea of Kemalism also takes its base from the six principles of Atatürk. Kemalism, also named Ataturkism, purposes the national sovereignty of the Turkish Republic by extensive political, social, cultural, and religious restructurings premeditated to reform the new Republic of Turkey by extracting from

---

[310] Taner Akçam, *From Empire to Republic: Turkish Nationalism and the Armenian Genocide*, Zed Books, London and New York, 2004, 52.
[311] Scruton 2007, 465.
[312] Ibid., 465.
[313] Sena Karasipahi, *Muslims in Modern Turkey*, I. B. Tauris, London and New York, 2009, 11.
[314] Scruton 2007, 366.

its Ottoman folklore and clinch Westernization.³¹⁵ The idea of Kemalism was regarded by the intellectuals as a key for reaching Western ideologies. As stated by Niyazi Berkes:

> In the eyes of the intellectuals, the West was the world of freedom, comfort, individual dignity, of reason, of decency, and of beauty and art. There was absolutely nothing in the old dissipated, rotten home environment and past to be liked, from which to derive inspiration, to love, with which to identify.³¹⁶

Establishing her study on "the formation and negotiation of Turkish modernity by comparing and contrasting Kemalism,"³¹⁷ Alev Çınar denotes Kemalism as "the founding ideology of the republic, which is based on the ideals of secularism, nationalism, and progress promoted by Mustafa Kemal Atatürk, with one of its main contenders, Islamism."³¹⁸ This perspective emphasizes the fact that Kemalism is a doctrine which regards the principles of Islam as obstacles to the removal of the older "dissipated, rotten past". It therefore signifies the secular regime and advocates the idea of Laicism.³¹⁹ According to M. Hakan Yavuz, "The Kemalist elite have always remained suspicious about the activities of religious groups and parties, seeing them as reacting against the modernizing and secularizing mission of Kemalism."³²⁰ Thus, the Kemalist ideologues have chosen secular/laic regimes as an alliance with their own thoughts. From that point of view, what Umut Azak articulates is a basic precept: "Secularism has been the central tenet of Kemalism, the official ideology of the modernizing political elite in the Republican period."³²¹

---

[315] Metin Heper, "Kemalism/Atatürkism" in *The Routledge Handbook of Modern Turkey*, Routledge, New York, 2012, 139–41.
[316] Berkes, 1998, 292.
[317] Alev Çınar, *Modernity, Islam, and Secularism in Turkey: Bodies, Places, and Time*, University of Minnesota Press, Minneapolis and London, 2005, 9.
[318] Ibid., 9.
[319] Umut Azak, *Islam and Secularism in Turkey*, I. B. Tauris, New York, 2010, 17.
[320] M. Hakan Yavuz, *Secularism and Muslim Democracy in Turkey*, Cambridge University Press, New York, 2009, 8.
[321] Azak, 2010, 9.

Having surveyed all of the above information, this study remains primarily concerned with the plays of George Bernard Shaw and Orhan Asena in close context with the political and ideological standpoints they espoused and those of the periods in which they lived. It goes on to discover how the dialogues of differently politicized playwrights exemplify dissimilar philosophies and show signs of the political and ideological concerns—such as Socialism, Communism, Nationalism, Laicism, and Kemalism—which shaped the evolution of British and Turkish politics and ideology. Thus, the examination of the political and ideological evolution in both countries principally serves to shed a light upon the interrelation between our chosen subjects' literature and the political scene of their time. George Bernard Shaw's Socialist and Communist, Nationalist ideologies, and Orhan Asena's Republicanist, Laic, and Kemalist ideologies will provide the context through which we may compare and contrast their literary agendas.

CHAPTER 2: POLITICS IN DRAMA

All significant drama is, in direct proportion to its significance, either *explicitly* or *implicitly* political.[322]

Paul A. Cantor, in *Literature and Politics: Understanding the Regime* (1995), says "In the classical view, literature will tend to reflect the spirit of the regime under which it is written, the dominant opinions and constitutive political principles."[323] This is true when the writers feel themselves under pressure from a strict group of rulers and when they believe that their writings include something rejecting or opposing the state control of the government, something that can be described as *etatism*.[324] This *etatism* both comprises the internal and international politics of the country and the politics in language, education, literature, arts, and all the other majors.[325] It could be the opposite; that is, the authors can also produce a number of political works to raise their reactions to government repression.[326]

The urge to write something of the *pros and cons* of the political status quo has been seen within literature since the very beginning of humanity. In world literatures, there has been almost no author who has not touched the political regimes or governmental policies of the period or country in which he or she has lived. Hence, "no book is genuinely free from political bias."[327] Drama, as a major form of literature, has been no exception. Many dramatists, directly or indirectly, have tackled the political agenda of their countries—for the most part to stimulate public self-awareness. In both British and Turkish Drama, politics has been a major consideration, too.

---

[322] Darko Suvin, "Modes of Political Drama" in *The Massachusetts Review*, Vol. 13, No. 3 (Summer, 1972), 311.
[323] Paul A. Cantor, "Literature and Politics: Understanding the Regime" in *PS: Political Science & Politics Volume* 28, Issue 02 (June 1995), 192.
[324] Ibid., 192.
[325] Ibid., 192.
[326] Clinton Omohundro, "Politics and Literature" in *Amalgam*, Issue 1 (2006), 29.
[327] George Orwell, *Why I Write?*, 1946, 2. http://web.calstatela.edu/faculty/jgarret/308/readings-4.pdf, Accessed: 04.04.2014.

Politics in British Drama

In British literature, there appears to be a highly political background to the shaping of many theatrical works. From the very beginning of the Medieval Era up to the Postmodern Era, British drama has witnessed—whether in great extent or small, directly or indirectly—political performances and writings that have projected such politics-based phenomena as regimes, authorities, struggles, power relations, class conflicts, cruelties, oppressions, the ruled and the rulers etc. (whose genres have been re-named within differing time frames).[328] Such works have occasionally been titled as mysteries, moralities, or civic plays; they have been, at various times, occasional, epic, theatre of cruelty, in-yer-face, theatre of the oppressed, or even comedy of menace, but all of these may legitimately be considered under the umbrella term of "political theatre."[329]

The reason why we use the word 'performance' must be clarified in order to distinguish between the texts and the acts. As expressed by Laurie Postlewate et al., in the introduction to *Acts and Texts* (2007):

> For the Middle Ages and Renaissance—before the dissemination of the printed (much less the broadcast) word—meaning and power were created and propagated through public performance. By performance we mean here the actual, physical, visual, and audible manifestations of bodies and voices which communicated to their publics through symbolic systems and codes.[330]

In Medieval British Drama, it is a fact that nearly all literary art forms have something to do with Christian religion; the basics of theatre and performance during this period reflect the authority of Christian religion which was "a skeleton of the drama which, for a brief moment,

---

[328] Martin Banham, *The Cambridge Guide to Theatre*, Cambridge University Press, Cambridge, 1998, 91, 179.
[329] Ibid., 704. See also: Amelia Hower Kritzer, *Political Theatre in Post-Thatcher Britain*, Palgrave Macmillan, 2008, 18,25, 28.
[330] Laurite Postlewate and Wim Hüsken, eds., *Acts and Texts*, Rodopi, Amsterdam and New York, 2007, 7.

combined the verbal, musical and visual arts with the beliefs and faith of Christendom."[331] Its power as a sub-branch of politics was utilized through that most authoritative institution: Christianity. Thus, the politics was, for the most part, addressed to the public through some theatric performances to create self-awareness. In this context, medieval drama and performance in British literature describe all theatre, stage shows and performances fashioned in Britain over that thousand-year period as reflecting the power and authority of Christendom and embrace a range of such Biblical genres as liturgical drama, miracle plays, mystery plays, morality plays, farces, and masques.[332]

Taking into consideration Cantor's words that "what is omitted from a work of literature may be as important as what is included,"[333] we reach the unavoidable conclusion that the subjects which the theatric performances of Medieval Era embraced were highly significant indicators of the power of the authoritative institution. Thus, the performances, for the most part, "focused on crusades against the threat to Christianity from pagan and heretical groups,"[334] in which the power holders, in a way, "began to pay more attention to the spiritual needs of its own flock at home."[335] So, the basic theatre forms during Medieval Era were mainly performed in times of feasts and ceremonies; accordingly, in a way they were considered as the "symbols of power".[336] The performances represented the religious rules of those in authority, and were broadcast according to their wishes.[337] Such

---

[331] Lynette R. Muir, *The Biblical Drama of Medieval Europe*, Cambridge University Press, Cambridge, 1995, 1.
[332] Lee A. Jacobus, *The Compact Bedford Introduction to Drama*, Bedford/St. Martin's, Boston and New York, 2005, 143–47.
[333] Cantor, 1995, 194.
[334] Muir, 1995, 4.
[335] Ibid., 4.
[336] Alejandro Cañeque, "On Cushions and Chairs: The Ritual Construction of Authority in New Spain" in *Acts and Texts*, ed. Laurite Postlewate and Wim Hüsken, Rodopi, Amsterdam and New York, 2007, 102.
[337] Jacobus, 2005, 143–47.

performances were therefore seen as counteracting the threat to Christianity posed by heretical groups.[338]

Randy Martin, in one of his reviews, states "what is termed 'political theatre' seeks to turn its own situation into a project, that is, to enact through performance an account of the difference to the world that its politics could make",[339] the inevitable form of drama in those days being performance. This staging and acting by a group of people was in the beginning rejected by the medieval authorities, specifically by the churches who considered them "immoral";[340] however, the power holders and the rulers saw the fruits of didactic theatre and performance, and as rulers realized its political potential, theatre became "neither the exercise of power by cosmetic means nor the mask of power, but as an integral part of power and politics."[341]

Comprising the periods of the 9th to 14th centuries, the liturgical plays (together with prophet plays, passion plays, mysteries, and miracles)[342] included "sung Latin dramatizations of biblical incidents from both Old and New Testaments outside of the usual range of Christmas and Easter plays"[343] which addressed the public audiences "to show how meaning is always socially produced."[344] Thus, "the references to biblical drama ... [did] not merely serve the function of giving life to the protagonists but, rather, [drew] attention to the central dilemma facing any religious dramatist in late medieval England."[345] In the 15th century, mysteries—deriving from Latin *mysterium* meaning "secret

---

[338] Ibid., 143–47.
[339] Randy Martin, *Performance as Political Act: The Embodied Self*, Bergin & Garvey Publishers, 1990, 176.
[340] Patricia Blocksome, "The Birth, Death and Resurrection of Theatre: Religion's Cyclical Relationship with the Stage" in *Communicating Vocation*, ed. Rebecca Blocksome and Nagypál Szabolcs, Bgöi&Wscf-Cesr, Wien-Budapest, 2009, 138, 144.
[341] Cañeque, 2007, 102.
[342] Dennis Kennedy, ed., *The Oxford Companion to Theatre and Performance*, Oxford University Press, New York, 2010, 351–52.
[343] Muir, 1995, 28.
[344] David Coleman, "Reviewed Work: Defining Acts: Drama and the Politics of Interpretation in Late Medieval England by Ruth Nisse" in *Mystics Quarterly*, Vol. 34, No. 1/2 (January/April 2008), 79.
[345] Ibid., 79.

rite, secret worship; a secret thing"[346]—prevailed among the medieval routines which often were dramatized by affiliates of expert groups. The reflections of mysteries embraced the religious idealism of some saints, and, in extraordinary cases, even corresponded to blasphemous issues. In these plays, the performance, for the most part, encompassed the rituals, reality, and myth which embraced the general condition of Christendom at that time and of the English monarchy.[347] These performances discovered "the idea of the 'state' as the essential concept that unified and gave cohesion to the political community—an entity with a life of its own, distinct from both rulers and ruled, and able, in consequence, to call upon the allegiances of ... [contrarian thoughts]".[348] Hence, the theatre of Medieval Era, as a mirror of politics, and as a significant agent of power, played no small part in moulding the bond of public affairs in medieval political culture.[349]

On the other hand, through the 16th century, with its political, social and cultural turbulence and with the improvements in science and philosophy, the liturgical plays were replaced with novel plays and performances, because "the number of performances recorded for the fourteenth and early fifteenth centuries is [was] limited, partly because of the disasters of war, famine and plague which ravaged the countries of Western Europe at this time."[350] The changes within the political atmosphere, improvements in science, and interchanges between cultures introduced a new phase of theatre in which the Renaissance blossomed.[351] In Elizabethan England, theatre became the most influential form of cultural introspection, illustrating human relationships and particularly the relationship between community and

---

[346] mystery, Online Ethymology Dictionary, http://www.etymonline.com/index.php?term=mystery, Accessed: 04.04.2014
[347] Jacobus, 2005, 145–46.
[348] Postlewate et al., 2007, 103.
[349] Jacobus, 2005, 143–47.
[350] Muir, 1995, 32.
[351] Norman Jones, "The Politics of Renaissance England" in *A Companion to Renaissance Drama*, ed. Arthur F. Kinney, Blackwell Publishers, Massachusetts, 2002, 13

the state.[352] It is crucial to note that theatre performances shaped the socio-political situation in England during the dynasty of Elizabeth I.[353] As Darko Suvin argues in *Modes of Political Drama* (1972):

> Since all dramas deal with human relationships and attitudes, and all human relations and attitudes presuppose a community as their context and molder (even if the stage figures are gods, talking animals, Martians or Robinson Crusoes), defining drama is an exercise basically in defining politics.[354]

Theatre as an exercise in defining politics revolutionized the stages of Elizabethan England[355] and produced a highly explicit characterization which contrasted with the classical Greek and Roman plays. Taking a famous motto from Shakespeare's *As You like It*—"All the world's a stage"—Arthur F. Kinney emphasizes the metamorphoses in the evolution of the Renaissance Theatre and stage performance when he states that, "In the Renaissance, all the world was a stage and all actions—from private prayers ... to staged narratives ... were essentially enactments or re-enactments."[356] These inferences are in a way in parallel with what Darko Suvin argues with the words, "It would not be exaggerating to state that theatre and drama, as communal arts, are ontologically political, if politics means the health or sickness of the community which determines all human relationships in it."[357] Thus, the enactments in the Renaissance drama texts reveal some abstract ontological rehearsal of politics. Accordingly, William Shakespeare, who pioneered the Elizabethan stage, with Thomas Kyd, Ben Jonson,

---

[352] Gary B. Goldstein, "Did Queen Elizabeth Use the Theatre for Social and Political Propaganda?" in *The Oxfordian*, Volume VII, 2004, 153.
[353] Kimberly Reynolds Rush, *"Princes Upon Stages" The Theatricalization of Monarchy in The Reign of Elizabeth I, 1558–1569*, Unpublished PhD Dissertation, Louisiana State University, May 2015, 6.
[354] Suvin, 1972, 309.
[355] José Manuel González Fernández De Sevilla, "Political Strategies of Drama in Renaissance England" in *Proceedings of the I National conference of the Spanish Society for English Renaissance Studies*, ed. Javier Sánchez, Zaragoza: SEDERI, 1990. (SEDERI: Yearbook of the Spanish and Portuguese Society for English Renaissance Studies), 90–91.
[356] Arthur F. Kinney, ed., *A Companion to Renaissance Drama*, Blackwell Publishers, Massachusetts, 2002, 1.
[357] Suvin, 1972, 311.

Christopher Marlowe, Thomas Middleton, John Webster, Sidney Fletcher, and some other playwrights portray the hidden "health or the sickness" of Elizabethan England during the Renaissance.[358]

Norman Jones, in *The Politics of Renaissance England* (2002), starts with these words: "The English Renaissance took place against a political backdrop dominated by international conflict, dynastic questions, religious tension and economic confusion."[359] With this in mind, it should not be thought exceptional for the drama of the time to include the turbulences of dynasty, the religious apprehension, and social turmoil, inequalities and injustices. One of the very first plays during Elizabethan Era, Thomas Kyd's *The Spanish Tragedy* (1582–92)—in which more than a few brutal murders are portrayed and one of its characters symbolizes an epitome of Revenge—illustrates a classical drama highly influenced by Seneca.[360] Nevertheless, *The Spanish Tragedy* conceals some kind of political message within its words in which the audiences or readers are invited to be aware of the corruption of law and justice. As Simon Barker and Hilary Hinds observe, the protagonist of the play, Hieronimo's "distracted tearing of the petitioners signals a despair over the functions of the law which some critics have seen as a parallel with the situation in contemporary England",[361] and they continue, "The empty box of the Pedringano subplot is a powerful sign of symbols of justice and redemption in the hands of the cynical."[362]

These observations have implications regarding the legal and justice system of the Elizabethan Era and the corresponding *mimesis* of corruption.[363] The idea of creating awareness in people has been a

---

[358] Harold Bloom, ed., *Elizabethan Drama*, Chelsea House Publishers, New York, 2004, 1–26.
[359] Jones, 2002, 13.
[360] Eugene D. Hill, "Senecan and Vergilian Perspectives in The Spanish Tragedy" in *Renaissance Historicism*, eds. Arthur F. Kinney and Dan S. Collins, The University of Massachusets Press, Massachusetts, 1987, 108–112.
[361] Simon Barker and Hilary Hinds, eds., *The Routledge Anthology of Renaissance Drama*, Routledge, New York, 2003, 35.
[362] Ibid., 35.
[363] González Fernández De Sevilla, 1990, 90–91.

continuous aim of playwrights; however, the materials they have used are generally based on the cultural and social alterations of the period in which they lived. This standpoint is something which is also addressed by Randy Martin, "there can be no generic model for political theatre, since its own aesthetic practice is contingent on the cultural field in which it arises and attempts to intervene."[364]

The impossibility of a "generic model" for political theatre lies in the changeable thoughts, ideologies, philosophies, and pressures which people have. As change is a basic factor in human evolution, it is also in the realm of ideology, because "no ideologies and institutions are really fixed, eternal and sacred."[365] These ideological and political metamorphoses are depicted on the Elizabethan stage with differing descriptions. The political climate, the anxiety and the intolerance of the period are all treated by Christopher Marlowe, too.[366] In *Edward II* (1594), Marlowe "offers compelling evidence of the way that the Elizabethan theatres provided a forum for the representation and analysis of political and social circumstances that had an immediate resonance for their audiences."[367] Though agreed to be one of the first history plays, *Edward II* politically disparages the kingship of Edward II, who is depicted "as a weak king unable to mediate between his personal desires and his public duty [which] set up a number of conflicts that might have seemed entirely relevant in late Tudor England."[368] The politics, here, is not found so much in the depiction of a weak king as in the idea of political thinking. Marlowe thus transmits a message in which he plants the idea of Machiavellian "common good" and underpins the Rousseauan "social contract" and urges them both upon the ruled and the rulers. He produces a communal system to call attention to the regime at a time when "religious and ideological

---

[364] Martin, 1990, 176.
[365] Suvin, 1972, 311.
[366] Barker et al., eds., 2003, 114.
[367] Ibid., 114.
[368] Ibid., 114.

disagreement threatened the peace and forced the king to seek new ways of resolving the tensions."[369]

Its dramatic enactment of the deposition and murder of a king, its investigation of the cycle and circles of sovereignty, and its examination of the power of rhetoric to shape social and political realities, all lead to a question that was constantly debated in Marlowe's time, especially as Elizabeth aged and the problem of the succession loomed: if a monarch's power is derived from God, what rights have their subjects?[370]

The images demonstrated within the plays unravel the religious and political anxieties of Elizabethan Era.[371] The problem of the threat to peace and political tensions was much later rewritten by Bertolt Brecht who recreated *Edward II* using his own epic techniques.[372] The fact that "*Edward II* emerges as a radical play that would have disturbed and challenged its Elizabethan audiences"[373] is not an end for Elizabethan political drama, because the problem of religion (the quarrels between Protestantism and Catholicism) and dynasty shaped the literary aura of the period; politics and religion were indissociable since "politics could not easily be separated from religion."[374]

William Shakespeare in particular, in his histories and tragedies, touches on the same political matters, and highlights the idea of political thinking, even if his political posture is not apparent.[375] As Andrew Hadfield addresses in *Shakespeare and Renaissance Politics*, "although no one would dispute that Shakespeare's plays and poetry

---

[369] Jones, 2002, 19.
[370] Barker et al., eds., 2003, 115.
[371] Jane Dall, "The Stage and the State: Shakespeare's Portrayal of Women and Sovereign Issues in Macbeth and Hamlet" in *The Hanover Historical Review*, Volume 8, 2000. http://history.hanover.edu/hhr/00/hhr00_2.html Accessed: 11.11.2014
[372] Louise J. Laboulle, "A Note on Bertolt Brecht's Adaptation of Marlowe's "Edward II" in *The Modern Language Review*, Vol. 54, No. 2 (Apr 1959), 214–218.
[373] Barker et al., eds., 2003, 115.
[374] Andrew Hadfield, *Shakespeare and Renaissance Politics*, Arden Shakespeare, London, 2004, 3.
[375] Alexander Leggatt, *Shakespeare's Political Drama*, Routledge, London and New York, 1988, vii–viii.

have a political significance and are informed by contemporary political ideas, events and debates, few would be able to state with any confidence exactly what political position Shakespeare adopted."[376] The same analysis is cited by Annabel Patterson, who believes that it may perhaps be that, "because Shakespeare himself remained enigmatic on political issues, typically challenging the English system of hereditary monarchy, the law, or the constitution at the opening of a play, only to reinstate the status quo by its ending,"[377] that our understanding of Shakespearian use of politics in his magnum opuses might be strengthened.

In *Richard II* (1595), *Henry IV* (1597), *Henry V* (1599), and *Henry VI* (1591) for instance, Shakespeare emphasizes the throne struggles among the English successors[378] which echoes the Machiavellian point of view stressed in *The Prince*: "a founder who is concerned with the common good, as distinguished from a tyrant, cannot be blamed if he commits murder in order to achieve his good end."[379] However, what Shakespeare underlines is the fact that it is not the "common good" that the kings are fighting for, but their own "self-good". According to Andrew Hadfield, "this stubborn reality of English history, reproduced faithfully from Shakespeare's sources..., does not simply haunt the surviving records of the reigns of English kings, but was also directly related to the situation of the incumbent monarch, Elizabeth I."[380] Shakespeare, through his historical narrations, props up a Hobbesian view of human nature concerning the idea of the tie between the State and individuals reflecting his view of "war of every man against every man."[381] Therefore, "Shakespeare's representation of kings of all history

---

[376] Hadfield, 2004, 12.
[377] Annabel Patterson "Political Thought and the Theatre, 1580–1630" in *A Companion to Renaissance Drama*, ed. Arthur F. Kinney, Blackwell Publishers, Massachusetts, 2002, 26.
[378] Hadfield, 2004, 36–77.
[379] Strauss, 1958, 44.
[380] Hadfield, 2004, 40.
[381] Hobbes, 1998, 85.

plays is governed by the understanding that it is what kings do rather than what they are or claim to be that is important."[382]

Shakespeare's political representations do not just comprise the fights for the sake of monarch or dynasty; various socio-cultural implications are also touched upon in his other plays.[383] In *Othello* (1603) and *Merchant of Venice* (1596-98), Shakespeare addresses a completely different issue from those of his histories. As Allan Bloom and Harry V. Jaffa, in *Shakespeare's Politics* (1981) argue:

> Othello and Shylock are the figures who are the most foreign to the context in which they move and to the audience to which they were intended. In a sense, it is Shakespeare's achievement in the two plays to have made these two men—who would normally have been mere objects of hatred and contempt—into human beings who are unforgettable for their strength of soul.[384]

Shakespeare, through these plays, stresses several highly significant political problems of the period: racism, xenophobia and religious persecution.[385] Concentrating on the community's readiness for these prejudices and political identification, Bloom and Jaffa observe "there was no liberal ideology which constrained intelligent citizens to suppress or alter their first feelings towards foreigners or those of another color in favor of an attitude based upon reflection or abstract conviction rather than emotion";[386] a factor which may support the notion that Shakespeare probably aimed to generate a moderate political readiness for the community.

However, it is not insignificant to stress that an African Moor and a convert to Judaism symbolize the portrayals of anti-Black (even anti-

---

[382] Hadfield, 2004, 56.
[383] Leggatt, 1988, vii–viii.
[384] Allan Bloom and Harry V. Jaffa, *Shakespeare's Politics*, University of Chicago, Chicago and London, 1981, 14.
[385] Mika Nyoni, "The Culture of Othering: An Interrogation of Shakespeare's Handling of Race and Ethnicity in the Merchant of Venice and Othello" in *Greener Journal of Art and Humanities* Vol. 1, No. 1 (December 2011), 1–10.
[386] Allan Bloom et al., 1981, 41.

Muslim) and anti-Semitic views which prevailed during the period.[387] The socio-political or socio-cultural state of any period may remain unchanged for a long time, as Darko Suvin argues: "During the rare times of several generations of political stability, the ideological premises and institutional frameworks of the community present themselves to the audience's mind as something fixed, sacred and possibly eternal."[388] Therefore, it requires much effort to eradicate this "sacredness" from the minds of the people. In the Elizabethan era, the reflections of "fixed, sacred biases and divine right" and "a natural ally of royal absolutism in politics" were on the stages of many playwrights.[389] On the other hand, denoting Shakespeare's *Hamlet* (between 1599–1602) and *King Lear* (1606) as the two greatest plays, R. A. Foakes, in *Hamlet Versus Lear*, unearths the direct or indirect ties of these two plays with politics. Foakes states that Hamlet "became in the nineteenth century an important symbolic political figure, usually typifying the liberal intellectual paralyzed in will and incapable of action",[390] and he continues, "By contrast, *King Lear* was depoliticized, even by the radical Hazlitt, perhaps at that time because of a possible association with the mad old monarch, George III."[391]

Being a contemporary of Shakespeare, Ben Jonson also touches upon one of the central issues of the period in his *The Masque of Blackness* in which the masquers are masquerading as Africans. In this play, together with its sequel of 1608, *The Masque of Beauty*, Jonson synthesizes the politics of race and gender by which "these are exposed as an integral part of one of the key processes whereby political power itself was produced and maintained."[392] Thus, through the symbolic creation of gender discrimination, Jonson imagines the interracial problems which are also publicized in Shakespeare's various plays.[393]

---

[387] Nyoni, 2011, 3–6.
[388] Suvin, 1972, 311.
[389] González Fernández De Sevilla, 1990, 90.
[390] R. A. Foakes, *Hamlet Versus Lear*, Cambridge University Press, Cambridge, 1993, 6.
[391] Ibid., 6.
[392] Barker et al., eds., 2003, 223.
[393] Ibid., 223.

Again, in *Alchemist* (1610), Jonson expresses some political truths of the period, denoting such basic political or ideological phenomena as "absolute wealth, absolute deprivation; prince vs. private subject; a monarchy or a republic ('free state')";[394] though Annabel Patterson believes that these "are nevertheless representative of the way in which drama and political thought are usually related in early modern England—that is to say, not very satisfactorily."[395] Jeanette D. Ferreira-Ross, in *Jonson's Satire of Puritanism in The Alchemist* (2008), pays attention to existing references and the bases on which Jonson depicted the sarcasm of "religious cant"[396] in *the Alchemist* to underline the religious policy of England. The reason behind the inclusion of these political spectacles into the writings has been, in the main, to provoke or stimulate the public, or to use literature as propaganda tool "by which the political propaganda imbued with religious affect would be most widely propagated."[397]

Unfortunately, after the initial blossoming of the Renaissance in 1642, the theatres of England remained closed for eighteen years.[398] During the Restoration Era, predominantly due to the closure of theatres, playwrights were not generally prolific in generating plays; instead, as an inventive genre of the period, comedy was hosted by English playhouses. As Gerald MacLean observes, the Restoration is regarded "as an uneasy, brief settlement within longer-term political negotiations among Crown, Parliament, Church, and people, the struggles over which continue through the Revolution of 1688 to reverberate well into the eighteenth century and beyond."[399] However, from 1660 onwards because of the changes in politics and religion "literature was already

---

[394] Patterson, 2002, 25.
[395] Ibid., 25.
[396] Jeanette D. Ferreira-Ross, "Jonson's Satire of Puritanism in The Alchemist" in *Sydney Studies in English*, 17, 2008, 22.
[397] Postlewate et al., 2007, 49.
[398] Jean I. Marsden, "Restoration Drama" in *The Oxford Encyclopedia of British Literature*, ed. David Scott Kastan, Oxford University Press, Oxford and New York, 2006, 335.
[399] Gerald Maclean, ed., *Culture and Society in The Stuart Restoration*, Cambridge University Press, Cambridge, 1995, 3.

thoroughly politicized in ways that would have been unthinkable."[400] Andrew R. Walkling expresses the same view when he says that, "much of the literature—particularly the drama—of Restoration England was explicitly political, both in its conception and in its rhetoric."[401] The Restoration comedy, titled as comedy of manners, dealt first and foremost with members of the political and social patriciates.[402] The very first woman comedy writer, Aphra Behn, was introduced to the English stages. In *The Rover* (1677), for instance, Behn introduces the political struggles against the Puritans; thus, *The Rover* may be interpreted as a means of considering Behn's "present-day" political stance.[403]

Another significant playwright of the Restoration Era is William Congreve.[404] Richard Braverman, in one of his essays, emphasizes that "Congreve was a political creature, and political concerns find their way, openly or subtly into his works."[405] In his famous comedy, *The Way of the World* (1700), Congreve, though indirectly, comes near to an exposé of new socio-economic order created by James II, which especially conceptualizes the communal outburst against new property law.[406]

> Produced in 1700, poised on the brink of the new century, ... *The Way of the World* is a comedy of manners notable for its sophisticated language, graceful economy and acid wit. But the play is nevertheless profoundly political, registering at its deepest

---

[400] Ibid., 10.
[401] Andrew R. Walkling, "Politics and the Restoration masque: the case of Dido and Aeneas" in *Culture and Society in The Stuart Restoration*, ed. Gerald Maclean, Cambridge University Press, Cambridge, 1995, 52.
[402] Deborah Payne Fisk, ed., *The Cambridge Companion to English Restoration Theatre*, Cambridge University Press, Cambridge, 2000, 48-49.
[403] Vanessa Coloura, "Cavalier Ideals, Exile and Spectacle in The Rover and The Second Half of the Rover" in *Heroines and Heroes*, ed. Christopher Hart, Midrash Publications, West Midlands, 2008, 25-26.
[404] Maclean, ed., 1995, 6.
[405] Richard Braverman, "Capital Relations and The Way of the World" in *ELH* Vol. 52, No. 1 (Spring, 1985), 133.
[406] Ibid., 133.

level the sweeping economy and social changes of the seventeenth century.[407]

Besides comedy of manners, the other noteworthy genre during the Restoration Era was masque. As Andrew R. Walkling states "Restoration masques, like their Jacobean and Caroline counterparts, were addressed primarily to members of the political and social elite and sought to advise that audience about important contemporary issues."[408] This is what Gerald MacLean observes: "Restoration literature is characteristically political—not only—because it commonly addresses social and political issues with an irreverent attitude toward established authority—"[409] (underlining the fact that the social elite are those who represent the authority) "but also—because of the ways in which reading and writing had made public debate increasingly central to the political experience of ordinary people living through the social and cultural changes of the 1640s and 1650s"[410] (highlighting the significance of these social and political matters reflected to the ordinary people through literature).

Aiming "to 'unpack' the allegory *of Dido and Aeneas* in order to reveal a compelling pattern of specific political allusion,"[411] Walking explains the political representations of masques in the Restoration Era. He discusses the basics of censorship, or the concealments produced during the performances of those masques. Walking considers:

> the masque establishes a complex of differing types of allegorization, a multi-tiered representational structure which allows for the allegorical portrayal both of actual political personages, such as the king, and of institutions or corporate bodies, such as England or the Church, by characters on stage.[412]

---

[407] Ibid., 133.
[408] Walkling, 1995, 52.
[409] Maclean, ed., 1995, 11
[410] Ibid., 11.
[411] Ibid., 55.
[412] Ibid., 56.

Thus, politics is once more acted upon through the performances of highly popular masques; that is to say, "the central economic and political issue of the play[s] [or masques] turns, as so much in the later seventeenth century does, on the nature of sovereignty, the ultimate locus of power in the civil state."[413]

From the end of seventeenth to the beginning of eighteenth century, the political representation in drama shifted too much, and was replaced with more tangible and concrete dramatic performances.[414] During the reign of George I, II, III and IV, (that is, throughout the Romantic Era), the foundation of modern British drama was laid. As David Krasner emphasizes: "Modern drama epitomizes individualistic self-expression, revealing its nascent beginnings (though not yet fully formed) in the romantic movement of the early nineteenth century."[415] Within the social and cultural habitat of England, major changes blossomed; there appeared a huge growth in population, an increase in the number of working class people, and a breakthrough in industrialization and an unexpected rise in the emergence of a middle class.[416] "As had been the case in Elizabethan times, theatre was still used in the Romantic period as an instrument of politics at the very highest level."[417] The economic turbulence, the new social, cultural, and political climate was, directly or indirectly, mirrored within the new genres. As Frederick Burwick stresses, "While melodrama, novelty acts, spectacle, and special effects on stage entertained and distracted, prostitutes and pickpockets were at work in the audience"[418] an observation which suitably reveals the tragicomic atmosphere of England during the period.

Due to the lack of theatre works, the revitalization of the performing of previous works was emphasized in this period, and the existing plays

---

[413] Braverman, 1985, 134.
[414] J. L. Styan, *Restoration Comedy in Performance*, Cambridge University Press, Cambridge, 1986, 2.
[415] David Krasner, *A History of Modern Drama Volume I*, Wiley-Blackwell, West Sussex, 2012, 6.
[416] David Worrall, *Theatric Revolution*, Oxford University Press Inc., New York, 2006, 15–22.
[417] Ibid., 211.
[418] Frederick Burwick, *Romantic Drama*, Cambridge University Press, Cambridge, 2009, 5.

reinterpreted in order to integrate the characteristics of the Romantic Movement.[419] Thus, the plays welcomed such basics of Romanticism as emotion and instinct, equality, subjectivity, individualism, and predominantly nationalism. With the onset of the French Revolution, which staggered national identity throughout Europe, English stages hosted a revival of these new performances.[420] As Burwick observes: "National and ethnic stereotypes were appropriated blatantly as stock characters: Negro, Jew, Scotsman, Irishman, Frenchman, German, Italian were often prefabricated from prejudice".[421] As a consequence, the politics of nationalism was staged in playhouses with the re-performances of various plays, particularly those of Shakespeare's plays. David Worrall, in *Theatric Revolution* (2006), underlines many initiatives of the period which suppress any performance which may have possibly been thought to be unpleasant, destructive, responsive, politically erroneous or problematic as dogged by authorities.[422] Here, Worrall announces the prohibition of some excerpts of staged drama, and says that the "closet drama" was popularized during Romantic Era,[423] and indeed, he continues, "There were also other more politicized movements at work which tended to radicalize the social role of drama"[424] counting "political Parliamentary reform of the electoral franchise"[425] as a primary one among others.

The revolutionary change within the scope of drama continued during the reign of Queen Victoria.[426] The modern introduction of Romantic drama was strengthened during the Victorian Era.[427] The revolution in

---

[419] Gerald Gillespie, ed., *Romantic Drama*, John Benjamins Publishing Co., Amsterdam and Philadelphia, 1994, 155–56.
[420] Burwick, 2009, 1–13.
[421] Ibid., 33.
[422] Worrall, 2006, 36–37.
[423] Ibid., 36–37.
[424] Ibid., 57.
[425] Ibid., 58.
[426] Anthony Jenkins, *The Making of Victorian Drama*, Cambridge University Press, Melbourne, 1991, 9 and 14.
[427] Ibid., 1–9.

Victorian drama was nothing more than the "modernity" within its political or ideological jurisdiction. As Darko Suvin articulates:

> In the modern epoch all aesthetically significant political drama has been on the revolutionary side; insofar as it has been significant and lasting, it is neither drama using politics for sensational subject-matter, nor (yet worse) politics using drama as a servant of whatever doctrine the powers-that-be happen to be promulgating.[428]

As Charles Dickens highlights in the very first paragraph of *A Tale of Two Cities* (1859), the Victorian Era "was the best of times, and the worst of times"[429] in respect with the social, cultural, economic, and political standpoint.[430] There appeared the huge impacts of industrialization; a huge population flourished in London, specifically those coming from rural areas.[431] During the reign of Queen Victoria, literature and theatre prospered as new playhouses were built and new theatre schools were founded. A number of political and social reforms were introduced. It was, by and large, an era which publicized the middle class, and began to confront the previous order of England.[432] Women challenged the notion of *Angels in the House*, antagonized against the old order, and produced highly fruitful literary works.[433]

Victorian drama, entitled as "verse or closet drama", for the most part projected the social problems of the period: the struggles of working class, the struggles of women against male dominance, the idea of equality, the problem of gender, education, religion, political turbulences, and civil liberties of classes.[434] In a way, the theatre of

---

[428] Suvin, 1972, 324.
[429] Charles Dickens, *A Tale of Two Cities*, Fictionwise e book, 3.
[430] James Eli Adams, *A History of Victorian Literature*, Wiley-Blackwell, West Sussex, 2009, 5.
[431] Ibid., 2–3.
[432] Ibid., 2.
[433] Ibid., 8.
[434] Grace Kehler, "Between Action and Inaction: The "Performance" of the Prima Donna in Eliot's Closet Drama" in *Victorian Recollections of Romanticism*, ed. Joel Faflak and Julia M. Wright, State University of New York Press, Albany, 2004, 66.

Victorian Era was a "theatre of ideas", as expressed by Anthony Jenkins, "the theatre itself had grown respectable and a drama of ideas, adapted (more or less) to middle class taste, had its place in that respectability."[435] The authors commonly endeavoured to give a picture of something new against the radicalism of Romanticism[436] which brought "a significant enabling factor in the deployment of drama, a change which amounted to a transition in the material basis of the national infrastructure of public expression."[437] However, in many writings of Victorian literature, the inescapable impacts of the previous era loom large. During the Victorian Era, "with all their limitations, the plays of Bulwer, Robertson, Gilbert, Jones, Pinero, and Wilde illustrate, in vivid ways, the differing conditions each writer sought to overcome."[438]

One of the foremost playwrights of the Victorian epoch, Oscar Wilde, in his well-known illustration of comedy of manners *The Importance of Being Earnest* (1895), "Wilde's most famous and—posthumously—most successful play,"[439] touches directly upon the political situation in England. As an Irish-born British playwright, "Wilde lived through an economic transition from industrial production to high mass consumption that would have global effects."[440] Drawing an outline of Victorian England, the play "exposes the immorality and hypocrisy, and the immense self-satisfaction, of the English ruling classes, and ... yet contrives to show glimpses of the charm and elegance, the allure, of a way of life which has no future."[441]

---

[435] Jenkins, 1991, 1.
[436] Joel Faflak and Julia M. Wright, eds., *Victorian Recollections of Romanticism*, State University of New York Press, Albany, 2004, 8 and 16.
[437] Worrall, 2006, 274.
[438] Jenkins, 1991, 29.
[439] Russel Jackson, "The Importance of Being Earnest" in *The Cambridge Companion to Oscar Wilde*, ed. Peter Raby, Cambridge University Press, Cambridge, 1997, 161.
[440] Regenia Gagnier, "Wilde and The Victorians" in *The Cambridge Companion to Oscar Wilde*, ed. Peter Raby, Cambridge University Press, Cambridge, 1997, 20.
[441] Peter Raby, ed., *The Cambridge Companion to Oscar Wilde*, Cambridge University Press, Cambridge, 1997, 154.

In view of Wilde's characters and dialogues, it would be appropriate to echo that the revolutionary purpose in his drama lies in the antagonism against traditional Victorian principles; for that reason, in *The Importance of Being Earnest*, Wilde puts across deep-seated politics. For instance, Ronald Knowles observes that "in *The Importance of Being Earnest* all food symbolizes the class distinction and separation of capitalist bourgeois society and the fissiparous distinctions of fashion within it,"[442] distinctions which institute the inequalities or class privileges succumbed within the Victorian socio-political state. On the other hand, Russell Jackson argues from the style and tone of Wilde's language that "it is in fact impossible to discuss the play's treatment of authority—its politics, in fact—without considering the style of the speakers."[443] Michael Patrick Gillespie discusses the same point addressing the contradictory evolutions within the play; to him "the entire structure of *The Importance of Being Earnest* rests upon diverse and often contradictory points of view, and the witty dialogue of its characters continually reinforces the complexity of that condition."[444] The suggestion of political opposition against conventional Victorianism comes into view within *The Importance of Being Earnest* in close contact with the reflection of women and their political stance.[445] In the play, "The women, in fact, create even more ambiguity and—in terms of societal norms—aberrance than do the men",[446] thus contrasting the cliché of Victorian way of life, and the politics of gendered roles, for "[though] it first invites and then frustrates traditional expectations, the play clearly encourages its audience to

---

[442] Ronald Knowles, "Bunburying with Bakhtin: A Carnivalesque Reading of the Importance of Being Earnest" in *Oscar Wilde*, ed. Harold Bloom, Infobase Publishing, 2011, 51.
[443] Russell Jackson, "The Importance of Being Earnest" in *The Cambridge Companion to Oscar Wilde*, ed. Peter Raby, Cambridge University Press, Cambridge, 1997, 169.
[444] Michael Patrick Gillespie, "The Victorian Impulse in Contemporary Audiences: The Regularization of the Importance of Being Earnest" in *Oscar Wilde*, ed. Harold Bloom, Infobase Publishing, 2011, 59–60.
[445] Gillespie, 2011, 63–64.
[446] Ibid., 64.

accommodate multiplicity when moving through the various stages of apprehension that one experiences."[447]

Regenia Gagnier states "the Victorians sought control of the physical world through the use of science and technology, with a faith in the objectivity of their knowledge, and they sought political emancipation, with a faith in the liberal tenets of individual freedom, equality and autonomy."[448] The thought of individual and liberal freedom and equality is the fundamental propaganda addressed by the other pioneer of Victorian drama, George Bernard Shaw, whose "whole way of thinking about life was transformed when, in September 1882, he listened to a lecture by Henry George, the American author of *Progress and Poverty*."[449] Shaw, in nearly all of his plays, tackles the social illnesses of communities, and the gender equality issue and the subject of poverty are basic to all his writings. As articulated by Jenkins, "That common topic and the politics of each decade—particularly as they touched the Woman Question—create a continuous sub-plot which vivifies each writer's struggle to come to terms with conventional or idiosyncratic ideals that barred the way to a drama of ideas."[450] Just like Oscar Wilde, Bernard Shaw is one of the greatest Irish dramatists, "whose speeches to the Fabian Society had restructured Wilde's aesthetic socialism, maintained that any kind of censorship denied man's right to question social, economic, and political conventions."[451] In many plays of Shaw, the characters "and all the others in [Wilde's] *The Importance of Being Earnest* stand, with their reformation of social institutions and perfect amour-propre, in Victorian garb vacillating between Modernism and post-Modernism."[452] The crucial political deportment of Shaw and the manifestation of his political ideologies within his plays will be further discussed in chapters three and four.

---

[447] Ibid., 62.
[448] Gagnier, 1997, 19.
[449] A. M. Gibbs, *A Bernard Shaw Chronology*, Palgrave, New York, 2001, 3.
[450] Jenkins, 1991, 29.
[451] Ibid., 29.
[452] Gillespie, 2011, 68.

The tone of revolution in Victorian theatre continued. At the end of 19th and through the beginning of 20th century, "ideas which possessed an entire century, like the status of women, a hero's idea of chivalric service, money's allure (which gaudy billboards might have alliterated as women, war, and wealth), [which] could not be examined seriously until the theatre learned to be serious about itself"[453] revolutionized with the contributions of some brave playwrights. Throughout the 20th century British drama and the playwrights were profoundly affected by "the massive social changes resulting from two world wars, the need for national reappraisal with loss of Britain's imperial role, together with the advances of technology and increasing urbanization."[454] Bernard Shaw and Henrik Ibsen are the principal pioneers of modern theatre, with Bernard Shaw himself being strongly affected by Ibsen.[455] However, within modern British drama, "Bernard Shaw dominates the theatre from 1890 right through to the Second World War, and his influence can still be felt up to the mid-1950s."[456] Christopher Innes, in *Modern British Drama* (1990), elucidates some of the political content not only Bernard Shaw's writings,[457] but also in John Galsworthy's political stage,[458] D. H. Lawrence's agitprop theatre,[459] Sean O'Casey's expressive plays,[460] John Arden's epic revelations,[461] David Edgar's agitprop and socialism,[462] Harold Pinter's comedy of menace,[463] Peter Barnes's politics of comedy,[464] and Carlyl Churchill's feminist plays.[465]

Since George Bernard Shaw's political presentations will be dealt with in detail in chapters three and four, here we shall, for the most part,

---

[453] Jenkins, 1991, 1–2.
[454] Innes, 1990, 1.
[455] Innes, 1990, 2–3.
[456] Ibid., 3.
[457] Ibid., 39.
[458] Ibid., 65.
[459] Ibid., 69.
[460] Ibid., 75.
[461] Ibid., 137.
[462] Ibid., 179.
[463] Ibid., 279.
[464] Ibid., 297.
[465] Ibid., 460.

assess those playwrights who touched politics other than Bernard Shaw. For instance with the depiction of prison conditions and with an urge to alter the contemporary political situation of Churchill's new Liberal government, John Galsworthy, through *Justice* (1910), "not only focused on public opinion, but had a central role in political decision-making."[466] Dramatizing "the rights of individual",[467] Galsworthy expressed a Shavian or "a Fabian perspective".[468] As Cary M. Mazer observes, in Galsworthy's depictions, "The political-economic dramas are always seen through the lens of the human agents forced to act within them, often at the expense of political analysis,"[469] and she continues, "Even in *Justice*, his most explicitly agitational play, Galsworthy's politics are Dickensian: seeking reform through exposing social ills, rather than contemplating, let alone proposing, systemic change."[470] D. H. Lawrence, "deliberately presenting 'the single human individual' in opposition to 'all these social beings' of Galsworthy's,… concentrates exclusively on personal relations and passions".[471] Having "no explicit political dimension",[472] Lawrence's plays pay attention to the notion that "the real is not idealized".[473] In Lawrence's agitprop, "The harshness of working class is emphasized".[474]

Being one of the contemporaries of D. H. Lawrence, Sean O'Casey depicts the working class; in *The Dublin Trilogy* (1920–26) his "direct use of political events struck a new note in British Drama".[475] As Ronald Ayling maintains, O'Casey's intention was to "startle, shock, even scandalize Irish audiences into questioning inherited political and

---

[466] Ibid., 65.
[467] Ibid., 65.
[468] Ibid., 66.
[469] Cary M. Mazer, "Granville Barker and the Court Dramatists" in *A Companion to Modern British and Irish Drama 1880–2005*, ed. Mary Luckhurst, Blackwell Publishing Ltd, Victoria, 2006, 79.
[470] Ibid., 80.
[471] Innes, 1990, 69.
[472] Ibid., 69.
[473] Ibid., 71.
[474] Ibid., 71.
[475] Ibid., 75.

religious beliefs and, indeed, reverential national attitudes on all levels of public life".[476] Though from a differing perspective, John Osborne also "startles", "shocks" and even "scandalizes" his audiences, striking the subject of social illness into their minds with his *Look Back in Anger* (1956). Hailed by Arthur Miller "as the only modern, English play",[477] *Look Back in Anger* portrays "four main characters [that] are clearly divided on class lines, in which sex equals status".[478] As Declan Kiberd expresses in *Reinventing England* (2006):

> *Look Back in Anger* is a protest against a society in which the age of heroes has been replaced by that of the installment plan, and in which the writing of tragedy has had to make way for farce. The struggle of a protagonist against an immovable object has given way to a struggle against a ridiculous object. What is presented is not the old revolt of the proletarian against a tyrannical aristocracy, but rather the complaint of a frustrated lower-middle class against the failure of its overlords to define any code at all, around which the community could conduct a debate about who should inherit England.[479]

The push for writing the socio-political and socio-cultural panorama of Britain divulges Osborne's "inversion of the Shavian model"[480] in which culture and politics are the chief mechanisms of the societal evolution. This view is addressed by Stephen Lacey, uttering "the significance of *Look Back in Anger* lay more in its impact on the realignment of culture and politics in the mid-point of the decade than in its direct contribution to the development of British drama and theatre."[481] That

---

[476] Jean Chothia, quoted in "Sean O'Casey's Powerful Fireworks" in *A Companion to Modern British and Irish Drama 1880–2005*, ed. Mary Luckhurst, Blackwell Publishing Ltd, Victoria, 2006, 125.
[477] Innes, quoted in, 1990, 98.
[478] Ibid., 99.
[479] Declan Kiberd, "Reinventing England" in *A Companion to Modern British and Irish Drama 1880–2005*, ed. Mary Luckhurst, Blackwell Publishing Ltd, Victoria, 2006, 29.
[480] Innes, 1990, 105.
[481] Stephen Lacey, "When Was the Golden Age? Narratives of Loss and Decline: John Osborne, Arnold Wesker and Rodney Ackland" in *A Companion to Modern British and Irish Drama 1880–2005*, ed. Mary Luckhurst, Blackwell Publishing Ltd, Victoria, 2006, 164.

kind of delineation is also dealt with by John Arden, in whose drama the social problems are melted within the political and epic traditions, revealing something Brechtian.[482] Mary Brewer accepts that "Arden has always been a political radical, wary of authority and overarching social institutions".[483] This idea is frequently depicted within his plays, because Arden was in the view that "any play that deals with people in a society must necessarily be a political one".[484] Christopher Innes, on the other hand, touches upon Arden's naturalistic portrayal of social hierarchies and order, and to him:

> The opposition between positive anarchy and negative order is basic to almost all of Arden's drama. Anarchy is approved as Dionysian (*The Workhouse Donkey*), individualistic (the "kink" in perfect philosophical circles, *Left-Handed Liberty*), intuitive, asymmetrical and curvilinear (*Ars Longa, The Hero Rises Up*), a Celtic and female principle (*Island of the Mighty*)—all adjectives which recur in Arden's critical writing. By contrast, order includes rationalism and logic, which are characterized as rectilinear, Roman and masculine, as well as moral repression and religious or class hierarchies.[485]

A contemporary of John Arden, Edward Bond is another playwright who "has adapted Brecht's principles".[486] Believing that "Literature is a social act,"[487] Bond attempts to justify the individualistic freedom in a way "to free the individual from social repression".[488] According to Michael Patterson, "Edward Bond is a playwright who perhaps more

---

[482] Innes, 1990, 137–40.
[483] Mary Brewer, "Empire and Class in the Theatre of John Arden and Margaretta D'Arcy" in *A Companion to Modern British and Irish Drama 1880-2005*, ed. Mary Luckhurst, Blackwell Publishing Ltd, Victoria, 2006, 156.
[484] Brewer, quoted in, 2006, 156.
[485] Innes, 1990, 142.
[486] Ibid., 156.
[487] Michael Patterson, quoted in "Edward Bond: Maker of Myths" in *A Companion to Modern British and Irish Drama 1880-2005*, ed. Mary Luckhurst, Blackwell Publishing Ltd, Victoria, 2006, 409.
[488] Innes, 1990, 162.

than any other contemporary British and Irish dramatist throws into relief the differences between the modes of communication of conventional politics and of the theatre".[489] This point of view is again addressed by Innes, who concludes that "all his plays are based on the same political analysis. Social institutions, originally developed for the protection of individuals, become self-perpetuating. Law and religion, mores and morality now have no function but moulding individuals to serve their needs".[490] Bond's political theatre is addressed by Patterson, who holds the view that, "Bond is an intensely political figure, anti-authoritarian, utterly committed to the relief of human suffering and to the alleviation of man's cruelty to man, occupying a position that might be loosely termed humane Marxism".[491]

Another name, David Edgar, is one of the other pioneers of British drama of "agitation and propaganda"[492] which was thought to be "self-consciously addressing the social, political and cultural state of the nation"[493] by Edgar himself. David Pattie observes the general condition of 20th century Britain within "a society trembling on the point of destruction"[494] in which "David Edgar's *Destiny* (1976) anatomized the conditions under which the radical right might begin to assume power".[495] These political depictions are the basic denotations that embraced Edgar's position and caused him to be viewed as a "political playwright".[496] Categorizing Edgar into political theatre experts, John Bull suggests:

---

[489] Patterson, 2006, 409.
[490] Innes, 1990, 163.
[491] Patterson, 2006, 410.
[492] Innes, 1990, 179–80.
[493] John Deeney, quoted in "David Hare and Political Playwriting: Between the Third Way and the Permanent Way" in *A Companion to Modern British and Irish Drama 1880–2005*, ed. Mary Luckhurst, Blackwell Publishing Ltd, Victoria, 2006, 506.
[494] David Pattie, "Theatre since 1968" in *A Companion to Modern British and Irish Drama 1880–2005*, ed. Mary Luckhurst, Blackwell Publishing Ltd, Victoria, 2006, 386.
[495] Ibid., 386.
[496] Maria DiCenzo, "John McGrath and Popular Political Theatre" in *A Companion to Modern British and Irish Drama 1880–2005*, ed. Mary Luckhurst, Blackwell Publishing Ltd, Victoria, 2006, 420.

> The great thread through all his work was politics, individual and collective, but the overall effect of his dramaturgies was to steer him away from the kind of socialist realism that had been a staple of the earlier generation of committed leftist writers such as Arnold Wesker, and left him with no obvious English model.[497]

The idea that Edgar's political depictions reveal a fresh kind of realism is stressed by Innes giving David Edgar's own statements:

> These qualities substantially justify Edgar's claim to have created a new style of realism, where spectators "would recognize the characters from the inside, but be able, simultaneously, like a sudden film-cut from close-up to wide-angle, to look at how these individual journeys were defined by the collective journey of an epoch".[498]

In this society that "trembled on the point of destruction", the interrelation between power and people reveals the conflicts of political ideologies. Placing David Hare among the "writers of the left",[499] Stephen Lacey discusses the destructive impact of World War II on the British stage, stressing the dichotomy between "European fascism"[500] and leftist writers. David Pattie regards David Hare's *Plenty* (1978) as a radical depiction of the politics which "echoed a wider sense of social disintegration in stories of individual, personal despair".[501] This social disintegration is addressed by Innes paying attention to Hare's "bleak depictions of modern society".[502] Maria DiCenzo counts David Hare among the "socialist and political playwrights",[503] and Innes stresses that Hare's social and populist ideology is revealed through his drama by his subtle depiction of "the absence of ideals and death of innocence

---

[497] John Bull, "Left in Front: David Edgar's Political Theatre" in *A Companion to Modern British and Irish Drama 1880–2005*, ed. Mary Luckhurst, Blackwell Publishing Ltd, Victoria, 2006, 442.
[498] Innes, 1990, 189.
[499] Lacey, 2006, 170.
[500] Ibid., 170.
[501] Pattie, 2006, 386.
[502] Innes, 1990, 205.
[503] DiCenzo, 2006, 420.

in modern society".[504] John Deeney, in *David Hare and Political Playwriting* (2006), emphasizes that Hare's writings pay a great attention to the direct depiction of British politics, from "wealth", "power", "national milieu", "capitalism", "Thatcherism", "postwar consensus",[505] to "bipolar opposites of Britain", "The Church of England", "the English legal system", and "the Labour party".[506] In one of his speeches, Hare explained why he used theatre as an agent of propaganda: "And I write about politics because the challenge of communism, in however debased and ugly a form, is to ask whether the criteria by which we have been brought up are right".[507]

Though regarded by Innes as "confusingly unpolitical",[508] Harold Pinter's plays also embrace the subjects of power, propaganda, and politics. Mary Luckhurst, in *Torture in the Plays of Pinter*, underlines the link between torture, governmental policies, and democracy[509] by which she sets the conclusion: "Pinter's fascination with power politics, cruelty and violence is clear in his earliest plays: *The Birthday Party* (1957) ... *The Room* (1957) ... *The Dumb Waiter* (1959) ... *The Caretaker* (1960) ... and *The Hothouse* (1958)".[510] Thus, Pinter's political representations evoke what Ruby Cohn calls the "system" that Pinter creates.[511] However, Innes understands this system in terms of a "a shift of attitude" rather than a "a change of theme", insisting that, "[Pinter's] political involvement represents a moral commitment, rather than a belief that the stage can change the world".[512] Though Pinter articulated that: "To engage in politics seemed to me futile",[513] his works written much later, namely *One for the Road* (1984) and

---

[504] Innes, 1990, 206.
[505] Deeney, 2006, 430.
[506] Ibid., 431.
[507] Deeney, quoted in, 2006, 432.
[508] Innes, 1990, 279.
[509] Mary Luckhurst, "Torture in the Plays of Pinter" in *A Companion to Modern British and Irish Drama 1880–2005*, ed. Mary Luckhurst, Blackwell Publishing Ltd, Victoria, 2006, 358.
[510] Ibid., 358-59.
[511] Ruby Cohn, "The World of Harold Pinter" in *The Tulane Drama Review*, Vol. 6, No. 3 (Mar 1962), 67.
[512] Innes, 1990, 280.
[513] Innes, quoted in, 1990, 280.

Mountain Language (1988), reveal openly political subjects.[514] David Pattie stresses that Pinter's last plays represent "the way in which power distorts and deforms both the powerful and the powerless."[515]

Being one of the contemporaries of Harold Pinter, a well-known feminist playwright, Caryl Churchill is among those who address the "power" phenomenon. Reflecting "sexual politics",[516] Churchill's *Cloud Nine* (1979) at the same time provokes "socialist feminist critiques of patriarchy and imperialism."[517] Kate Dorney, in *The Changing Language of Modern British Drama* (2009), writes:

> she generally displays more awareness of the power dynamics of interaction.... In common with Brenton, Hare and Edgar, Churchill's characters are never lost for words, but the explicit analysis of language and power suggests this is because the people she is writing about are already in a marginalized position and need someone to speak on their behalf, so they might as well have someone speaking articulately.[518]

The modern portrayal of power, politics, autocracy, agitation, torture, and propaganda has been shaped through the depictions of many playwrights. Though the settings, *zeitgeist*, characterization, set and stage-crafts are all unique to their own origin, drama has been unitedly seen as a tool or agent to protest against "undesirable realities". In the history of British Drama, the emergence of politics and power has witnessed some evolutionary improvements encompassing the social, cultural, economic, and political changes in society.[519]

---

[514] Ibid., 283.
[515] Pattie, 2006, 390.
[516] Innes, 1990, 461.
[517] Elin Diamond, "Caryl Churchill: Feeling Global" in *A Companion to Modern British and Irish Drama 1880–2005*, ed. Mary Luckhurst, Blackwell Publishing Ltd, Victoria, 2006, 476.
[518] Kate Dorney, *The Changing Language of Modern English Drama 1945–2005*, Palgrave Macmillan, Hampshire, 2009, 159.
[519] Christopher Innes, *Modern British Drama*, Cambridge University Press, Cambridge, 1990, xxxiv–484.

Politics in Turkish Drama[520]

Metin And classifies the history of Turkish theatre into four vital eras; the first era of the Turkish theatre is the "Traditional Turkish Theatre" which "over the centuries, in both villages, and in cities, was improved by the Turkish people with their own creative power, far from foreign influences, and having its own origin".[521] The second era is titled as "Turkish Theatre in the Tanzimat[522] and Istibdat[523] Era" which comprises the years 1839–1908; the third one is titled as "Turkish Theatre in the Meşrutiyet[524] Era" which overlaps the years 1908–1923; and the last one is entitled as "Republican Turkish Theatre" which encompasses the period 1923–1973.[525] The subsequent period of Turkish Drama, which comprises the years starting from 1973 until the present day, is referred to either as Republican Turkish Drama or (by some scholars) as Modern Turkish Drama.

Many researchers and intellectuals including Refik Ahmet Sevengil, Niyazi Akı, Metin And, Özdemir Nutku, Melahat Özgü, Sevda Şener, Ayşegül Yüksel, and Aslıhan Ünlü (among others) have dealt with the origins of Turkish Drama and have contributed to bringing the theatric manuscripts and sources to the modern generation.[526] The origins of traditional drama have been linked to pre-Ottoman and even to pre-

---

[520] All the Turkish quotations in this part have been translated by the author into English.
[521] Metin And, *Meşrutiyet Döneminde Türk Tiyatrosu*, Türkiye İş Bankası Kültür Yayınları, Ankara, 1971, 7.
[522] "The period from 1839 to 1876 is known in Ottoman history as the Tanzimat (literally, reorganization) and marks the most intensive phase of nineteenth century Ottoman reformist activity. During these years, the inspiration for reforms came not from the sultans but from Europeanized Ottoman bureaucrats, the French knowers, who were shaped by the institutions established by Mahmud II" (Cleveland et al., 82).
[523] It literally means "the period of autocracy". It encompasses the reign of Abdulaziz and Abdulhamid II.
[524] "Figuratively speaking, the Ottoman Empire entered the twentieth century on 23 July 1908, the day Sultan Abdülhamid II (r.1876–1909) restored the constitution he had shelved thirty years earlier" (Ahmed 49).
[525] Ibid., 7.
[526] See Sevengil's *Tanzimat Tiyatrosu*, Akı's *Türk Tiyatro Edebiyatı Tarihi*, And's *Geleneksel Türk Tiyatrosu* and other works, Nutku's *Dünya Tiyatrosu Tarihi*, Şener's *Gelişim Sürecinde Türk Tiyatrosu*, Yüksel's *Haldun Taner Tiyatrosu*, Ünlü's *Türk Tiyatrosunun Antropolojisi*.

Islam Turkic lifestyles and cultural milieu.[527] Just like any other nation's theatric evolution, the first theatric performances of the Turkish people were held within some significant days which welcomed certain "rituals", "ceremonies", and "festivities".[528] These "theatrical plays", for the most part, took their origin from "ceremonies held in the name of God for such reasons as the product fertility, plenty of offspring of animals, and revival of nature".[529] Sevda Şener, in *Moliere ve Türk Komedyası* (1974), believes that the traditional Turkish theatrical plays are "folk motives influenced by the eulogia of the generating and alive power of nature".[530] Aslıhan Ünlü articulates that these theatrical plays were predominantly performed by pre-Islamic Turkic tribes who, for the most part, applied basic tenets of Shamanism;[531] however, Özdemir Nutku, pointing out that various parallel theatrical plays were very much affected by Islamic, Anatolian, and Seljuk heritages, establishes in *Dünya Tiyatrosu Tarihi* (1993) that traditional Turkish theatre was fashioned after the conquest of Istanbul; and hence the original influences behind traditional theatre were largely shaped through Islamic and Ottomanic culture and art.[532]

Nutku observes that along with increased trade opportunities, the cultural exchange with European countries improved, and thus the Ottoman Empire united Asia and Europe, gathering Muslims and Christians under the rule of a single state.[533] Taking Nutku's studies as a standpoint, we observe that the traditional Turkish drama—which can also be termed Ottoman Drama—began in the 15th century and continued its progression till the end of the 17th century in the Ottoman

---

[527] Enver Töre, "Türk Tiyatrosunun Kaynakları" in *Turkish Studies International Periodical For the Languages*, Literature and History of Turkish or Turkic, Volume 4, Nos. I–II (Winter 2009), 2183–85.
[528] Ünlü, 2006, 65–66.
[529] Ibid., 66.
[530] Sevda Şener, "Moliere ve Türk Komedyası" in *Tiyatro Araştırmaları Dergisi*, Sayı: 5, 1974, 26.
[531] Ünlü, 2006, 55–57.
[532] Özdemir Nutku, *Dünya Tiyatrosu Tarihi*, Cilt 1, Remzi Kitabevi, İstanbul, 1993, 193–94.
[533] Ibid., 194.

Turkey.[534] To Özdemir Nutku, of all Islamic countries, Turkey is the one in which the most developed theatrical plays have been performed, and the one that has generated and reformulated theatrical genres from homegrown plays.[535] From the 15th to 17th century, in the Ottoman Empire, it may be observed that the theatrical performances were in the form of "festivities" or "ceremonies" in which artists, illusionists, jugglers, magicians, acrobats, etc. were the basic performers.[536] The reasons for these festivities or ceremonies were changeable: the emergence of military expedition, the birth and circumcision of the sultan's children, victories and triumphs, and some other private conditions.[537] Being completely unwritten, these theatrical plays mirrored the "autocracy" and "power" of the governors.[538] The goal of each ceremony was a political one. Sibel Özbudun expresses this view by laying emphasis on the definition of ceremony: "ceremonies are practices that enable the government to enhance its existence through mythology/cosmogony and to reinforce hierarchy".[539] These ceremonies were thus political performances that gathered a great number of people; as a consequence, "one of the other aims of these festivities and ceremonies was to bring together a majority of people from all classes, and all faiths, and enable a collective participation which is fundamental to the art of drama."[540]

Aslıhan Ünlü, in *Türk Tiyatrosunun Antolojisi* (2006), says that traditional Turkish theatre consists of the dramatic demonstrations in Ottoman festivities, the stories told by encomiasts (*meddah*), *Karagöz* shadow plays, and light comedies (*ortaoyunu*).[541] Metin And, in *Türk Tiyatrosunun Evreleri* (1983) states that one of the foremost genres of

---

[534] Ibid., 194.
[535] Ibid., 194.
[536] Ibid., 194.
[537] Nazlı Miraç Ümit, "Çadırlardan Saraylara Türk Tiyatrosunun Sahneleri" in Art-Sanat Journal Vol 1 (2014), 49–50.
[538] Serdar Öztürk, "Karagoz Co-Opted: Turkish Shadow Theatre of the Early Republic (1923-1945)" in *Asian Theatre Journal*, Volume 23, Number 2 (Fall 2006), 294.
[539] Sibel Özbudun, *Ayinden Törene*, Anahtar Yayınları, İstanbul, 1997, 120.
[540] Nutku, 1993, 194.
[541] Ünlü, 2006, 73.

the traditional theatrical plays was eulogy show in Ottoman culture and entertainment life that was performed by *Meddah*s.[542] While Metin And signifies that *Meddah* is "a narrative form",[543] Özdemir Nutku conveys that *Meddah* can be considered as "a solo performance"[544] which greatly affects people and educates them. Though there is insufficient data on the narratives of *Meddah*s, from the scripts of And and Nutku we may conclude that these story-tellers generally narrated "heroic epics, religious issues and historical events",[545] and that their narrations were "imitative, realistic, and illusionistic"[546] in terms of their subject matter. However, from Metin And's research we learn that in the 18th century, *Meddah*s were appointed as policy-makers in government circles.[547] The same information is revealed by Özdemir Nutku, and to him, in the 18th century, the storytellers did politics while narrating stories in the coffee houses; in a way, *Meddah*s had taken on the task of being the official gazette that announced the new decisions of the Sultan or viziers to the public.[548]

Being another genre of traditional drama, puppet shows (*kukla*) are considered to have come from Central Asia much before the introduction of shadow shows (*gölge oyunu*) and light comedies (*ortaoyunu*).[549] Despite the fact that there seem to be no marks of political depiction in these puppet shows, two characters named *İbiş* and *İhtiyar,* representing respectively a "master" and a "slave",[550] evoke Hegel's master-slave dialectic.

After the introduction of puppet shows, shadow plays (*gölge oyunu*) became prominent. Shadow plays (*Gölge Oyunu*) are thought to have

---

[542] Metin And (a), *Türk Tiyatrosunun Evreleri*, Turhan Kitabevi, Ankara, 1983, 73.
[543] Ibid., 73.
[544] Nutku, 1993, 197.
[545] Ibid., 197.
[546] And (a), 1983, 73.
[547] Ibid., 79.
[548] Nutku, 1993, 199.
[549] And (a), 1983, 83.
[550] Ibid., 89.

been brought to Turkey from Egypt in the 16th century.[551] More commonly recognized as *Karagöz*, these shadow plays took their definitive form in the 17th century.[552] From the descriptions of Özdemir Nutku in *Dünya Tiyatrosu Tarihi,* we find out that in *Karagöz shadow plays*, there is a white screen, and an oil lamp between the screen and the person making the animation.[553] Making a deep analysis of *Karagöz* in *Türk Tiyatrosunun Evreleri*, Metin And states that it presented a pivotal political satire.[554] Though Karagöz is not a playwright, but just a speaker of a shadowy performer, Louis Énault, in *Constantinople et la Turquie* (1855), states:

> In a country where power is absolute, Karagheuz represents an unlimited freedom; it is a vaudevillian having less censorship, a newspaper without bail, being toneless and disobedient. Not even any character throughout the empire, except for the Sultan, whose person is sacred and whose doings are unassailable, escapes his satirical sarcasms.... The people applaud him and the government tolerates. [555]

Serdar Öztürk reveals "the political stance of the *Karagöz* had always been that of the little guy criticizing the powerful".[556] Though *Karagöz* was depicting the daily life and therefore the societal life of Turkish society,[557] it was also a representation of governmental policies of the existing Ottoman Sultans. In one of his articles titled *Karagöz* published in *Encyclopedia of World Drama* (1984), Metin And highlights that in *Karagöz* shadow plays the numerous plots include parodies of trade and tradition, the portrayal of customs, intrigues of some kind, protecting woman, love affairs, familial affairs, popular

---

[551] Nutku, 1993, 201.
[552] And (a), 1983, 95.
[553] Nutku, 1993, 201
[554] And (a), 1983, 96–97.
[555] Louis Énault, *Constantinople et la Turquie*, L. Hachette, Paris, 1855, 367. The original script was in French; it was translated into English by the writer of the thesis.
[556] Öztürk, 2006, 294.
[557] Nutku, 1993, 203.

stories, and legends.[558] Nonetheless, And observes that the emergence of *Karagöz* was political in origin, in that the aim was to draw the attention of the Sultan to the corruptions of viziers and ministers.[559] It is revealing that after "the depictions of the dethroning of Abdulhamit II and public rejoicing following the adoption of the new constitution of 1908",[560] "in 1911, the authorities banned all political references in *Karagöz* performances".[561]

The other major genre of the traditional Turkish Theatre is *ortaoyunu* (light comedies) which differs from *Karagöz* in that in *ortaoyunu* the characters are all on the stage, that is, there are no shadow shows, but live performances. Thus, *ortaoyunu* can be considered as the principal constituent of modern Turkish drama. Nutku reveals that the light comedies which were thought to have something to do with the guild of janissaries and *Ahi* guilds—members of a Turkish-Islamic guild— could also be named as *Meydan Oyunu* or *Yeni Dünya Oyunu*.[562] These members were the supporters of the Ottoman Empire not only in cultural matters, but social, military, economic, and political terms. Sevinç Sokullu, in her article titled *Geleneksel Türk Tiyatrosunun Ulusal Tiyatromuza Kaynaklığı Üzerinde Yeniden Durmak* (2009), also establishes that the light comedies (*Ortaoyunu*) were not just a tool of cultural entertainment, but an agent of political satire through which— by addressing the ministers—the sultans were mocked.[563] Rejecting the view of "theatre's appealing only to a limited crowd of people that are, for the most part from ruling class," Sokullu articulates:

> the political satires in the light comedies (*ortaoyunu*) were limited to a function that aimed to appeal to a certain privileged

---

[558] Metin And, "Karagöz" in *Encyclopedia of World Drama*, ed. Stanley Hochman, McGraw-Hill, USA, 1984, 130.
[559] Ibid., 132.
[560] Ibid., 132.
[561] Ibid., 132.
[562] Nutku, 1993, 196.
[563] Sevinç Sokullu, "Geleneksel Türk Tiyatrosunun Ulusal Tiyatromuza Kaynaklığı Üzerinde Yeniden Durmak" in *Tiyatro Araştırmaları Dergisi*, Sayı: 28, 2009, 155.

class, and so it could be said that these comedies undertook such a mission which did not go beyond entertainment. However, what makes the theatre different from entertainment is that the former reflects the conscience of the public.[564]

In the light of the wide range of data from Metin And's *Geleneksel Türk Tiyatrosu*, we know that *ortaoyunu* in the very beginning was nearly totally verbal, and the characters generally imitated some animals through which they staged the first live comedies.[565] In many of his findings based on the notes of various foreign travellers and ambassadors, Metin And reveals that women were banned from appearing on stage, instead men, dressed in women's clothes, played female roles in *ortaoyunu*.[566] In the very beginning, such statesmen as Istanbul Lords, Janissary Aghas and such Grand Viziers as Ragıp Pasha were imitated, and with the proclamation of Second Constitutional Period (*İkinci Meşrutiyet*) high state officials and statesmen were again imitated.[567] Evaluating all the three genres of traditional Turkish drama in his *The Communication Process in Turkish Traditional Performances* (1988), Metin And expresses that "The early performances of story tellers or theatrical troupes contained political satire, jokes and imitation of high officials, even of prime ministers".[568] Thus, he, in a way, points out that all these imitations were political satires and ironies produced by the period's artists.

Until the end of 18th century, *ortaoyunu* was staged and improved progressively; however, in the 19th century, *ortaoyunu* was highly affected by western drama; at the end of this influence and change, the *tuluat* theatre (a kind of improvisational drama which was the mixture of *ortaoyunu* and western theatre) was introduced.[569] Though there appeared many objections against this new genre of drama, many

---

[564] Ibid., 155.
[565] Metin And, *Geleneksel Türk Tiyatrosu*, İnkılap Kitabevi, İstanbul, 1985, 337–44.
[566] Ibid., 348–53.
[567] Ibid., 371.
[568] Metin And, "The Communication Process in Turkish Traditional Performances" in *Tiyatro Araştırmaları Dergisi*, Sayı: 8, 1988, 44.
[569] And, 1985, 372.

supporters of the west welcomed "western" drama;[570] for the first time women figures, though not Muslim, were permitted to perform on stages. This period also corresponds to the *Tanzimat Era* which was the first innovative factor of Ottoman Turkey's Westernization movement. As Sait S. Halman discloses "[Tanzimat] also assumed the task of giving voice to civil disobedience. Its practitioners, despite censorship, often acted as provocateurs and agitators for reform and social innovation and as propagators of rebellion against tyranny".[571] After the proclamation of the Tanzimat Epoch in 1839, the first samples of intermingling the Ottomanic *ortaoyunu* with Western drama were introduced to the Ottoman stages. This period was also the one that embraced many constructions of playhouses, theatre buildings.[572] The vast majority of the Ottoman Sultans supported the theatre, and even they struggled to reintegrate a variety of representations of western drama into the society.[573] However, there was no written text. As Metin And emphasizes, "One of the two most important distinctions between Western theatre and our traditional theatre was the theatre building and the stage; as for the other, it was a written text."[574] Until the introduction of the first play of Turkish drama in 1859, which was Ibrahim Şinasi's *Şair Evlenmesi*, the first written texts in Turkish were either translations or adaptations of western plays.[575]

Two significant figures of *Tanzimat* and *İstibdat* drama are İbrahim Şinasi and Namık Kemal. As a journalist, poet, and essayist, and at the order of the Sultan of the period, Şinasi wrote *Şair Evlenmesi* (Marriage of the Poet) in 1859 to be staged in Dolmabahçe Palace Theatre.[576] Thus, the first Turkish play was introduced. In *On Dokuzuncu Asır*

---

[570] Ibid., 381–82.
[571] Talat S. Halman, *A Milenium of Turkish Literature*, ed. Jayne L. Warner, Syracuse University Press, New York, 2011, 65.
[572] Metin And, *Tanzimat ve İstibdat Döneminde Türk Tiyatrosu*, İş Bankası Kültür Yayınları, Ankara, 1972, 18.
[573] Ibid., 20–29.
[574] Ibid., 59.
[575] Ibid., 59.
[576] Ibid., 258.

Türk Edebiyatı Tarihi (2013), Ahmet Hamdi Tanpınar reveals some conflicting views on Şinasi's political stance; whilst he is considered to be a follower of Western ideologies, a supporter of Tanzimat and its canons,[577] he is also thought to have been on good terms with the existing government.[578] Tanpınar observes that in one of his speeches Şinasi said that, "we were slaves in the hands of tyranny and captivity; Reshid Pasha's law freed us by putting the Sultan in his place."[579] Özdemir Nutku also points out Şinasi's tendency to support Constitutionalism (*Meşrutiyet*), noting that in one of the newspapers of the period titled *Tercüman-ı Ahval*, Şinasi protested against the rulers by saying that, "supporting the State with the troops and taxes, and fulfilling the amendments of the State, the nations could check whether they were ruled goodly or badly, and should have acquired the right to voice their thoughts in written or spoken ways."[580]

One of the other most important political debates in this period was the question of the impact of Islam upon the social structure, and the thought of freedom introduced by westernization. Şinasi, in his *Seele*, articulates that "The essence of civilization lies in reason. It is the case in western civilization. In the past, it was the case in Muslim civilization, too. Unfortunately, superstitions invaded and changed its nature."[581] Though there were not many political reflections in *Şair Evlenmesi*, Şinasi sarcastically lampoons bigotry by addressing a religious figure, Ebullaklaka. Characterizing an ignorant and deceitful *imam*, Ebullaklaka is a person who represents both bigotry and zealotry. According to the notes of Tanpınar, some foreign scholars, specifically Gordlevski, believe that, by the characterization of Ebullaklaka, Şinasi refers to the notorious Vehbi Molla who was a member of Ministry of Education of the era.[582] Thus, in a way, Şinasi

---

[577] Ahmet Hamdi Tanpınar, *On Dokuzuncu Asır Türk Edebiyatı Tarihi*, ed. Abdullah Uçman, Dergah Yayınları, İstanbul, 2013, 203.
[578] Ibid., 191.
[579] Ibid., 204.
[580] Nutku, quoted in, 1993, 359.
[581] Tanpınar, quoted in, 2013, 207.
[582] Ibid., 210.

mocks the religious ideology of the Ottoman Empire, in which Islam plays a significant part.

Sait S. Halman and Jane L. Warner, in *A Millennium of Turkish Literature* (2011), state that in Ottoman Empire "In more recent times, the focal targets of satire have been morals and manners, cant, political norms, and politicians themselves."[583] Giving a great significance to "morality" and "ethics",[584] Namık Kemal was another figure who in the main propped up nationalism and addressed such social and political issues as "patriotism, Islamic union, and human rights".[585] The fact that his many works are ideological[586] makes Namık Kemal a nationalist-propagandist who aims to nurture people with ideas of "patriotism and national consciousness".[587] Believing that "drama is a school that teaches ethics,"[588] Kemal provokes "a new phase in human understanding, and changing the meaning behind the presence of men on the Earth."[589] Being his best-known play, *Vatan Yahut Silistre* (Fatherland or Silistra) (1872) was such an agitprop that established nationalist consciousness. The same play was the reason for the playwrights' exile to Cyprus. After its presentation in Gedikpasha Theatre, the theatre was closed, and increased pressure was placed on playwriting, staging, and playwrights.[590] Although the press had been reluctant to publicize these productions during the reign of Abdulaziz, this play put an end to this hesitation.[591]

Touching upon historical issues in many of his plays, including *Celaleddin Harzemşah* (1874) and *Akif Bey* (1874), Namık Kemal over and over again, though sometimes sarcastically, depicted the Ottoman

---

[583] Halman, 2011, 31.
[584] Nutku, 1993, 360.
[585] Tanpınar, 2013, 373.
[586] Ibid., 373.
[587] Ünlü, 2006, 116.
[588] Nutku, 1993, 361.
[589] Niyazi Akı, XIX. *Yüzyıl Türk Tiyatrosunda Devrin Hayat ve İnsanı*, Atatürk Üniversitesi Yayınları, Erzurum, 1974, 29.
[590] Ünlü, 2006, 118.
[591] Tanpınar, 2013, 375.

dynasty, the fights for the throne, political turmoil, infidelities, and betrayals of the viziers and commanders.[592] However, as his political interest grew, he depicted much of what he saw in the community politically in his plays, especially in *Gülnihal* (1875) in which he mostly described, as Tanpınar observes, "the struggle for freedom against Abdulaziz's reign".[593] Regarded as a "Tanzimat child; a man of reform rather than revolution"[594] by Ahmet Hamdi Tanpınar, Namık Kemal conveyed life to the theatre to awaken the social consciousness, because he believed that "it is the consciousness that perceives the drama".[595]

After Namık Kemal's revolutionary and freedom-provoking plays, other playwrights began to write along similar lines. As members of the Young Ottomans (*Genç Osmanlılar*), Namık Kemal and his friends "wanted to save through liberal reforms and the temptation to return, given a chance to influence policy from within,"[596] and so, "they certainly influenced, albeit indirectly, the introduction of the Ottoman constitution in 1876, and the Ottoman constitutional movement, which was to oppose the autocratic rule of the sultan after 1878, based itself on their writings".[597] Again, Erik Jan Zurcher, in his other book titled *The Young Turk Legacy* (2010), states:

> When one reads the passage about the constitutional revolution of 1876, one could be forgiven for thinking that it was Namık Kemal's play *The Fatherland or Silistria* which brought down the old regime, and not the famine in Anatolia, the insurrection in the Balkans or the financial crisis of the state.[598]

Thus, a new phase for Ottoman Turkey began: the *Meşrutiyet Era*, which highly affected theatre as well; primarily because the plays which had been censored or banned during the autocracy period were now

---

[592] Ibid., 375–94.
[593] Ibid., 380.
[594] Ibid., 381.
[595] Nutku, quoted in, 1993, 361.
[596] Erik J. Zürcher, *Turkey: A Modern History*, I. B. Tauris, New York, 2007, 70.
[597] Ibid., 70.
[598] Erik J. Zürcher, *The Young Turk Legacy and Nation Building*, I. B. Tauris, New York, 2010, 45.

staged, and thus theatre became an agent of the depiction of enthusiasm for freedom.[599] The atmosphere of freedom brought much encouragement to the playwrights and, though there were various playwrights whose plays were published or staged during the *Meşrutiyet Era*, some writers, scholars and critics complained of well-made plays.[600] Influenced by Tanzimat drama, and European (especially French) drama,[601] the theatre during that period addressed mainly the Ottoman Constitutional Movement, the 1908 revolution, the wrongdoings during the autocratic period, the political and social turmoil, and the injustices in the legal system.[602] According to Metin And, the most interesting characteristic of the plays in the Meşrutiyet Era is way in which the playwrights so frequently dealt with political issues; a significant number of the plays being written in documentary genre.[603]

Many playwrights produced several plays during the Meşrutiyet Era. The main political ideologies that influenced drama were Turkism, Islamism, and Ottomanism,[604] besides Westernism and Socialism.[605] In an effort to set a new political and legal order, theatre reflected the *Zeitgeist,* the political realities and social turbulences. The most notable and efficient playwrights of the era were İbnürrefik Ahmet Nuri and Musahipzade Celal who were also proficient writers during the Republican Era.[606] The other prominent figures were Hüseyin Suat Yalçın, Mehmet Rauf, Halit Ziya Uşaklıgil, Safvet Nezihi, and Yusuf Ziya Ortaç among others.[607]

Metin And, in *Meşrutiyet Dönemi Türk Tiyatrosu* (1971), suggests that nearly all the plays written in that period were "documentary" rather

---

[599] Ünlü, 2006, 118.
[600] And, 1971, 101.
[601] Ibid., 115.
[602] Ibid., 186.
[603] Ibid., 181.
[604] Ünlü, 2006, 118.
[605] And, 1971, 198.
[606] Ibid., 110.
[607] Ibid., 101–108.

than historical plays, since all the characters were true to real life, being selected from that exact period, and the particular issues dealt with were documented via actual records, letters, resolutions, government reviews, speeches, statements, and actual events.[608] Thus, what writers echoed was in the main attributed to the general feeling of the era, which was highly political. From Metin And's observations we learn that of all the political plays written during that time, the one that aroused the most interest among people was Hüseyin Kami's *Sabah-ı Hürriyet* (1908) which was staged immediately after the proclamation of the Second Constitutional Period in 1908.[609]

Being the two most significant preliminary phases of the era, autocracy (*İstibdat*) and freedom (*Hürriyet*) were the main themes of such plays as M. Sezai's *Mithat Paşa Yahut Hükm-i İdam* (1912), Hüseyin Suat's *Şehbal Yahut İstibdadın Son Perdesi* (1908), Mehmet Burhanettin's *Fehim Paşa* (1912), İbnülcemal Ahmet Tevfik's *İstibdadın Son Günü Yahut Zavallı Valide* (1908), Kazım Nami's *Nasıl Oldu?* (1926), Hasan Nazmi's *Genç Zabit yahut İstibdat Zulümleri* (1910), Selanikli Hilmi's *Menfiler yahut Felaket-i İstibdat* (1911).[610] On the other hand, some playwrights touched upon the "legacy of Young Turks"; and it was addressed by such playwrights as Şehbenderzade Ahmet Hilmi in *İstibdadın Vahşetleri yahut Bir Fedainin Ölümü* (1911), and Sait Hikmet in *Mazi ve Ati*, Aka Gündüz in *Aşk ve İstibdat*.[611]

Another momentous political event of the period was the Armenian riots of 1895, and in his play titled *Ermeni Mazlumları yahut Fedekar Bir Türk Zabiti* (1906), Mehmet İhsan sought to justify the Armenians.[612] One of the other most noteworthy political events of the era was the 31st March Incident (*31 Mart Vakası*) which was addressed by Cenap Şehabettin in his one-act play *Yalan* (1917).[613] Written in

---

[608] Ibid., 182.
[609] Ibid., 184.
[610] Ibid., 185–90.
[611] Ibid., 190–91.
[612] Ibid., 193.
[613] Ibid., 195.

French, Selim Bey's *La Chute d'un Sultan* (*Bir Sultanın Düşüşü*) was another play that portrayed the 31st March Incident.[614] Meanwhile, Reşat Nuri Güntekin's *Gönül* addressed the ideological conflicts among political parties.[615] Other prominent playwrights, as noted by Özdemir Nutku in *Dünya Tiyatrosu Tarihi*, were Abdulhak Hamit and Şemsettin Sami.[616] Abdulhak Hamit, in *İlhan* (1913), *Turhan* (1916) and *Liberte* (1912), handled such issues as the politics of Central Asia, 14th century conditions and the policies of the palaces.[617] Şemsettin Sami, on the other hand, dealt with political turmoil that drove a wedge between the Sultan and public in *Gave* (1876).[618]

Counted among the playwrights of the Tanzimat Era, Namık Kemal also wrote in Meşrutiyet as well, and the forthcoming Republican Theatre was largely affected by his writings. In *Young Turk Legacy*, Zurcher, considering Atatürk's speech (*Nutuk*) (1927), points out that Atatürk "modelled his style on that of the great mid-nineteenth century writer and politician Namık Kemal";[619] this denotes Namık Kemal's incontrovertible impact on Turkish nationalism and patriotism. Niyazi Berkes observes that "The last phase of the Tanzimat witnessed the first signs of innovations in language and script, journalism and literature. The latter two became the vehicles of the earliest liberal ideas and of nebulous nationalist concepts".[620] These liberal ideas and nationalist concepts were also strengthened through the writings of some figures during the Meşrutiyet Era. With the formation of the "nationalist" spirit, a Republican Turkey emerged under the rule of Mustafa Kemal Pasha in 1923. Thus, it was not only the internal and external problems that prompted the downfall of the Ottoman Empire, but some notorious writers like İbrahim Şinasi, Namık Kemal, Ziya Gökalp,

---

[614] Ibid., 196.
[615] Ibid., 198.
[616] Nutku, 1993, 364–65.
[617] Ibid., 364.
[618] Ibid., 365–66.
[619] Zürcher, 2010, 8.
[620] Berkes, 1998, 192.

Ahmet Mithat, Şemsettin Sami, among many others; whose principal anticipation was, "that a modern Turkish literature would be born, based on the models of Western literature."[621]

Undoubtedly, as a golden age of literature and more narrowly drama, the Republican Era was the most productive period of literature. In *Cumhuriyet Dönemi Türk Tiyatrosu* (1983), Metin And establishes that Republican Turkish drama, just like Tanzimat and Meşrutiyet drama, was strongly affected by the traditional Turkish Theatre and European Drama.[622] In *Elli Yılın Türk Tiyatrosu* (1973), And establishes that the earliest Republican writers were by and large influenced by Maeterlinck's and Ibsen's social realism, Strindberg's psychological realism, and German expressionism.[623] Aslıhan Ünlü emphasizes that during the earlier Republican Era, to establish the new ideology and to popularize Kemalist ideology, a Cultural Revolution was started in every aspect; and theatre was an influential carrier of that Cultural Revolution.[624] Therefore, the major political ideologies of Republican drama were Turkism, Kemalism, Kemalist Laicism, Secularism, Nationalism, and Socialism. Indeed, these political ideologies were touched upon in nearly every play.

Due to the political turmoil of the Republican period, numerous political and ideological literary works were written by dozens of different names. In the very beginning of this era, from 1923 to 1940 onwards, many playwrights dealt with socio-political and socio-cultural depictions of the community. For instance, Reşat Nuri Güntekin's *Hülleci* (1933) lampoons "religion exploiters"[625] in a way which characterizes the socio-political reflection of Islamic values. The most influential political figure of the Republican Era was Mustafa Kemal Atatürk, the founder of Turkish Republic. His pioneering of the

---

[621] Ibid., 198.
[622] Metin And (b), *Cumhuriyet Dönemi Türk Tiyatrosu*, Türkiye iş Bankası Kültür Yayınları, Ankara, 1983, 423.
[623] Metin And, *Elli Yılın Türk Tiyatrosu*, Türkiye iş Bankası Kültür Yayınları, İstanbul, 1973, 448.
[624] Ünlü, 2006, 120.
[625] And, 1973, 523.

modern country of Turkey made him a national hero, and this is the major issue dealt with in *Gazi Mustafa Kemal* (1926) by Hayri Muhittin Dalkılıç.[626]

Halit Fahri Ozansoy, in *On Yılın Destanı* (1921), celebrates and eulogizes the Turkish War of Independence and Atatürk's monumental reforms.[627] Faruk Nafız Çamlıbel also celebrates the Republic by his *Canavar* (1925) through which he invites the readers to compare and contrast the pre-Republican and post-Republican disparities.[628] Çamlıbel, in his second play titled *Akın* (1932), glorifies the Turkish race[629] by which he backs up the ideology of Turkism. Yakup Kadri Karaosmanoğlu, in *Sağanak* (1929), addresses the revolutions and the clashes between religion and secularism.[630] Just like Ibsen and Shaw, Hüseyin Rahmi Gürpınar, in *Kadın Erkekleşince* (1933), tackles with the "woman question" and he touches upon the political impact of Westernism, reforms, and revolutions upon women.[631] Another noteworthy playwright Musahipzade Celal, produced a number of plays; one of which, *Bir Kavuk Devrildi* (1930), lampoons the ruled and the ruling class, whilst his *Pazartesi-Perşembe* (1931), ridicules bureaucracy and the corruption of officials,[632] and his later *Genç Osman* (1937) encompasses the dethronement of the reformist Sultan and his being killed by *ulema*.[633] Nazım Hikmet's *Kafatası* (1932) deals with economy-politics by which the playwright criticizes the capitalist economic order.[634] The eulogy of Turkism and the honor of the Turkish War of Independence are again addressed by Necip Fazıl Kısakürek in

---

[626] Ibid., 524.
[627] Ibid., 529.
[628] Ibid., 529.
[629] Ibid., 531.
[630] Ibid., 531.
[631] Ibid., 531.
[632] Ibid., 533.
[633] Ibid., 533.
[634] Ibid., 536.

his *Tohum* (1935) in which he depicts the liberation of Maraş province from French occupation.[635]

The plays of some of the above-mentioned playwrights were staged from 1940 to 1950; however other new playwrights also emerged during this time.[636] Such writers as Sedat Simavi, Ahmet Muhip Dranas, Ahmet Kutsi Tecer, Cevat Fehmi Başkut, Nahit Sırrı Örik, Oktay Rıfat, and Sabahattin Kudret Aksal were the most prominent among these.[637] Sedat Simavi's *Hürriyet Apartmanı* (1940) reflects the apotheosis of liberty (*hürriyet*) by concentrating on the proclamation of independence.[638] Oktay Rıfat's *Kadınlar Arasında* (1966) tackles economic politics and the impact of Second World War on the global economic depression.[639]

From 1950 onwards, some more rewarding plays were pioneered. As Metin And puts it, during 1950s and 1960s, with the establishment of *Küçük Sahne* (Miniature Stage) and *Devlet Tiyatrosu* (State Theatre), there was a favorable environment for the development of playwriting.[640] Written in this period, Reşat Nuri Güntekin's *Tanrıdağ Ziyafeti* (1954) is a political comedy tackling the hypocrisy of the ministers towards the leadership of countries ruled by monarchy.[641] Cevat Fehmi Başkut's *Sana Rey Veriyorum* (1950) depicts the reforms in the socio-political life brought by the multi-party system[642]. The repercussions of economic policy are addressed in *Harput'ta Bir Amerikalı* written by the same playwright.[643]

The political mayhem during the rule of Ottoman Sultan Mehmet the Conqueror is dealt with in Nazım Kurşunlu's *Fatih* (1941) which was

---

[635] Ibid., 536.
[636] Ibid., 543–47.
[637] Ibid., 547.
[638] Ibid., 547.
[639] Ibid., 552.
[640] Ibid., 553.
[641] Ibid., 555.
[642] Ibid., 557.
[643] Ibid., 557.

written in honor of the 500th anniversary of the conquest of İstanbul.[644] Selahattin Batu portrays three Turkish statesmen: Oğuzkhan, Mete, and Atatürk in *Oğuzata* (1955)[645] in which he glorifies Turkism and its ideology. Orhan Asena's *Korku* and *Hürrem Sultan* are his other political and ideological plays. Haldun Taner's *Günün Adamı* (1957) outlines the multi-party system.[646] In Refik Erduran's *Cengizhan'ın Bisikleti* (1959), the readers are invited to the politics of comedy by which he stages the gaining of civil law and the new values in new Turkey.[647]

The years between 1960 and 1970 were years during which Turkish theatre matured.[648] The fact that the 1961 Turkish Constitution enabled the authors a freer environment is the basic reason behind both qualitative maturity and numerical saturation in playwriting.[649] The political plays written during this time were realistic depictions that either mocked or glorified the existing socio-political or socio-cultural conditions. Written at that time, Güngör Dilmen Kalyoncu's *İttihat ve Terakki* (1969)[650] glorifies the idealism of some groups and depicts the impracticality of the ideology of Turkism. Orhan Asena's *Tohum ve Toprak* revolves around a reformist Pasha named Alemdar Pasha, and the way in which self-seekers and reactionists scheme against him.[651] Recep Bilginer's *İsyancılar* (1964) deals with the relationship between the ruling and the ruled classes through the depiction of exploitation by agha (village rulers);[652] the same playwright, in *Gazeteciden Dost* (1962), describes a dirty and gossipy world order consisting of politicians.[653]

---

[644] Ibid., 563.
[645] Ibid., 566.
[646] Ibid., 570.
[647] Ibid., 572.
[648] Ibid., 575.
[649] Ibid., 575.
[650] Ibid., 578.
[651] Ibid., 578.
[652] Ibid., 590.
[653] Ibid., 601.

Turgut Özakman's *Ulusal Kolej Disiplin Kurulu* (1966) and Rıfat Ilgaz's *Hababam Sınıfı (1957)* critique the politics of the education system and misjudgments in education institutions.[654] Çetin Altan's *Dilekçe* (1962), Necati Cumalı's *Masalar* (1969), and Recep Bilginer's *Ben Devletim* (1965) disapprove of the public officials who do not do their jobs properly.[655] Ali Tahsin's *Haysiyetli Milli Kalkınma ve Hak Hukuk Partisi* (1969) lampoons the political life; Cevat Fehmi Başkut's *Hacıyatmaz* (1960) probes the struggle for power during the multi-party system; Çetin Altan's *Komisyon* (1969) sheds light on the contemporary political system and lifestyle; Refik Erduran's *Kartal Tekmesi* (1966) deals with a capitalist family considering the political régime and political events of the era.[656] Sermet Çağan's *Ayak Bacak Fabrikası* (1963) exemplifies the exploitation of human beings by the governing power in respect with religion, economy, and politics.[657] Aydın Engin's *Devr-i Süleyman* (1967) is yet another example of the diverse political satires of the period.[658]

From 1970 onwards, there appeared some prolific authors. During that time, some playwrights wrote about the Turkish War of Independence.[659] For instance, Erol Toy's *Parti Pehlivanı* (1970), İsmet Küntay's *Tozlu Çizmeler* (1970), and Engin Orbey's *Birinci Kurtuluş* (1979) are among the plays that concentrated on this war.[660] Turan Oflazoğlu, in *IV Murat* (1970), dramatizes the lust for power.[661] Ayşegül Yüksel, in *Haldun Taner Tiyatrosu*, expresses that Taner's *Eşeğin Gölgesi* (1965) is his sharpest political satire,[662] which although written in 1965 was not performed until the 1970s and 80s. Yüksel classifies Haldun Taner's such plays as *Çıktık Açık Alınla* (1977),[663]

---

[654] Ibid., 601.
[655] Ibid., 603.
[656] Ibid., 605.
[657] Ibid., 613.
[658] Ibid., 617.
[659] And (b), 1983, 466 and 490.
[660] And, 1973, 621.
[661] Ibid., 627.
[662] Ayşegül Yüksel, *Haldun Taner Tiyatrosu*, Bilgi yayınevi, İstanbul, 1986, 92.
[663] Ibid., 135.

Gözlerimi Kaparım Vazifemi Yaparım (1964), *Zilli Zarife* (1966), *Vatan Kurtaran Şaban* (1967),[664] and *Keşanlı Ali Destanı* (1964)[665] as political satires. From 1980s to the present Turkey, such figures as Memet Baydur, Murathan Mungan, Oğuz Atay, Tuncer Cücenoğlu, Ülkü Ayvaz, and Ferhan Şensoy among many others have produced some creative plays. Sevda Şener, in her article titled *Memet Baydur Tiyatrosu,* implies that Baydur's *Cumhuriyet Kızı* (1988) is a depiction of political satire in which the professors characterized the faculty members who were kicked out of the university by law number 1402 from the Turkish Higher Education Council (*YÖK*).[666] In *Gelişim Sürecinde Türk Tiyatrosu*, Şener deals with the same play and accuses Memet Baydur of writing in a way that is sympathetic with the coup d'état of 12 September 1980.[667]

Throughout the history of drama, there have been extensive presentations, performances, and shows concentrating on such concerns as modern-day events, cultural reforms, political turmoil, and governmental policies fundamental to the social order and stability; thus, political theatre, from its very earliest origin to today, has aimed to promote self-awareness, consciousness, and communal revolution. In the history of both British and Turkish drama, political satires and politics itself have been presented and depicted not only within traditional performances but also in modern stages by differing artists ranging from the oral literature mentoring acrobats, Meddahs, Karagöz shadow shows, strolling players on feast days revealing Miracles, Moralities, and Mysteries, religious ceremonies, and other performances to written literature encompassing modern staging of epic drama, agitprop, and political drama. From the classical period to today, the central aim of theatre has been to plant the idea of self-awareness into people's minds through those ritualistic and societal

---

[664] Ibid., 168.
[665] Ibid., 214.
[666] Sevda Şener, "Memet Baydur Tiyatrosu" in *Tiyatro Araştırmaları Dergisi Sayı*. 31, 2011, 116.
[667] Sevda Şener, *Gelişim Sürecinde Türk Tiyatrosu*, Mitos-Boyut Yayınları, İstanbul, 2011, 219.

performances that augment the significance of the political questions.[668]

---

[668] Jerzy Grotowski, *Towards a Poor Theatre*, ed. Eugenio Barba, Routledge, New York, 2002, 57.

CHAPTER 3: BERNARD SHAW AND ORHAN ASENA

Discussing the Paris Commune movement between 1848 and 1940, Michel Foucault, in conversation with Gilles Deleuze on *Intellectuals and Power*,[669] stated "The intellectual spoke the truth to those who had yet to see it, in the name of those who were forbidden to speak the truth: he was conscience, consciousness, and eloquence".[670] By describing the "intellectual" in this way, Foucault emphasized what Deleuze also said, that the thing which is fundamental to the intellectual is "the indignity of speaking for others".[671] In another interview on *Truth, Power, Self*, Foucault revealed his view that "to change something in the minds of people—that's the role of an intellectual".[672] The political posture of many intellectuals, scholars, philosophers, statesmen, activists, etc. comes from their "indignity of speaking for others", and their insistence "to change something in the minds of people", as does the political evolution in their own life. This is true for both George Bernard Shaw and Orhan Asena.

The idea of "speaking for others" was the basic grounds for Shaw's being regarded "as a public minded author"[673] a designation which reveals his intellectual wit, as he is here making a discrimination between his roles as "G. B. S., the journalist, and Bernard Shaw, the dramatist".[674] Shaw's literary career was exceedingly prolific; he was not only "the indefatigable champion of social justice"[675] but also a "political reformer, novelist, art critic, musical critic, dramatic critic,

---

[669] Foucault, New York, 1977, 207.
[670] Ibid., 207.
[671] Ibid., 209.
[672] L. H. Martin et al., quoted in *Technologies of the Self: A Seminar with Michel Foucault*, Tavistock, London, 1988, 9.
[673] Wilbur Dwight Dunkel, "George Bernard Shaw" in *The Sewanee Review* Vol. 50, No. 2 (Apr-Jun 1942), 255.
[674] Ibid., 256.
[675] Arnold Bennet, "Three Plays for Puritans" in *George Bernard Shaw*, ed. T. F. Evans, Routledge, London and New York, 1976, 93.

vestryman,"[676] whose standing was "a case of intellect almost pure."[677] His political thinking always oscillated between conflicting views, ranging from Fabianism, Socialism, and Communism to dictatorship and even anti-democratic movements. In every masterpiece, through the depictions of certain characters, he emphasized his statement that "I was a downstart and the son of a downstart",[678] revealing his struggle against poverty and economic turbulence.

Orhan Asena, on the other hand, was one of the prolific authors of Republican Turkey—called by Sami Çağdaş the "Shakespeare of the Turkish Theatre."[679] Orhan Asena is a great man who introduced 54 plays, 12 scenarios, 2 musical comedies, and 2 librettos.[680] Asena is considered to have been a successful playwright who aimed to address the issues of daily life concerning historical customs and traditions by projecting social and political events.[681] He was a man of ideas who was again a "speaker for others". He was a foremost humanist, a socialist, and a well-educated public speaker stressing the national and secular phases of modern Turkey by eulogizing Kemalist tradition. His political thinking fluctuated from time to time, but he never gave up the principles of Mustafa Kemal and those of nationalism.[682]

In this chapter, I shall focus on the changes in the political thinking of Bernard Shaw and Orhan Asena. This analysis will cover their life and career and feature connected illustrations taken from some contemporary witnesses. Last but not least, their political writings,

---

[676] Ibid., 94.
[677] Ibid., 93.
[678] Arthur Ganz, quoted in George Bernard Shaw, Macmillan, Hong Kong, 1983, 7.
[679] Hami Çağdaş, "Türk Tiyatrosunun Shakespeare'i Öldü" in *Hürriyet Daily News*, http://hurarsiv.hurriyet.com.tr/goster/ShowNew.aspx?id=-226855, 2001, Accessed: 12.10.2014.
[680] Hülya Nutku, "Cumhuritet Tarihimizin Yakın Tanığı Bir Yazar: Orhan Asena" in *Bütün Dünya*, Başkent Üniversitesi Kültür Yayını, 2000, 23.
[681] Ibid., 21.
[682] This fluctuation appears within his plays in many of which differing topics are held. For instance, he dealt with Mustafa Kemal Atatürk and his way of life in *Korku* (1956) and *Tanrılar ve İnsanlar* (1959), and in his child play *Mustafa* (1963), projecting the ideologies of Republican way of life and Turkish nationalim. Nevertheless, after his departure to Germany, he dealt with socialist and communist milieu prevaling Chile in *Şili'de Av* (1975), *Ölü Kentin Nabzı* (1978), and *Bir Başkana Ağıt* (1979–80).

specifically their selected plays, will be examined in terms of their changing political visions; here the plays will only be categorized in terms of political views, whilst the actual political contents of each play will be examined more closely in the fourth chapter.

Political Evolution in Bernard Shaw

Arthur Ganz considers Shaw "as the most notable English-speaking playwright since Shakespeare ... a public figure ... artist, prophet, and clown".[683] When considering Shaw's literary productions, we can never surpass W. H. Auden's observation that, "Surely, George Bernard Shaw possessed more energy, physical and mental, than any other man who ever lived. I am not surprised to learn that he suffered from migraine: How else could nature persuade him to take a rest?"[684] James Huneeker, on the other hand, reveals that Shaw was even regarded by some as a non-human machine, saying that "Shaw was said to be a syndicate; the fabrication of some clever charlatan; a pen, not a human".[685] Alternatively, R. N. Roy, in the preface to *Historical Plays*, regards Shaw as "a gigantic figure who bestrode 'modern thought like a colossus'".[686]

Shaw's ideology and political thinking were not limited to the *Zeitgeist* of Victorianism; they were highly influenced by his living conditions, his lifestyle, his readings, and the groups to which he had some vital contacts.[687] His political thinking and his ideologies comprised the economic, religious, socio-cultural, and governmental linkages which produced overtly differing approaches.[688] Born in Dublin in 1856 into a

---

[683] Ganz, 1983, 5.
[684] Kauffmann, quoted in, 1986, 54.
[685] James Huneeker, "A Word On the Dramatic Opinions and Essays of Bernard Shaw" in *Dramatic Opinions and Essays with an Apology Vol I (Bernard Shaw)*, Brentano's Rosings Digital Publications, New York, 6.
[686] R. N. Roy, *George Bernard Shaw's Historical Plays*, Macmillan, London, 1976, ix.
[687] Gareth Griffith, *Socialism and Superior Brains: The Political Thought of George Bernard Shaw*, Routledge, New York, 1993, 23–100.
[688] Gilbert Keith Chesterton, *George Bernard Shaw*, John Lane, New York, 1909, 53–86.

Protestant family[689]—"the Protestant class whose ancestors were mostly British settlers in Ireland"[690]—George Bernard Shaw "as resident propagandist and original thinker, often tackling neglected themes".[691] Being an Irishman, (as quoted by Gilbert K. Chesterton, Shaw once said "I am a typical Irishman; my family came from Yorkshire"),[692] Shaw "certainly [had] all the virtues and all the powers that go with this original quality in Ireland."[693] Shaw, in the preface to his *John Bull's Other Island*, stresses that "When I say that I am an Irishman I mean that I was born in Ireland, and that my native language is the English of Swift and not the unspeakable jargon of mid-XIXth century London newspapers."[694] The link to Swift is addressed by Chesterton, saying that:

> There is a great deal of Jonathan Swift in Bernard Shaw. Shaw is like Swift, for instance, in combining extravagant fancy with a curious sort of coldness. But he is most like Swift in that very quality which Thackeray said was impossible in an Irishman, benevolent bullying, a pity touched with contempt, and a habit of knocking men down for their own good.[695]

It is necessary to emphasize Shaw's birth country, Ireland, since it would not be surprising to conclude that Shaw's political identity originated from Shaw's birth-place and background; since during that time Ireland was "a country in which the political conflicts are at least genuine; they are about something. They are about patriotism, about religion, or about money: the three great realities."[696] These three factors were the basis of evolution in Shaw's political views. Thus, this

---

[689] Griffith, 1993, 23.
[690] Ganz, 1983, 6.
[691] Griffith, 1993, 1.
[692] Chesterton, 1909, 20.
[693] Ibid., 24.
[694] George Bernard Shaw, *Preface to John Bull's Other Island and Major Barbara*, Brentano's, New York, 1907, viii.
[695] Chesterton, 1909, 40.
[696] Ibid., 31.

part of the chapter will consider the political evolution in Shaw's views regarding these three factors: patriotism, religion, and money.

Shaw's patriotism, his religious metamorphoses, and his dealings with economic matters came after his voyage to London. As Ernest A. Boyd conveys "his escape to London lifted Shaw not only out of the family environment but also out of that atmosphere of political and religious concentration which made all but a few Irishman incapable of disinterested thinking."[697] Thus, it is probable that Shaw's propagandist and rebellious identity may be a part of his "early set[ting] sail for England in search of fame, fortune and identity in 1876."[698] Though it is a fact that Bernard Shaw had a rebellious identity before arriving England, which is clear from his own statements, such as "it is true that one of my grandfathers was an Orangeman; but then his sister was an abbess; and his uncle, I am proud to say, was *hanged as a rebel* [italics used to emphasize]",[699] his views on patriotism and the political mannerism mutated after his arrival to London. In saying that "I am a genuine typical Irishman of the Danish, Norman, Cromwellian, and (of course) Scotch invasions"[700] Shaw discloses the affiliation between his Irish identity and his Englishness. Shaw believed that "Ireland is the only spot on earth which still produces the ideal Englishman of history".[701] However, though Ernest A. Boyd discloses that "being under no necessity of declaring himself for or against England, as would have been necessary in Ireland, he was able to assume the air of impartiality,"[702] Gilbert K. Chesterton nevertheless considers Shaw as a man who is "so unlike the English image of Ireland that the English have actually fallen back on the pretence that he was not Irish at all."[703]

---

[697] Ernest A. Boyd, *Appreciations and Depreciations*, The Talbot Press Ltd., Dublin, 1918, 105-106.
[698] Griffith, 1993, 24.
[699] Shaw, 1907, viii.
[700] Ibid., viii.
[701] Ibid., viii.
[702] Boyd, 1918, 106.
[703] Chesterton, 1909, 39.

J. Hackett, on the other hand, in *George versus Bernard*, states that "he is pointed to proudly by the Britons who believe he is English, as the greatest living dramatist, and claimed eagerly by others who think he is Irish, as a sample of the genius which sprouts so readily on their native soil."[704] Shaw himself, selecting the phrase "God's Englishman"[705] to refer to those who are considered as English although they are Irish, articulates that "England cannot do without its Irish and its Scots today, because it cannot do without at least a little sanity".[706] William Lyon Phelps, in *Essays on Modern Dramatists*, writes that Shaw "sees only the evil side of patriotism, he hates war, he reduces Napoleon, Caesar and Shakespeare to ordinary dimensions, he believes that nothing that glitters is really gold."[707] The clashes between Irish and English identities, identity confusions, and the dominant groups within his society, who were for the most part English, had a great impact on Shaw's pioneering of an intellectual movement: the Irish Literary Revival.[708] Chesterton relates that "when one is oppressed it is a mark of chivalry to hurt oneself in order to hurt the oppressor,"[709] and this is what Shaw fought for throughout his life.

In all this it will not be difficult to see the Irishman in Bernard Shaw. Though personally one of the kindest men in the world, he frequently wrote in order to hurt; not because he hated any particular man (he was hardly angry and animal enough for that), but because he really hated certain ideas. He provokes; he will not let people alone. One might even say that he bullies, only that this would be unfair, because he always wishes the other man to hit back.[710]

---

[704] J. Hackett, *Shaw: George versus Bernard*, Sheed and Ward, New York, 14.
[705] Shaw, 1907, ix.
[706] Ibid., ix.
[707] William Lyon Phelps, *Essays on Modern Dramatists*, The Macmillan Company, New York, 1921, 70.
[708] Boyd, 1918, 103.
[709] Chesterton, 1909, 27.
[710] Ibid., 28.

Whether English or Irish, Bernard Shaw "has spent his life trying to make people listen to him".[711] He certainly did not embrace the eulogy of Englishness, but rather as is put forward by Phelps, "Shaw's chief happiness comes from the thought that he was born to set it [the world] right. No one has ever had so good a time lecturing humanity."[712] The core thing he stressed was his understanding of the brain and reason, "Perhaps no man of our time ... has lived so exclusively the life of reason."[713] Phelps moreover considers that reason was for Shaw a powerful weapon: "Rousseau's weapon being Sentiment and Shaw's Reason".[714] Being "one of the master intellectuals of his age, a prince in the universe of progressive thought,"[715] "Bernard Shaw entered England as an alien, as an invader, as a conqueror. In other words, he entered England as an Irishman".[716] In his preface to *John Bull's Other Island* (1904), Shaw derogates the English community by saying that:

> The successful Englishman of today, when he is not a transplanted Scotchman or Irishman, often turns out on investigation to be, if not an American, an Italian, or a Jew, at least to be depending on the brains, the nervous energy, and the freedom from romantic illusions (often called cynicism) of such foreigners for the management of his sources of income.[717]

Thus, Shaw "cannot be expected to exhibit the virtues of a people, but only (as Ibsen would say) of an enemy of the people".[718] His Irish identity was another reason behind his oscillation between reason and religion. Shaw believed that "faith in reason as a prime motor is no longer the criterion of the sound mind, any more than the faith in the

---

[711] Hackett, 73.
[712] Phelps, 1921, 69.
[713] Ibid., 69.
[714] Ibid., 86.
[715] Griffith, 1993, 2.
[716] Chesterton, 1909, 33.
[717] Shaw, 1907, vii.
[718] Chesterton, 1909, 38.

Bible is the criterion of righteous intention".[719] That's the main point that takes us to Shaw's religious identity. Arthur Ganz expresses that in 1869 Shaw was sent to the Central Model Boys' School in which the children of lower-middle class Catholics were educated,[720] and Ganz continues, "To a child of the Ascendancy, the loss of social status was horrifying",[721] (Shaw being "born into the Ascendancy, the Protestant class whose ancestors were mostly British settlers in Ireland").[722] However, as is revealed by Chesterton, "there can surely be no question that Bernard Shaw's Protestant Education in a Catholic country has made a great deal of difference to his mind."[723] Ernest A. Boyd conveys the same view, "Needless to say,... Irish loyalism and Irish Protestantism being the inseparable twin products of anglicized Ireland. Naturally transplantation, and the special circumstances of Shaw's career, have modified them equally".[724]

The fact that "the 1880s was a period of 'ideological cluster', not unlike the 1960s"[725] was a key factor that refurbished Shaw's political and ideological stance "from socialism to theosophy".[726] Here, it will not be inconvenient to convey Griffith's statements on Shaw's stance: "as an artist he sought to present a dialogue on the diversities of the world, whereas as an ideologist he sought instead to offer a discourse on its unities. Hence the uniqueness of art must be acknowledged when Shaw's political argument is under discussion."[727] Shaw's ideology concerning religion had developed continuously; it may be well-established by Chesterton that "Bernard Shaw comes of a Puritan middle-class family of the most solid respectability,"[728] yet it is also crucial to note that Shaw ridiculed "human conceit and most

---

[719] Shaw, 1913, 20.
[720] Ganz, 1983, 11.
[721] Ibid., 11.
[722] Ibid., 6.
[723] Chesterton, 1909, 42.
[724] Boyd, 1918, 114.
[725] Griffith, 1993, 24.
[726] Ibid., 24.
[727] Ibid., 13.
[728] Chesterton, 1909, 55.

dogmas"[729] in a way which reflected his metamorphosed "faith". Probing Shaw's views on religion in *George versus Bernard*, J. Hackett considers Shaw an outsider who "usually wants to discredit the creed which conflicts with his own, and it will always be found that his tendency to distort truth is directly proportional to the weakness of his own position".[730] Thus, the search for the truth urges Shaw to reject any religious view, and to apply some new views instead. As is revealed by Shaw's own words:

> Civilization cannot be saved by people not only crude enough to believe these things, but irreligious enough to believe that such a belief constitutes a religion. The education of children cannot safely be left in their hands. If dwindling sects like the Church of England, the Church of Rome, the Greek Church, and the rest, persist in trying to cramp the human mind within the limits of these grotesque perversions of natural truths and poetic metaphors, then they must be ruthlessly banished from the schools until they either perish in general contempt, or discover the soul that is hidden in every dogma.[731]

Considering Shaw's words, it is credible to ascertain what Hackett observes, saying that "so many certainties have been disturbed of late that people are beginning to put their trust in the belief that belief is not to be trusted".[732] As Hackett reveals, Shaw was highly affected by Henri Bergson who led Shaw to embrace Life Force and Creative Evolution[733] which had "some certain similar points of view independently, and each brought them to a focus in his own way".[734] Based on "the facts put forward, from time to time, in favor of the theory of the gradual evolution of species"[735] the idea of Creative

---

[729] Phelps, 1921, 89.
[730] Hackett, 28.
[731] R. Finch, quoted in *A Shaw Anthology*, Raplace Publications, USA and Great Britain, 2010, 115.
[732] Hackett, 30.
[733] Ibid., 34–35.
[734] Ibid., 34.
[735] Ibid., 35.

Evolution emerged in about 1859 "when *The Origins of Species* was published by Charles Darwin, and when for the first time the theory of evolution was dealt with in a thorough and scientific manner".[736] As Griffith notes, "Darwinism had caused a generational rift in consciousness and in its wake there followed a wave of radicalism"[737] that "marked the coming of a great reaction from the smug commercialism and materialism of the mid-Victorian epoch, and a preparation for the new universe of the twentieth century."[738]

Within the framework of Creative Evolution and Life Force theories or theologies, Shaw tried to find some concrete answers to the exact meaning of life. He searched for the meaning of life; he, many years before the pamphlet of Terry Eagleton's *The Meaning of Life (2007)*, focused on the flux of time which uncovers the gist behind the life itself. In Preface to *Back to Methuselah*, Shaw, believing that he wrote it "as a contribution to the modern Bible",[739] reveals the hidden creeds of life: "that human life is continuous and immortal,"[740] "that God is without 'body, parts, or passions', or as we say, an *Élan Vital* or Life Force",[741] that "sense of the kinship of all forms of life is all that is needed to make Evolution not only a conceivable theory, but an inspiring one."[742] Thus, from these words, it is inferred that Shaw's new theology or religion comprises a wide range of life forms which underpin his ideas of "reason, freedom, free thought, and not being bound to any divine religion", as Henri Bergson believes: "Life is the effort made by energy to become free. It uses the powers and properties of matter, storing itself up and releasing itself in free action and in so doing becoming more free".[743] Perhaps it was because of such a free way of thinking that Shaw once said "I was wholly unmoved by their

---

[736] Ibid., 35.
[737] Griffith, 1993, 24.
[738] Griffith, quoted in, 1993, 24.
[739] George Bernard Shaw, *Back to Methuselah*, 1st World Library, Fairfield, 2007, 22.
[740] Ibid., 36.
[741] Ibid., 49.
[742] Ibid., 73.
[743] Hackett, quoted in, 40.

eloquence; and felt bound to inform that I was, on the whole, an atheist".[744] In one of his letters to Tolstoy, Shaw wrote:

> To me God does not yet exist; but there is a creative force constantly struggling to evolve an executive organ of godlike knowledge and power; that is, to achieve omnipotence and omniscience; and every man and woman born is a fresh attempt to achieve this object.[745]

That kind of free thinking may have some visible impacts on the political ideologies employed by Shaw. That's why Shaw's perspective on the phenomenon of religion—in other words, his isolating himself from such divine beliefs as Protestantism, Puritanism, Christianity, Catholicism, and/or Methodism—sheds significant light on his approval of such politics-based ideologies as Fabianism, Socialism, Feminism, and Communism.[746] As Pathak observes:

> A philosophy of life must have its affirmations with appropriate action to make faith effective. ... He moved on to his ideas of the Life Force, an immanent vitalism of the spirit. Materialism he rejected. His faith in Creative Evolution, through which the Life force promoted change through choice could fairly be called a religion.[747]

Shaw's manifesto on the institutionalization of Socialism was recognized in 1882 in the tracts which were published in 1893 under the title of *The Fabian Society* (1906), in which Shaw defined the "whys, whats and hows" of Fabianism within a few words: "the reconstruction of society in accordance with the highest moral possibilities,"[748] as well as stressing the basis of Fabianism:

---

[744] Chesterton, quoted in, 1909, 75.
[745] Kauffmann, quoted in, 1986, 61.
[746] D. N. Pathak, *George Bernard Shaw: His Religion and Values*, Mittal Publications, Delhi, 1985, 23-31.
[747] Ibid., 14.
[748] George Bernard Shaw, *The Fabian Society: Its Early History*, The Fabian Society, London, 1906, 3.

> The Fabian Society was warlike in its origin: it came into existence through a schism in an earlier society for the peaceful regeneration of the race by the cultivation of perfection of individual character. Certain characters of that circle, modestly feeling that the revolution would have to wait an unreasonably long time if postponed until they personally had attained perfection, set up the banner of Socialism militant; seceded from the Regenerators; and established themselves independently as the Fabian Society.[749]

Though there are many concurrent characteristics of Fabianism and Socialism, Shaw went in search of the small particulars of the two movements: for instance, during the emergence of the Fabian Society there were two different constitutions named the Social Democratic Federation and the Socialist League,[750] and Shaw explained the exact reason for forming a separate society with the following words: "the apparent reason was that we were then middle-class all through, rank and file as well as leaders, whereas the League and Federation were quite proletarian in their rank and file".[751] In another statement, he emphasized that "the object of our campaign, with its watchwords, 'EDUCATE, AGITATE, ORGANIZE', was to bring about a tremendous smash-up of existing society, to be succeeded by complete Socialism".[752] The main discussion was on the "inclusiveness of money" within the boundaries of the society, and Shaw wrote: "In 1884, we were discussing whether money should be permitted under Socialism, or whether labor notes would not be a more becoming currency for us",[753] and he continued, "and I myself actually debated the point with a Fabian who had elaborated a pass-book system to supersede both methods".[754]

---

[749] Ibid., 3–4.
[750] Ibid., 4.
[751] Ibid., 4.
[752] Ibid., 4.
[753] Ibid., 3.
[754] Ibid., 3.

Money (income) was a basic tool for Shaw to employ on behalf of Socialism and fight against poverty.[755] The fact that Shaw was not from a well to do family taught him to "never deceive himself about the need for money, having known for too long the frustrations of his class";[756] for "his class was that ephemeral social entity known as 'the Shabby Genteel, the Poor Relations, the Gentlemen who are no Gentlemen."[757] Thus his writings and all his plays projected the idea of poverty and its unavoidable impacts on the harsh conditions of human beings; Shaw emphasized his goals in writing plays, and in his letter to Lady Colin Campbell on 4 May 1983, he stated: "a 'play' may be a playing with ideas instead of a feast sham of emotions compounded from dog-eared prescriptions".[758] These ideas improved through his exploration of Socialism; Shaw got the hints of Socialism with his participation in the conference lectured by Henry George in 1882 on his book *Progress and Poverty*.[759] In his letter to Hamlin Garland, Shaw stated, "I knew he [Henry George] was an American because ... he spoke of Liberty, Justice, Truth, Natural Law, and other strange eighteenth century superstitions",[760] reflecting his anger against the conditions in Britain, and he continued, "The result of my hearing that speech, ... was that I plunged into a course of economic study, and a very early stage of it became a Socialist."[761] In another letter, Shaw stated that "I read *Progress and Poverty*, and went to a meeting of the Democratic Federation.... They told me I was a novice, and that I should read Karl Marx's *Capital*. ... I immediately became a Socialist".[762]

---

[755] George Bernard Shaw, *The Intelligent Woman's Guide to Socialism, Capitalism, Sovietism and Fascism*, Alma Classics Ltd, Surrey, 2012, 17.
[756] Ganz, 1983, 7.
[757] Griffith, 1993, 23.
[758] Dan H. Laurence, ed., *Bernard Shaw Theatrics*, University of Toronto Press, Toronto, 1995, 10.
[759] Schwartzman, 1990, 114.
[760] Daniel T. Rodgers, quoted in *Contested Truths*, Harvard University Press, Canada, 1987, 37.
[761] Michael Silagi and Susan N. Faulkner, quoted in "Henry George and Europe: As Dissident Economist and Path-Breaking Philosopher, He Was a Catalyst for British Social Reform" in *American Journal of Economics and Sociology*, Vol. 48, No. 1 (Jan 1989), 119.
[762] Schwartzman, quoted in, 1990, 118.

Griffith, composing the most thriving data on Shaw's political thought and Socialism in *Socialism and Superior Brains*, maintains that, "Hatred of idleness and of poverty was the central motif of his Socialism; their eradication, its denouement",[763] and continues, "Poverty, according to famous dictum from *Major Barbara*, was the greatest of evils and the worst of crimes."[764] According to Schwartzman:

> Being a Fabian (evolutionary) Socialist (or Communist, as he later called himself), Shaw disagreed with George's "Remedy", blaming both Land and Capital for the existing social disparity. He advocated, instead of a Single Tax on land values, the appropriation by the State of both rent and interest.[765]

Thus, Shaw believed that "socialism's first duty was to secure sufficiency of means for the masses".[766] To Shaw, "the essential principle of socialism is that man shall honestly labor for those who labor for them, each man replacing what he consumes, none profiting at his fellows' expense, and all profiting alike by the most economical division of labor."[767] Therefore, Shaw's Fabian League was "composed of Socialists who believe[d] that Socialism may be most quickly and most surely realized by utilizing the political power already possessed by the people".[768] In order to overcome the social illnesses, and "such socially useless production Ruskin called *illth*",[769] Shaw and his supporters "raged against emigration, National Insurance, Co-operation, Trade-Unionism, old fashioned Radicalism, and everything else that was not Socialism".[770] In *The Fabian Society*, it is emphasized "The Fabian Society is composed of Socialists"[771] and that "aims at the

---

[763] Griffith, 1993, 28.
[764] Ibid., 28.
[765] Schwartzman , 1990, 118.
[766] Griffith, 1993, 28.
[767] Griffith, quoted in, 1993, 29.
[768] Shaw, 1906, 13.
[769] Griffith, 1993, 30.
[770] Ibid., 15–16.
[771] Shaw, 1906, 31.

re-organization of the society by the emancipation of Land and Industrial Capital from individual and class ownership, and the vesting of them in the community for the general benefit".[772] Within its general rules, under the title of *General Socialism in its various aspects*, the lecturer William Morris—also a forerunner of Fabian Society—holds Communism as an interrelated phenomenon to Socialism,[773] and Morris believes "the first duty of Socialists is to educate the people to understand what their present position is, and what their future might be, and to keep the principle of Socialism steadily before them."[774] Believing that Communism covers a "true and complete Socialism", Morris underpinned the idea that it is practically impossible that "the betterment of the working people might go and yet stop at last without having made any progress on the direct road to Communism." Shaw, agreeing with Morris, once announced himself to be a Communist:

> What more can I do for Communism than I am doing? ... I have gone around the world ... shouting that I am a Communist ... I have given every scrap of my support for what is worth to Russia.... There is no public man in England more completely committed to Communism, and in particular to the support of the Russian system, than I.[775]

Shaw's search for equal life standards and his aiming at the "ethos of tolerance, ... the crucial intellectualism and ... exclusiveness"[776] led him also to "turn upon mutual intellectual interests in Ibsen and a concern for the relationship between socialism and sexual equality".[777] Chesterton reveals that "Bernard Shaw (being honestly eager to put himself on the modern side in everything) put himself on the side of what is called the feminist movement; the proposal to give the two

---

[772] Ibid., 31.
[773] Ibid., 32.
[774] Ibid., 12.
[775] Schwartzman, quoted in, 1990, 123.
[776] Griffith, 1993, 32.
[777] Ibid., 33.

sexes not merely equal social privileges, but identical".[778] In one of his other statements, Chesterton stresses:

> Indeed, almost every one of Bernard Shaw's earlier plays might be called an argument between a man and a woman, in which the woman is thumped and thrashed and outwitted until she admits that she is the equal of her conqueror.[779]

To sum up, regarding the literature reviews, it is seen that "when Shaw first burst into London, a young, red-haired Irishman, announced himself as an atheist, an anarchist, and a vegetarian",[780] and then, "within months of his conversion to socialism, the poor, self–educated outsider found himself at the center of the small stage which sufficed for the socialist movement".[781] He eulogized the Creative Evolution and Life Force theories believing that his "greatest and surest successes as a public speaker have been on religious subjects to religious audiences";[782] "by the end of 1888, Shaw was editing *Fabian Essays*, the success of which made him a national celebrity in socialist circles".[783] He made clear that "the achievement of Socialism economically involves the transfer of rent from the class which now appropriates it to the whole people,"[784] and so maintained:

> This is the true joy in life, the being used for a purpose recognized by yourself as a mighty one; the being thoroughly worn out before you are thrown on the scrap heap; the being a force of Nature instead of a feverish selfish little clod of ailments and grievances complaining that the world will not devote itself to making you happy.[785]

---

[778] Chesterton, 1909, 64.
[779] Ibid., 67.
[780] Edwin E. Slosson, *Six Major Prophets*, Little Brown and Company, Boston, 1917, 28.
[781] Griffith, 1993, 32.
[782] Slosson, quoted in, 1917, 29-30.
[783] Griffith, 1993, 44.
[784] Ibid., 43.
[785] Harold Bloom, quoted in *Dramatists and Dramas*, Chalsea House Publishers, Philadelphia, 2005, 161.

Therefore, Shaw protested against every "feverish selfish little clod of ailments and grievances"; his words reflected "the love of justice and the hatred of shams"[786] which made him "the indefatigable champion of social justice, not because he has a passion for social justice, but because he has an intellectual perception of it, because his aquiline eyesight instantly sees through all delusions, deceptions, and hypocrisies".[787] Shaw was a prolific playwright whose political stance embraced such political thoughts as Socialism, Communism, and Feminism and such spiritual ideologies as Creative Evolution, Life Force, and *Übermensch*.[788] According to Stanley Kauffman, Shaw, at the age of 93, announced that *Shakes versus Shav* (1949) "in all actuarial possibility is my last play",[789] he, as it turned out, was speaking the truth—he died at the age of 94.[790]

Political Evolution in Orhan Asena

The most extensive study on the biography of Orhan Asena so far written is by Prof. Hülya Nutku, whose work, titled *Cumhuriyet'in 75. Yılında 75 Yılın Tanığı Bir Yazar: Orhan Asena,* was awarded the Greatest Prize in Biography by the Turkish Ministry of Culture in 1998,[791] and provides us with certain details about the playwright's life. Orhan Asena was born in 1922 in Diyarbakır.[792] Before starting primary

---

[786] Bennet, 1976, 99.
[787] Ibid., 93.
[788] Most Nietzsche scholars prefer to render the term *Übermensch* as "superman" or "overman". Some prefer to leave the word in the original since there is no good English equivalent. Detwiller (1990), in his book *Nietzsche and the Politics of Aristocratic Radicalism*, argues that the word "superman" allows us to tie the translation to others words use "super" like "superhuman" or "superhistorical". However, others scholars such us Kaufman (1974) prefer to connect the *Übermensch* with *Uberwindung* in its sense of overcoming. As Nietzsche notes in the firs speech, prophet Zarathustra made to the people began: "I teach you the overman. Man is something that should be overcome (*Uberwunden*). What have you done to overcome him?" *(Thus Spoke Zarathustra*, 1966, 3). Taken from Ingrid Flórez Fortich, "Nietzsche's Übermensch: The Notion Of A Higher Aristocracy Of The Future" in *Civilizar* 10 (18): 75–80 (2010), 76.
[789] Kauffmann, quoted in, 1986, 58.
[790] Ibid., 58.
[791] Hülya Nutku, *Cumhuriyet'in 75. Yılında 75 Yılın Tanığı Bir Yazar: Orhan Asena*, Kültür Bakanlığı Yayınları, Ankara, 1998.
[792] Ibid., 1.

school, it was noted that he could recite Süleyman Çelebi's *Mawlid* (written in 15th century), and some parts of *Siyer-i Nebi* (prophetic biography of the prophet Mohammed PBUH).[793] Asena was greatly influenced by what his grandmother and grandfather read to him during his childhood, including some readings on *Tutiname, Altıparmak Tarihi, Kısası Enbiya, Cengizhan* and *Harzem Şahı Celalettin,* and he learnt something of *Ölmüş Kadının Evrak-ı Metrukesi* (1905) and *Nedret* (1922) by Güzide Sabri Aygün, *Zavallı Necdet* (1902) by Saffet Nezihi, such translations as *Tunçtan Kızlar* written by Xavier de Montepin written in 1856 and translated by Mehmed Tevfik in 1892, *Monte Kristo* (1844) by Alexander Dumas, and *Sefiller* (*Les Misérables,* 1862) by Victor Hugo.[794]

Being a relative of Ziya Gökalp, who was a well-known figure pioneering the ideal of Turkism, Asena witnessed many of the historical events which emerged in Turkey at that time.[795] For instance, he witnessed the repercussions of the 31st March Incident in Diyarbakır,[796] an incident which was "the crucial episode of the counter revolution of 1909".[797] Asena, in his childhood, firstly dealt with poetry; he got great marks in history and social sciences,[798] and was highly affected by Faruk Nafiz Çamlıbel's poetry, attempting to mirror his style of rhymed poetry and the poems written in metre.[799] Though his grandfather was a well-known agha within the circles of Diyarbakır, his father M. Celalettin Asena was, on the contrary, an ordinary officer who was driven to drink and gambling. From the writings of Hülya Nutku, we find out that during Orhan Asena's early years, Diyarbakır had witnessed a great economic depression which was the mirror image of the Great Depression in the world.[800] Thus, this economic turmoil

---

[793] Ibid., 1.
[794] Ibid., 1–2.
[795] Ibid., 3–5.
[796] Ibid., 3.
[797] Zürcher, 2007, 368.
[798] Nutku, 1998, 3.
[799] Ibid., 3.
[800] Ibid., 5.

radically affected the Asenas; their life changed dramatically.[801] In 1945, Asena graduated from medical faculty[802] and after his marriage to Neriman Asena, the couple had two sons, Bora and Aydın.[803]

Asena's literary career began when he first published his poems in the magazine *Dicle Kaynağı*, and then he published some of his short stories in such periodicals as *Yeni Mecmua, Yücel, Çınaraltı, Varlık, Yeni İstanbul,* and *Yaratış*.[804] In 1941, his first poetry book, *Masal*, was published.[805] When he was a high school student, he wrote a few such amateur plays including *İntikam* and *Tamara* till he saw *Zehirli Kucak* which caused him not to write any plays until his attendance at university.[806] Asena, in one speech, said: "I frequently read Dostoyevsky. I bought all his works and read them thoroughly. That's why my first critical play was *Bir Ölü Dolaşıyor*".[807] Then, he wrote *Yeşil Türbe Sokağı* in 1952.[808] But his rise as a playwright was based on *Gılgamış (Tanrılar ve İnsanlar)* which was written in 1952 and first performed in 1954 in Ankara Büyük Tiyatro.[809] With that play, Asena introduced a new style of drama which comprised both the Republican era and the political turbulences of the period.

In one of his writings, Asena stressed "A feeling, a dream, a thought, a subject is evidently not created out of nothing. It is, whether conscious or unconscious, a kind of reflection of the environment, the society, or the life in which the artists live".[810] This comment provides us, no doubt, with certain clues as to the contents of his political and socio-cultural plays. After writing *Yeşil Türbe Sokağı*, Asena revealed "And six months later, I went to Ankara. The Republican People's Party

---

[801] Ibid., 5.
[802] Ibid., 6.
[803] Ibid., 7.
[804] Ibid., 7.
[805] Ibid., 7.
[806] Ibid., 7.
[807] Ibid., quoted in, 9.
[808] Ibid., 8.
[809] Ibid., 9.
[810] Orhan Asena, "Yaratı ve Üreti" in *Çağdaş Türk Dili Dergisi*, Cilt 1, Sayı 5, Temmuz 1988, 222.

(RPP)[811] lost the elections, the Democratic Party (DP)[812] won the elections, there was pressure and I was amazed by this";[813] a comment which echoes his political leanings during this period. Indeed, Asena's political ideologies were highly connected to the period's social turbulence and political unrest. In 1950, "The DP won 53 percent of the popular vote and 84 percent of the parliamentary seats, in contrast to the RPP's 40 percent of the vote and 14 percent of the seats".[814] Considering this political atmosphere, it is important to emphasize that Asena supported the RPP because of the party's Kemalist vision and its stress on Mustafa Kemal's philosophy, which "named six principles in the 1930s, showing a general direction with roots in realism. They were: Republicanism, Nationalism, Populism, Reformism, Secularism and Statism".[815]

The fact that the RPP was composed of a society pioneered by Mustafa Kemal Atatürk was the basic factor that urged Asena to support them. As revealed by Frank Tachau, "the People's Party (later the Republican People's Party, or RPP) in 1923, ... was the sole party of the authoritarian regime that prevailed for the next 27 years, after the declaration of the Republic of Turkey"[816] under the rule of Atatürk. Metin And, in *Cumhuriyet Dönemi Türk Tiyatrosu*, stresses that

---

[811] Cumhuriyet Halk Partisi. Major Turkish political party 1923–80. Formally terminated in 1982 by decision of the National Security Council. Obedient to Kemal Atatürk's charismatic authority and modernization programme. Held dictatorial single-party rule 1923–46 and continued in power under the multiparty system until 1950, when it lost free general elections and became an opposition party. Led several coalition governments in the 1960s and 1970s. Ideology was Ottoman patriotism and Islamism, rather than Turkish nationalism. Sought to preserve the offices of caliphate and sultanate, secure the integrity of the Ottoman motherland, and safeguard national independence. Rallied people through religion. Taken from John L. Esposito, ed., *The Oxford Dictionary of Islam*, Oxford University Press, New York, 2003, 264.
[812] Demokrat Parti. Ruled Turkey 1950–60. Lifted prior ban on call to prayer in Arabic. Permitted radio broadcasts of religious programs. Reintroduced Islamic instruction in schools. Encouraged religious activity as a distraction from the economic downturn of the 1950s. Facilitated the resurgence of Islam, especially at the popular level, in Turkey. Taken from Esposito, ed., 2003, 66.
[813] Nutku, quoted in, 1998, 10.
[814] Frank Tachau, "Turkish Political Parties and Elections: Half a Century of Multiparty Democracy" in *Turkish Studies*, Vol. 1, No.1 (Spring 2000), 130.
[815] Türkkaya Ataöv, "The Principles of Kemalism" in *The Turkish Yearbook of International Relations*, Milletlerarası Münasebetler Türk Yıllığı, Cilt: 20, 1980, 28.
[816] Tachau, 2000, 129.

Atatürk, with modern Turkey now a Republic, paid great attention to art and literature, especially to the theatre.[817] He would frequently go to the theatre and speak to the artists about their work.[818] Indeed, in one of his speeches, Atatürk said: "Gentlemen! You may all become deputies.... You may all become proxies.... You can even become presidents.... But you cannot become artists!"[819] Hence some consider Atatürk to be "the first dramaturge of Turkey".[820] Atatürk, from the very early years of the Republican Turkey to its maturity, recognized the idea that the theatre must perform a public service and that it must be preserved and supported by the public authority.[821] In another dialogue, Atatürk said that "The theatre is the mirror image of a country's cultural level".[822] These statements reflect the fact that Atatürk was an art-lover and because of his stance towards the theatre, the playwrights and the artists felt admiration for him and supported many of his policies.[823] The fact that Atatürk was the founder of the Turkish Republic and the power holder of the RPP led most playwrights and artists to support his political party, and Asena was no exception. Asena, to reflect his admiration for Atatürk, wrote many poems, and dramatic works; for instance, in 1991, he wrote a poem titled *Atatürk Bir Çıkıştır, Varış Değil* (*Atatürk is a Starting, Not a Finish*):

> Atatürk is a starting, not a finish,
> Finish means being exhausted, Atatürk is inexhaustible,
> Finish means death, Atatürk never dies.
> I am dead; Ataturk will be missing just once without me,
> You are born, he/she is born, and others are born;

---

[817] And (b), 1983, 5.
[818] Ibid., 7.
[819] Ibid., quoted in, 7.
[820] Ibid., 7.
[821] Ibid., 11.
[822] Ibid., quoted in, 11.
[823] Seda Bayındır Uluskan, *Atatürk'ün Sosyal ve Kültürel Politikaları*, Korza Basım, Ankara, 2010, 422–23.

With you, a thousand is born, a thousand multiplies, a thousand emerges,
The earth revolves, life continues, lives Ataturk. [824]

In his children's play titled *Mustafa* (1993), Asena documented the historical biography of Mustafa Kemal Atatürk by which he aimed to educate the children and impress Kemalist perspectives upon them.[825] İnci Enginün, in one of her articles, emphasizes that in *Mustafa* Asena portrays the childhood days of Atatürk—the founder of the Turkish Republic—encompassing his childhood till his entry into military secondary schools, and stresses that Asena, through *Mustafa,* depicts Atatürk's rebellious manners against injustices, thereby which giving some clues pertaining to his future position and principles.[826] Asena's love for Mustafa Kemal Atatürk and his support of Kemalist perspectives were also mirrored in *Gılgamış* (1959) and *Korku* (1956).

Asena, in one of his lectures, said that Prof. Rene Giraud—who translated *Gılgamış* into French—remarked in the foreword, "Obviously, Atatürk is the Gilgamesh of the generation of Orhan Asena,"[827] and considering that word of Giraud, Asena continued, "No matter how Gilgamesh took the gods on himself for the sake of human beings, was not it Ataturk who had taken the imperialist powers imagined as modern gods, the sultan of authority and power, obsolete institutions, bodies, the Caliphate alliance on himself?"[828] Hülya Nutku, discusses the way in which *Korku* Asena depicted something of Atatürk and she says: "Ironically, those who had not realized that Gılgamesh was Atatürk were nevertheless able to recognize the hero in *Korku:* it was Atatürk".[829]

---

[824] Orhan Asena, *Atatürk Bir Çıkıştır, Varış Değil!*, Ankara, 24.9.1991, http://www.turkishnews.com/Ataturk/siirleri/s6.htm Accessed: 01.04.2013.
[825] Ayşe Ulusoy Tunçel, "Tiyatro Eserlerinde Oyun Kişisi Olarak Atatürk" in *Journal of Turkish World Studies*, Xiii/1 (Yaz 2013), 124–26.
[826] İnci Enginün, "Orhan Asena'nın Oyunları" in *İstanbul Üniversitesi Türk Dili ve Edebiyatı Dergisi*, Cil 28, 1998, 245.
[827] Nutku, quoted in, 1998, 20.
[828] Ibid., 20.
[829] Ibid., 26.

Apart from these nostalgic portrayals, Asena also revealed the political problems of the period in which he lived. The unrest in the country led Asena to protest against the widespread injustices and wrongs across the country. Asena's protest approved itself during the government of Adnan Menderes, a period known as pre-coup period in Turkey. As noted by Teresa Cicierska Chtapowa, Asena wrote two plays two years after 1954, the two years which were "the period that reached its largest size of the Menderes dictatorship consuming the hopes of the all progressive forces and attempting to destroy Atatürk's revolutions".[830] The coup d'état of 1960[831] was a major problem for many writers. Though Asena, as noted by Hülya Nutku, first went to Germany in 1964 in order to specialize and became an expert in his field, remaining there for more than two years,[832] after turning back to Turkey he could not concentrate on his studies and again fled to Germany in 1971, just after the 12 March coup d'état[833] of Turkish military.[834] Asena, for his imperative departure, said:

> I had talked big, because I went there [Germany] once more, even to stay for six years. Rather, I was forced to go. Turkey had reached the dead-end on March 12th, Turkey was stuck [in a difficult situation]. It was such a period that Demirel was again the only alternative power. That is, it was the irresponsibility period which led to the 12th March. It was such a period in which even our freedom to be silent was taken from us. Men were put into prison not because of what they wrote, but because of what

---

[830] Ibid., quoted in, 1998, 27.
[831] The 1960 coup in Turkey grew out of tensions engendered by a widespread belief that the Democrat Party government of Adnan Menderes and Celal Bayar was about to return to one-party rule by abolishing Ataturk's party led by former President Ismet Inonu. The military move in 1960 thus represented, in the minds of most of its initiators, a move to save the state. Taken from George S. Harris, "Military Coups and Turkish Democracy, 1960–1980" in *Turkish Studies* Vol. 12, No. 2 (June 2011), 203.
[832] Ibid., 78.
[833] This "coup by memorandum" demanded that a cabinet of technocrats be formed to cope with leftist terrorists. Otherwise, the generals threatened to use "the authority of law to protect the Turkish Republic" by taking over the government directly. S. Demirel and his cabinet quickly resigned. Harris, 2011, 206.
[834] Ibid., 78.

they read, and what they thought. It was a period in which the books were burnt.[835]

It is possible to perceive the manifestations of this seditionist spirit in many of his plays. In *Gılgamış* (1952), *Tohum ve Toprak* (1964), *Hürrem Sultan* (1960), *Simavnalı Şeyh Bedrettin* (1969), *Yıldız Yargılanması* (1983), *Şili'de Av* (1975), *Atçalı Kel Mehmet* (1970), and *Ya Devlet Başa Ya Kuzgun Leşe* (1983), Asena partially reflects the politics of the period—albeit dressing this up with the "colors" of history—thus emphasizing his political point of view. Consequently, we conclude that Asena's urgent departure was not just an escape from the pressures of the 12th March coup d'état of Turkish military in 1970; it was something to do with his own libertarian mannerism. During the time he was in Germany, Asena wrote three significant plays collected under the name of the Chile trilogy: *Şili'de Av* (1975), *Ölü Kentin Nabzı* (1979) and *Bir Başkana Ağıt* (1980).[836] This trilogy dealt with the political events which occurred in Chile in 1973, though Asena was highly affected by what Joseph Lawrensky wrote in his *Allende*.[837] The state of siege in Turkey was a major factor in Orhan Asena's turning to deal instead with the problems in Chile,[838] where he identified himself with Salvador Allende and projected three well-made plays reflecting Allende's tragedy. It was in 1970 that Turkey faced a great coup d'état, and interestingly, "In 1970, the people of the South American republic of Chile elected Salvador Allende Gossens president in an event that was perceived across the Third World as a major democratic and socialist revolution".[839] The fact that Salvador Allende was a "a member of the Popular Unity coalition and a Marxist pledged to support the right of unions to organize, redistribute land to landless peasants and

---

[835] Ibid., quoted in, 78.
[836] Ibid., 79.
[837] Hülya Nutku, "Orhan Asena'nın Oyun Yazarlığının Gelişimi ve Oyunları" in *Orhan Asena: Toplu Oyunları 1*, Boyut Yayınları, İstanbul, 1992, 24.
[838] Nutku, 1998, 81.
[839] Charles De Jesus and John Heitner, "U.S. Imperialism Defeats Salvador Allende and Democracy in Chile", 1. http://people.hofstra.edu/alan_j_singer/CoursePacks/USImperialismDefeatsSalvador AllendeandDemocracyinChile.pdf, Accessed: 09.09.2014.

the nationalization of foreign-owned private industry"[840] must have affected Asena so much that he aimed to address his tragedies within his plays. Indeed, to Asena, "if the problems are up to date and the interpretations are oriented towards today, historical or geographic variances do not change the actuality of the event or person".[841]

In *Şili'de Av*, Asena ironically referred to the witch-hunt in Turkey, as Hülya Nutku reveals, "Now, the hunting outside is a ruthless human prey. As far as they are aware, people are in a fight against the changing conditions of their country".[842] In *Ölü Kentin Nabzı* (1977), Asena outlined the social problems and conflicts within a Turkish city, the pressures of a fascist rule, and a dead city, a city tired and diminished.[843] In *Bir Başkana Ağıt* (1979) Asena portrayed the leader of Unidad Popular and the president of Chile: Salvador Allende. However, because of the success of Allende, some Chilean power holders and other supporters in the country were worried. They were worried because Salvador Allende managed to be supported by the society.[844] The play ended with the coup d'état of the military forces. As can be concluded, Asena made an analogy between Chile and Turkey and he, in some ways, identified Atatürk with Allende by eulogizing the socialism and humanism of Salvador Allende, as well as emphasizing the public's love and support for him. From the Chile trilogy, we may arrive at the idea that Asena admired the socialism of Allende, and by his artistic depiction he correlated this with the situation in Turkey. On the other hand, as Chtapowa expresses "In all the plays of this author, the common point or the common denominator is his deep humanism. For Asena, man is always the starting point. Man—with his inexhaustible wealth of possibilities!"[845]

---

[840] Ibid., 1.
[841] Nutku, 1998, 73.
[842] Ibid., 84.
[843] Ibid., 86–87.
[844] Nutku, 1992, 41.
[845] Nutku, quoted in, 1998, 27.

The playwright's other political play, no doubt, is his first historical play and the first one of the "Power Quadruples (*İktidar Dörtlemesi*)": *Hürrem Sultan* (1958). The play reflected the classical throne struggles of the Ottoman Empire, *Hürrem Sultan* also echoed the period in which the play was written. As Asena revealed:

> Let's try to recall the period ... many writers were in prison. There was a serious look in the press. It was the first time that I had dealt with historical topics. Turkey was more or less in a condition similar to that of the conflict between Suleiman the Magnificent and Prince Mustafa. There was a battle between the ruling and opposition sides which would result in one of them being beheaded. Many such values as democracy, human rights, freedom of ideas—adopted hitherto by the government—were put aside. In short, we were going through a crisis.[846]

Similarly, in *Tohum ve Toprak* (1964) Asena documented the coup d'état in Turkey, "the first coup in the Turkish Republic, in 1960, [which] represented a water-shed in its politics".[847] Focusing thematically on the killing of Alemdar Mustafa Pasha, who was introduced as a saviour in *Tohum ve Toprak,* Asena reflected on the common destinies, sufferings, and loneliness of the revolutionaries who sought to shed light on society, but who were eventually annihilated by the bigger and stronger dark powers.[848] Orhan Asena, for *Tohum ve Toprak*, said: "I confess that what urged me to deal with that topic was my anticipation of the loneliness of May 27th and those who supported it and yet were left alone".[849] In *Simavnalı Şeyh Bedrettin* (1969), Asena tackled the idea of a "more powerful but unjust order" and systematically depicted the conflict between the state and public by projecting Şeyh Bedrettin as a socialist and revolutionary.[850] In the

---

[846] Ibid., quoted in, 46.
[847] Umit Cizre Sakallioglu, "Parameters and Strategies of Islam-State Interaction in Republican Turkey" in *International Journal of Middle East Studies*, Vol. 28, No. 2 (May 1996), 238.
[848] Nutku, 1998, 53.
[849] Ibid., 53.
[850] Ibid., 68–71.

same way, his socialist standpoint was reestablished in *Atçalı Kel Mehmet* (1970) in which the conflict between the leader and the public was the main feature.[851] One of Asena's other would-be-political masterpieces is *16 Mart 1920* (1974) which was again written in Germany.[852] In one of his writings in 1979, Asena wrote: "I was a playwright. I could sound my voice only on the stage. They closed the stages. To stay—in an uneasy even a threatening environment—to be seen to be intimidated, to keep quiet were really hard. I would go and write there [Germany]".[853] Asena's *16 Mart 1920* was written for the 50th Anniversary of the Turkish Republic, and in it Asena stressed the significance of republicanism; he revealed his nationalist and Kemalist vision through his tribute to the War of Independence.[854] He characterized such nationalist figures as Mustafa Kemal, İsmet İnönü, Halide Edip Adıvar, Adnan Adıvar etc. by which he reflected the Kemalist, nationalist, and republican mannerisms. In the 1980s, Asena became more directly involved in politics,[855] and we reach the conclusion that the 12th September 1980 Turkish coup d'état became to the means through which he became at last able to address directly the historical issues through which he represented the problems of 1980s Turkey.

In his *İktidar Dörtlemesi: Roksolon* (1985), *Hürrem Sultan* (1960), *Ya Devlet Başa Ya Kuzgun Leşe* (1982), and *Sığıntı* (1986), Asena dealt entirely with political matters, as he expressed: "I depicted the vicious cycle of fear-crime-fear-crime, and in order to write this, I needed to live during pre- and post- 12th September."[856] In *Yıldız Yargılanması* (1983), at the suggestion of the journalist Uğur Mumcu, Asena depicted Mithat Pasha by portraying the period of autocracy under the rule of

---

[851] Ibid., 73.
[852] Ibid., 79.
[853] Ibid., 44.
[854] Ibid., 92.
[855] Ibid., 105.
[856] Ibid., quoted in, 109.

Ottoman Abdulaziz and Abdulhamit.[857] As might be expected, Asena used the techniques of the theatre of cruelty to represent the unjust state of the legal system and its political clashes. Lastly, in 1987, Asena wrote *Ankara 1920* by which he again tackled a political issue which was of great importance in terms of the War of Independence. In the play Asena portrayed the revolts of Cerkez Ethem.[858]

To sum up, Orhan Asena was faced with many differing political situations; he witnessed a number of coups d'état in Turkey. His love for Republican thought, his love for Mustafa Kemal Atatürk and his Kemalist perspectives, his love for the nation-state never changed. He did not accept the religion-based norms of the governments ruled by Adnan Menderes, Celal Bayar, and Necmettin Erbakan. For the sake of his liberal standpoint, he departed from Turkey and lived in Germany for a very long time. All his political and ideological ideas found their way into his plays.

---

[857] Ibid., 130.
[858] The Istanbul government also tried to organize armed resistance to the nationalists, with support from the somewhat sceptical British. They used exactly the same kind of bands of irregulars as the nationalists did. Circassian Ahmet Anzavur led the most important of these in the region of Balıkesir, but they were suppressed, though with some difficulty, by *Çerkez* (Circassian) Ethem's bands on behalf of the nationalists. Zurcher, 2004, 131, 152.

CHAPTER 4: POLITICAL LANGUAGES OF SHAW AND ASENA

Andrew Heywood, in *Political Theory*, emphasizes the point that "language is often used as a political weapon; words are seldom neutral but carry political and ideological baggage".[859] It is no wonder that "we live in a world saturated with divisive political language—a world of metaphors and adjectives that conjure up archetypal images of good and evil, of impending war and celestial conquest".[860] Let's take Harold Pinter's following questions into consideration:

> Does reality essentially remain outside language, separate, obdurate, alien, not susceptible to description? Is an accurate and vital correspondence between what is and our perception of it impossible? Or is that we are obliged to use language only in order to obscure and distort reality—to distort what happens—because we fear it?[861]

The response is either yes or no. Though George Orwell, in *Politics and the English Language* (1968), said "language is a natural growth and not an instrument which we shape for our own purposes,"[862] he also believed that "all issues are political issues, and politics itself is a mass of lies, evasions, folly, hatred, and schizophrenia"[863] in which "language merely reflects existing social conditions".[864] Thus, language reflects the reality; that is, the life itself. When George Orwell said that "Political language—and with variations this is true of all political parties, from Conservatives to Anarchists—is designed to make lies sound truthful

---

[859] Heywood, 2004, 14.
[860] Gregory Shafer, "Political Language, Democracy, and the Language Arts Class" in *English Journal* 103.2 (2013), 30.
[861] Nadine Gordimer, quoted in *Living in Hope and History*, Bloomsbury Publishing, London, 1999, 12.
[862] Sonia Orwell And Ian Angus, eds., *The Collected Essays, Journalism And Letters Of George Orwell*, Vol IV, Secker And Warburg, London, 1968, 127.
[863] Ibid., 137.
[864] Ibid., 137.

and murder respectable, and to give an appearance of solidity to pure wind",[865] he was emphasizing the disguised agenda of real life. In a way, Orwell gave the answer to the questions raised by Harold Pinter.

Concentrating on the link between ideology and language, Thomas Ricento suggests that it is ideology that helps us understand language politics;[866] the language is shaped through the ideologies employed by the writers. This is just what Orwell signifies with the following: "if thought corrupts language, language can also corrupt thought".[867] In this regard it would not be an exaggeration to describe language as being rather like a liquid which takes the shape of the vessel into which it is poured. Thoughts shape language and vice versa.

In all of their writings, both Shaw and Asena employ some kind of political language which addresses what Aristotle in *Politics* calls the power of lingual elocution; "the power of speech is intended to set forth the expedient and inexpedient, and therefore likewise the just and the unjust".[868] In this chapter, regarding all the thoughts above, we will concentrate upon the direct and indirect use of political language employed by Bernard Shaw and Orhan Asena. Accordingly, Shaw's *Arms and the Man, Mrs Warren's Profession, Major Barbara, Pygmalion, Widowers' Houses, Candida*; Orhan Asena's *Hürrem Sultan, Ya Devlet Başa Ya Kuzgun Leşe, Tanrılar ve İnsanlar, Şili Üçlemesi, Tohum ve Toprak,* and *Korku* are to be examined to determine how the political language of each work may be described.

Political Language of Bernard Shaw

Regarding Shaw, Richard Burton, in *The Man and The Mask* (1916), writes:

---

[865] Ibid., 137.
[866] Thomas Ricento, ed., *Ideology, Politics and Language Policies*, John Benjamins Publishing Company, Amsterdam and Philadelphia, 2000, 3-14.
[867] Orwell et al., eds., London, 1968, 137.
[868] Anthony F. Lang, Jr, ed., quoted in *Political Theory and International Affairs*, Praeger, Westport, 2004, 30.

> The proof of his genuineness as thinker and writer lies in an open-minded examination of his works, approaching them with a fortifying comprehension of his personality and private history; also, as especially important, with a clear-eyed realization of certain peculiarities in his way of conveying his message.[869]

The fact that Shaw "conveyed his messages" through an Orwellian standpoint by "merely reflecting existing social conditions" is not a simple proof of his "genuineness as a thinker"; as he reveals in preface to *Major Barbara* "I, the dramatist whose business it is to shew the connection between things that seem apart and unrelated in the haphazard order of events in real life, have contrived to make it known".[870] Thus, Shaw's urge to transmit his political messages reflects his idealism. As Griffith comments, "Shaw's political thought, like Plato's, was haunted by his idealism, by his perfectionist desire to transcend the sordid realm of conflict".[871] Therefore, Shaw goes in search of reality by politically corrupting idealism, as Richard M. Ohmann remarks:

> Shaw embraces Ibsenism because he sees in it the exposure of ideals to the cold light of day. The idealist hides from fact because he hates himself; the realist sees in ideals "only something to blind us, something to numb us, something to murder self in us, something whereby, instead of resisting death, we can disarm it by committing suicide" (QI, 34).[872]

The Platonic view is strengthened by Shaw's own words in *Quintessence of Ibsenism*: "If the term realist is objected to on account of some of its modern associations, I can only recommend you, if you must associate it with something else than my own description of its

---

[869] Richard Burton, *Bernard Shaw: The Man and The Mask*, Henry Holt and Company, New York, 1916, 34.
[870] George Bernard Shaw, *Pygmalion and Major Barbara*, Bantam Dell, New York, 1992, 35.
[871] Griffith, 1993, 61.
[872] Richard M. Ohmann, *Shaw: The Style and The Man*, Wesleyan University Press, Middletown Connecticut, 1962, 105.

meaning (I do not deal in definitions), to associate it, not with Zola and Maupassant, but with Plato."[873] This politics of idealism and realism—which is distinguished through the words "build[ing] a play not on pathos, but on bathos"[874] by Chesterton—is evidently emphasized within the melodrama *Arms and the Man* in which "Shaw only objects to [the romantic war and the romantic love] in so far as they are ideal; that is in so far as they are idealized".[875] Just as what Shaw emphasizes in his preface to *Plays Pleasant and Unpleasant* with the words "the romantic morality of the critics and the realistic morality of the plays,"[876] the eulogy of idealism and the representation of realism are politically underlined through *Arms and the Man*. As Shaw explains:

> I am quite aware that the much criticized Swiss officer in *Arms and the Man* is not a conventional stage soldier. He suffers from want of food and sleep; his nerves go to pieces after three days under fire, ending in the horrors of a rout and pursuit; he has found by experience that it is more important to have a few bits of chocolate to eat in the field than cartridges for his revolver.[877]

According to Shaw—as is reflected in *Quintessence of Ibsenism*—to the idealists "human nature, naturally corrupt, is held back from ruinous excesses only by self-denying conformity to the ideals",[878] whilst "to the other [he means the realists] these ideals are only swaddling clothes which man has outgrown, and which insufferably impede his movements."[879] However, to Shaw, the proportions are not equal; as mentioned in *Back to Methuselah* (1922): "I seem a man like other men because nine-tenths of me is common humanity. But the other tenth is a faculty for seeing things as they really are."[880] This clarification again

---

[873] Shaw, 1913, 27.
[874] Chesterton, 1909, 115.
[875] Ibid., 118.
[876] George Bernard Shaw, *Plays Pleasant and Unpleasant II*, Grant Richards, London, 1898, xvi.
[877] Ibid., xvi.
[878] Shaw, 1913, 28.
[879] Ibid., 29.
[880] Griffith, quoted in 1993, 3.

reminds us the politics of realism uttered by Bluntschli in *Arms and the Man*: "life isn't a farce, but something quite sensible and serious."[881]

The idealized or illusionary way of life is concurrently depicted by Shaw; this standpoint is stressed by Richard M. Ohmann: "Shaw's 'unpleasant' plays, too, consist mainly in the stripping away of illusions—Trench's illusions about the innocence of interest, the Petkoff's about war, Morell's about women and marriage and so on",[882] and he continues, "Mrs Warren, who has most reason to doubt the saccharine Victorian world-view, gives the lie to society most convincingly, the more so because she is trying to justify herself to her daughter".[883] That's why, Griffith is strongly right to announce that "Fundamentally, Shaw made the problems involved in translating theory into practice, in relating the ideas of doctrine to the complex realities of power politics, the central theme of the drama",[884] because, just like other plays, in *Mrs Warren's Profession* Shaw blends idealism with realism and makes use of politics of "the dirty trade of harlotry"[885] which is a realistically political and/or politically realistic practice of Victorian life. This is not an ideal/ism; yet, "it is a really sharp exposition of the dangers of 'idealism', the sacrifice of people to principles, and Shaw is even wiser in his suggestion that this excessive idealism exists nowhere so strongly as in the world of physical science."[886]

When Shaw, in his lectures in *the Fabian Society,* stated that "I had to come to the point of being able to deliver separate lectures ... on ... Liberalism, Socialism, Communism, ... Democracy, the Division of Society into Classes, and the Suitability of Human Nature to Systems of Just Distribution,"[887] "he shows that the scientist tends to be more

---

[881] George Bernard Shaw, *Arms and the Man*, Grant Richards, London, 1898, 66.
[882] Ohmann, 1962, 104.
[883] Ibid., 104.
[884] Griffith, 1993, 61.
[885] Chesterton, 1909, 134.
[886] Ibid., 128.
[887] Shaw, 1906, 17.

concerned about the sickness than about the sick man; but it was certainly in his mind to suggest here also that the idealist is more concerned about the sin than about the sinner".[888] Accordingly, Shaw believes:

> The realist declares that when a man abnegates the will to live and be free in a world of the living and free, seeking only to conform to ideals for the sake of being, not himself, but 'a good man', then he is morally dead and rotten, and must be left unheeded to abide his resurrection, if that by good luck arrive before his bodily death.[889]

This explanation is evidently verified through *Mrs Warren's Profession* in which Shaw, as a socialist, projects the politics of "the profession of prostitution to indict capitalism."[890] As can be seen from John Allett's research, "Prostitution was not made illegal in England until 1839, and even then it continued to have some public sympathy,"[891] a factor which was the main target for Shaw's realistic political language.

In *Mrs Warren's Profession*, this case is plainly described by Crofts: "If you're going to pick and choose your acquaintances on moral principles, you'd better clear out of this country, unless you want to cut yourself out of all decent society",[892] and as Vivie Warren bemoans: "When I think of the society that tolerates you, and the laws that protect you—when I think of how helpless nine out of ten young girls would be in the hands of you and my mother—the unmentionable woman and her capitalist bully."[893]

Thus political language is persistently employed as a weapon by either Mrs Warren or her daughter Vivie. For example, when Vivie asks her mother whether she is ashamed of her profession, the answer given

---

[888] Chesterton, 1909, 128.
[889] Shaw, 1913, 29.
[890] John Allett, "Mrs. Warren's Profession" and The Politics of Prostitution" in *Shaw and History*, ed. Gale K. Larson, The Pennsylvania State University Press, Pennsylvania, 1999, 23.
[891] Ibid., 23.
[892] George Bernard Shaw, *Mrs. Warren's Profession*, Brentano's Publishers, New York, 1905, 221.
[893] Ibid., 222.

reflects something which covers two differing points: public sympathy for prostitution and the politics of gender dichotomy; "If people arrange the world that way for women, there's no good pretending it's arranged the other way. No: I never was a bit ashamed really."[894] Such use of political language illustrates what Shaw stresses in *Quintessence of Ibsenism*: "This being so, it is not surprising that our society, being directly dominated by men, comes to regard Woman, not as an end in herself like Man, but solely as a means of ministering to his appetite."[895] When Mrs Warren questions her life with such forthright questions as: "Do you think I was brought up like you? Able to pick and choose my own way of life? Do you think I did what I did because I liked it, or thought it right, or wouldn't rather have gone to college and been a lady if I'd had the chance?"[896] she underlines the issue of power politics. Shaw thus affirms that "to treat a person as a means instead of an end is to deny that person's right to live."[897] Consequently, *Mrs Warren's Profession* reveals what Griffith refers to as "the association between capitalism, poverty and prostitution,"[898] and it also highlights "the issue of the White Slave Trade of the period in which young British girls were shipped out to work in the legalized brothels on the continent".[899]

Shaw's believable portrayal of the gender equality through the political depiction of the woman's body and Mrs Warren's sympathy for this profession described "the subtle ways in which capitalism manipulates female sexuality,"[900] and that sympathy "was especially the case among the lower classes who had yet to be afforded the luxury of finger-

---

[894] Ibid., 206.
[895] Shaw, 1913, 34.
[896] Shaw, 1905, 200.
[897] Shaw, 1913, 34.
[898] Griffith, 1993, 174.
[899] Ibid., 174.
[900] Ibid., 174.

pointing 'the fallen woman' as the 'living violation of bourgeois notions of female sexual propriety'".[901]

The fact that Shaw exclaims "I was a Socialist, detesting our anarchical scramble for money, and believing in equality as the only possible permanent basis of social organization, discipline, subordination, good manners and selection of fit persons for high functions"[902] is another reference to what Mrs Warren tries to justify within the following words: "How could you keep your self-respect in such starvation and slavery? And what's a woman worth? What's life worth? Without self-respect!"[903] This exclamation is, in a way, a political or propagandist justification of the normalization of Liz's pejorative statement: "wearing out your [women's] health and your appearance for other people's profit".[904]

The most striking political stanza is uttered again by Mrs Warren saying that "The only way for a woman to provide for herself decently is for her to be good to some man that can afford to be good to her",[905] which metaphorically celebrates the patriarchy of Victorian England and the idea of the "womanly woman".[906] Vivie's use of such expressions as "conventional authority"[907] and "conventional superiority"[908] are some reflections of political addresses made by Shaw to urge the idea of realist feminism against the illusion/utopia or the ideal of femininity.

Shaw's paradoxical subject matter: bad mother and good daughter, wealth and poverty, and masculinity and femininity, mirror these clashes between realism and idealism. According to William Lyon Phelps, "Shaw's method, like the method of many great teachers, is the

---

[901] Allett, 1999, 23.
[902] Jean Reynolds, quoted in *Pygmalion's Wordplay: The Postmodern Shaw*, University Press of Florida, Gainesville, 1999, 21.
[903] Shaw, 1905, 205.
[904] Ibid., 202.
[905] Ibid., 205.
[906] Shaw, 1913, 30–34.
[907] Shaw, 1905, 200.
[908] Ibid., 200.

paradox",[909] because "as a realist, he believed human nature was complex, a mixed bag of potential for good and harm, and something which had to be understood on its own terms instead of those imposed on it by dogmatic moralists."[910] That kind of paradox is palpably accentuated through *Major Barbara,* in which Lady Britomart typifies someone who had been poor, but who dehumanized the poor herself once she became rich. "It is only in the middle classes, Stephen, that people get into a state of dumb helpless horror when they find that there are wicked people in the world. In our class, we have to decide what is to be done with wicked people; and nothing should disturb our self-possession."[911] From Griffith's following elucidation "Certainly, in *Major Barbara* the emphasis was on strict hierarchy in working relations",[912] we reach the view that politics triumphs over the ideology of power politics. What I mean to say is that politics considers an Eagletonian approach which "would seem to make reference not only to belief systems, but to questions of power".[913] The paradox is manifestly witnessed within the characterization of Lady Britomart by whom Shaw projected his socialism; "hatred of idleness and of poverty was the central motif of his socialism; their eradication, its denouement."[914] Here, Shaw attempts to figure out what he clarifies in his preface to *Major Barbara*:

> the greatest of evils and the worst of crimes is poverty, and that our first duty—a duty to which every other consideration should be sacrificed—is not to be poor. "Poor but honest," "the respectable poor," and such phrases are as intolerable and as immoral as "drunken but amiable," "fraudulent but a good after-dinner speaker," "splendidly criminal," or the like.[915]

---

[909] Phelps, 1921, 84.
[910] Griffith, 1993, 17.
[911] George Bernard Shaw, *Major Barbara*, Dover Publications Inc., Mineola New York, 2002, 5.
[912] Griffith, 1993, 89.
[913] Eagleton, 1991, 5.
[914] Griffith, 1993, 28.
[915] Shaw, 2014, 5.

This perspective draws attention to the enigmas twisted within *Major Barbara* "with its contrast between the scenes at the Salvation Army shelter and those at Undershaft's munitions factory in the final act".[916] It is very ostensible that Shaw brings three momentous elements (religion–poverty–power) together to proclaim that "the ignorance and corruption of the poor were entailed in the logic of capitalism"[917] and that "the relationship between thought and action, aims and means, arriving, seemingly, at the negative conclusion that capitalism is too powerful, culturally and politically [and even religiously], to be undermined by the radical."[918] Shaw "was convinced of the essential changeability of human nature, only in one change was due mainly to the operations of individual will,"[919] a point which causes Andrew Undershaft to highlight "the malleability of man in relation to the processes of social engineering,"[920] as denoted by Lady Brit's use of femininity or feminism as a tool of power politics:

> A woman has to bring up her children; and that means to restrain them, to deny them things they want, to set them tasks, to punish them when they do wrong, to do all the unpleasant things. And then the father, who has nothing to do but pet them and spoil them, comes in when all her work is done and steals their affection from her.[921]

The concealed ideology or power politics in what Lady Brit utters above reveals that "Ideology is less a matter of the inherent linguistic properties of a pronouncement than a question of who is saying what to whom for what purposes".[922] Such a viewpoint is methodically characterized by Bernard Shaw to strengthen his language politics and characterization, as he wrote in *Quintessence of Ibsenism,* "Unless Woman repudiates her womanliness, her duty to her husband, to her

---

[916] Griffith, 1993, 88.
[917] Ibid., 85.
[918] Ibid., 62.
[919] Ibid., 17.
[920] Ibid., 17.
[921] Shaw, 2002, 19.
[922] Eagleton, 1991, 9.

children, to the society, to the law, and to everyone but herself, she cannot emancipate herself."[923] Lady Brit, though eager for money and wealth, exemplifies "a woman who repudiates her womanliness", and thus her character illuminates the clash between feminist ideals and romantic politics.

The same idea is again addressed by Shaw when he says that "Woman's reasoning is that she begins to fall into all the errors which men are just learning to mistrust."[924] In order to make known all the three elements—religion, poverty, and power—and their political reflections, Shaw composed *Major Barbara* of a lot of would-be hero or heroine characters. In one of his letters to Wendy Hiller on 4 December 1940, Shaw wrote that "In Barbara ... all the other characters are her [Barbara's] rivals professionally; and Sybil Thorndike can do a tremendous lot with half a dozen lines, especially in a religious part which suits her own saintly temperament."[925]

Furthermore, Chesterton believes that "*Major Barbara* contains a strong religious element"[926] and that *Major Barbara* expresses the poverty which "is a crime; that it is a crime to endure it, a crime to be content with it, that it is the mother of all crimes of brutality, corruption, and fear."[927] When Andrew Undershaft says that "there are two things necessary to Salvation"[928], these are "Money and gunpowder",[929] readers, are aware that Andrew Undershaft is doing nothing more than what Lady Brit does. Brit is obsessed with money; Shaw points out in the preface to *Major Barbara* "What is new, as far as I know, is that article in Undershaft's religion which recognizes in Money the first need and in poverty the vilest sin of man and society."[930] "In short, he

---

[923] Shaw, 1913, 37.
[924] Ibid., 18.
[925] Dan H. Laurence, *Bernard Shaw: Collected Letters 1926–1950*, Max Reinhardt, London, 1988, 589.
[926] Chesterton, 1909, 191.
[927] Ibid., 192.
[928] Shaw, 2002, 34.
[929] Ibid., 34.
[930] Shaw, 2014, 9.

[Bernard Shaw] maintained here what he had maintained elsewhere: that what the people at this moment require is not more patriotism or more art or more religion or more morality or more sociology, but simply more money,"[931] a point which is addressed by Undershaft as follows:

> UNDERSHAFT: I fed you and clothed you and housed you. I took care that you should have Money enough to live handsomely—more than enough; so that you could be wasteful, careless, generous. That saved your soul from the seven deadly sins.
>
> BARBARA: [*bewildered*] The seven deadly sins!
>
> UNDERSHAFT: Yes, the deadly seven. [*Counting on his fingers*] Food, clothing, firing, rent, taxes, respectability and children. Nothing can lift those seven millstones from Man's neck but money; and the spirit cannot soar until the millstones are lifted. I lifted them from your spirit. I enabled Barbara to become Major Barbara; and I saved her from the crime of poverty.[932]

What Shaw did in his plays might have been rooted in the view that politics or ideology "is a matter of 'discourse' rather than 'language'. It concerns the actual uses of language between particular human subjects for the production of specific effects".[933] As Chesterton observes "This ... is not a question of thinking for himself; it would be highly immodest to think for anybody else. Nor is it any instinctive licence or egoism; ... he is a man of peculiarly acute public conscience".[934] Perhaps, just because of this, Shaw, in one of his letters to E. Strauss stated that "You find that several of my characters are myself. ... And of course it is true in the sense that Hamlet and Macbeth are both

---

[931] Chesterton, 1909, 192.
[932] Shaw, 2014, 72–73.
[933] Eagleton, 1991, 9.
[934] Ibid., 177.

Shakespeare. They both speak his language, and cannot think nor feel anything outside his consciousness."[935]

On the other hand, in an undated letter to O. B. Clarence in 1942, Bernard Shaw wrote "When they told me that the public would not endure long speeches I told them ... that the public liked nothing better; and that its favorite subjects were politics and religion".[936] Therefore, in nearly all of his plays he tackled political problems and used a political language because he believed that "As a socialist, it is my business to state social problems and to solve them".[937] For instance, in *Pygmalion*, Shaw projects a professor whose "true objective was the provision of a full, accurate, legible script for ... [a] noble but ill-dressed language";[938] however, "The author of *Pygmalion* was too perceptive an observer of social mores to imagine that the relationship could be explain solely in economic terms."[939] Here, it is particularly of import to note that "In all his writing and thinking [as it is in *Pygmalion*], Shaw uses speech as all first-class literary persons do, to enforce his thought by an appeal to its radical meanings. ... Shaw does it primarily for the purpose of mental shock and stimulation of the intellect into thinking".[940] For example, when the note taker announces that "A woman who utters such depressing and disgusting sounds has no right to be anywhere—no right to live"[941] the readers are invited to "a mental shock and stimulation of the intellect into thinking" by which the metaphorical agenda is demonstrated: Shaw's "discussion of the relationship between dialect and class in *Pygmalion* raised important and neglected issues in socialism. In creating a new speech for Eliza, Higgins claimed he was 'filling up the deepest gulf that separates class

---

[935] Laurence, 1988, 633.
[936] Ibid., 657.
[937] Ibid., 633.
[938] Shaw, 1992, 181.
[939] Griffith, 1993, 81.
[940] Burton, 1916, 191.
[941] George Bernard Shaw, *Pygmalion*, The Electronic Classics Series, Hazleton, 2013, 16.

from class and soul from soul'".⁹⁴² In addition, Shaw wished to depict, as Richard Burton explains:

> [that] not only is poverty the matter with the poor; uselessness is the matter with the rich; meaning, that if the rich become useful, which, by the way, some of them do, there is no objection to their being rich unless that in so becoming they unfairly block the rights of others, namely, the poor.⁹⁴³

This point of view is continually depicted within the words of Alfred Doolittle who always considers the significance of "middle-class morality" and this political stance reveals the relationship between poverty and the implication of "uselessness". When Alfred Doolittle says that "I'll have to learn to speak middle class language from you, instead of speaking proper English,"⁹⁴⁴ Shaw figuratively penetrates a political or ideological meaning by which "people assume superiority and grade social distinction".⁹⁴⁵

Alternatively, Frederick W. MacDowell, in his review on *Bernard Shaw and the Socialist Theatre* (1996), puts forward that "Shaw's plays are most often a debate among several individuals, with the truth not being lodged in a single 'raisonneur' but emerging from a synthesis of contrasting ideas and values expressed by the different characters."⁹⁴⁶ Such is the case with *Pygmalion*. These "syntheses of contrasting ideas and values" are degraded into two conflicting sexes: woman and man. The clashes between Eliza and Professor Higgins typify Shaw's orthodox vision of gender equality. Chesterton lays emphasis on this as follows: "Indeed, almost every one of Bernard Shaw's earlier plays might be called an argument between a man and a woman, in which the woman is thumped and thrashed and outwitted until she admits

---

⁹⁴² Griffith, 1993, 87.
⁹⁴³ Burton, 1916, 197.
⁹⁴⁴ Shaw, 1992, 272.
⁹⁴⁵ Burton, 1916, 178.
⁹⁴⁶ Frederick W. McDowell, "Bernard Shaw: Socialist and Dramatist" in *Shaw* Vol. 16, Unpublished Shaw (1996), 230.

that she is the equal of her conqueror."⁹⁴⁷ Though Shaw projects gender equality through "man and woman arguments", his depiction of "the strong, dynamic woman of the plays were said to have inspired many women to break the bonds of their Victorian upbringing."⁹⁴⁸ With the propaganda on behalf of "New Woman'" Shaw, through his support to feminist movements,⁹⁴⁹ underpins the very idea of socialism by which he conveys the ideological repercussions of socialist views; when Eliza jumps on Higgins with these words: "You told me, you know, that when a child is brought to a foreign country, it picks up the language in a few weeks, and forgets its own. Well, I am a child in your country. I have forgotten my own language, and can speak nothing but yours,"⁹⁵⁰ Shaw figuratively expresses the dominance of man over woman and so describes the political power of Victorian patriarchy and the ideological reflection of "the woman's position as a product of male, middle class society."⁹⁵¹

In one of his letters to Lady Rhondda on 12ᵗʰ August 1932, Shaw stated that "I am quite sure that women who are going to change things are those who ... will see Capitalism damned before they will spend their lives plastering its sores and trying to clean up its masses in the name of 'womanly charity'".⁹⁵² By "womanly charity" Shaw is alluding to Eliza's outcry against the "sympathy of a man" in order to echo a feminist ideology, in which the "general meaning of ideology turns on ideas and beliefs (whether true or false) which symbolize the conditions and life experiences of a specific, socially significant group or class."⁹⁵³ The fact that "Bernard Shaw (being honestly eager to put himself on the modern side in everything) put himself on the side of what is called the feminist movement; the proposal to give the two sexes not merely

---

⁹⁴⁷ Chesterton, 1909, 67.
⁹⁴⁸ Griffith, 1993, 157.
⁹⁴⁹ Ibid., 157.
⁹⁵⁰ Shaw, 2013, 74.
⁹⁵¹ Griffith, quoted in, 1993, 158.
⁹⁵² Laurence, 1988, 302.
⁹⁵³ Eagleton, 1991, 29.

equal social privileges, but identical"[954] was the major factor behind his depiction of such female characters as Candida, Eliza, Mrs Warren, Vivie Warren, Barbara, Cleopatra etc., because Shaw had "no difficulty as a playwright, in making female *dramatis personae* as easily as male ones,"[955] believing as he did that "The sexes wear different boots and bonnets, not different souls."[956] That's why, in his letter to Emmeline Pethick-Lawrence on 4th July 1933, Bernard Shaw stated that "women should agitate for a proportion of women on every governing body, whether elected, co-opted, nominated, or picked up in the street like a coroner's jury, provided only their sex was unquestionable",[957] through which Shaw projected the independence of women. Such kind of political or ideological metaphor lies under the dialogues of Eliza and Higgins:

> LIZA: You think I like you to say that. But I haven't forgot what you said a minute ago; and I won't be coaxed round as if I was a baby or a puppy. If I can't have kindness, I'll have independence.
>
> HIGGINS: Independence? That's middle class blasphemy. We are all dependent on one another, every soul of us on earth.[958]

With the words above, Shaw does not target "the dependency of the two sexes on each other", but "the desire to undermine the Victorian ideal of the self-sacrificing womanly woman"[959] and the idea of being free. Higgins sacrifices a middle-class woman by camouflaging himself as a phonetics professor for the sake of the eulogy of proper pronunciation of the English dialect. By pretending to be a person in need of nobody else, thus echoing the political dichotomy of "womanly woman" expressed in *Quintessence of Ibsenism*: "No one ever feel helpless by the side of the self-helper; whilst the self-sacrificer is always

---

[954] Chesterton, 1909, 64.
[955] J. Ellen Gainor, quoted in *Shaw's Daughters: Dramatic and Narrative Constructions of Gender*, University of Michigan Press, Ann Arbor, 1991, 89.
[956] Griffith, 1993, 161.
[957] Laurence, 1988, 346–47.
[958] Shaw, 2013, 81.
[959] Griffith, 1993, 162.

a drag, a responsibility, a reproach, an everlasting and unnatural trouble with whom no really strong soul can live".[960]

Aristotle, in his *Politics*, says that a man as a husband "over a wife he rules in the manner of a statesman, over children in that of a king; for by nature the male is more fitted to be in command than the female, unless conditions in some respect contravene nature",[961] an idea which Shaw parodys in *Candida*. The dialogues among Eugene, Candida and Morell divulge such kind of paradoxical "ruling of a man over a wife":

> CANDIDA: (With emphatic warning) Take care, James. Eugene, I asked you to go. Are you going?
>
> MORELL: (Putting his foot down) He shall not go. I wish him to remain.
>
> MARCHBANKS: I'll go. I'll do whatever you want. (He turns to the door)
>
> CANDIDA: Stop! (He obeys). Didn't you hear James say he wished you to stay? James is master here. Don't you know that?[962]

When Morell exclaims that "I have nothing to offer you but my strength for your defense, my honesty of purpose for your surety, my ability and industry for your livelihood, and my authority and position for your dignity, that is all it becomes a man to offer to a woman",[963] Shaw again purports some political or ideological Aristotelian view that "The skill of household-management proved to have three parts, one being the skill of a master, ... next that of a father, and a third marital".[964] Thus, Shaw concludes *Candida* with the metaphoric statements of Candida herself: "I make him master here, though he does not know it, ... And when he thought I might go away with you,

---

[960] Shaw, 1913, 31–32.
[961] Aristotle, *Politics*, trans. Trevor J. Saunders, Clarendon Press, Oxford, 1995, 18.
[962] George Bernard Shaw, *Candida*, Grant Richards, London, 1898, 145.
[963] Ibid., 148.
[964] Aristotle. 1995, 18.

his only anxiety was—what should become of me!"⁹⁶⁵ even though, in fact, Morell is depicted to be "a man whose sermons were mere phrases that he cheated himself and others every day,"⁹⁶⁶ being "trapped in a web of feminine mystery and machination without any real hope of escape".⁹⁶⁷

Similarly, Griffith observes that "The portraits of women in Shaw's early plays often expressed the complications involved in the process of emancipation".⁹⁶⁸ One of the best examples of this kind of "process of emancipation" is characterized by Blanche within *Widowers' Houses.*⁹⁶⁹ However, the way for that kind of emancipation is available with what Sartorius calls "a reasonable guarantee",⁹⁷⁰ because Sartorius himself is "a gentleman of considerable wealth and position",⁹⁷¹ and his daughter, Blanche, in order to emancipate herself, "will inherit the bulk of her father's fortune, and will be liberally treated on her marriage."⁹⁷² The paradox that is figured out by Shaw is a manifestation of an ideological rationalization by which he again purports to be "a Socialist for the obvious reason that poverty was cruel".⁹⁷³ With Blanche's saying that "Oh, I hate the poor. At least I hate those dirty, drunken, disreputable people who live like pigs",⁹⁷⁴ Shaw aims to express the dichotomy of poverty and emancipation; a political argument in which there appears a dominant ideology that "can do this either by falsifying social reality, suppressing and excluding certain unwelcome features of it, or suggesting that these features cannot be avoided".⁹⁷⁵ Sartorius "excludes certain unwelcome features of the general society", namely the poor, believing that "when people are very poor, you cannot help

---

⁹⁶⁵ Shaw, 1898, 150.
⁹⁶⁶ Griffith, 1993, 54.
⁹⁶⁷ Shaw, 1898, 159.
⁹⁶⁸ Griffith, 1993, 167.
⁹⁶⁹ Ibid., 167.
⁹⁷⁰ George Bernard Shaw, *Widowers' Houses*, Brentano's Publishers, New York, 1905, 17.
⁹⁷¹ Ibid., 23.
⁹⁷² Ibid., 23.
⁹⁷³ Chesterton, 1909, 80.
⁹⁷⁴ Shaw, 1905, 62–63.
⁹⁷⁵ Eagleton, 1991, 27.

them, no matter how much you may sympathize with them. It does them more harm than good in the long run".[976]

As Griffith suggests, for Shaw "socialism's first duty was to secure sufficiency of means for the masses",[977] and thereby, "Financial security would be assured in the new economic order, an order where men would 'fight for ideas, not for bread and butter' at one end and for corrupt and stolen luxury at the other".[978] When Cokane says "Life here is an idyll—a perfect idyll",[979] and that "the love of money is the root of all evil",[980] we reach the Shavian conclusion that "Every economic problem will be found to rest on a moral problem: you cannot get away from it",[981] and "A man must live"[982] to fight for his ideas and get away from immorality. On the other hand, though Griffith believes that "Blanche is both the ultimate defender of the rule of property and the perverse expositor of the Shavian doctrine of selfishness,"[983] Shaw targets Trench as an "offender" by use of the following words in Preface to *Plays, Pleasant and Unpleasant*: "In 'Widowers' Houses' I have shown middle class respectability and younger son gentility fattening on the poverty of the slum as flies fatten on the filth."[984] Trench, with the following words: "Well, it appears that the dirtier a place is, the more rent you get; and the decenter it is, the more compensation you get"[985] exemplifies "middle class respectability and younger son gentility" all the way through, a political behaviour which "Peter Sloterdijk calls 'enlightened false consciousness', which lives by false values but is ironically aware of doing so, and so which can hardly be

---

[976] Shaw, 1905, 46.
[977] Griffith, 1993, 28.
[978] Ibid., 29.
[979] Shaw, 1905, 37.
[980] Ibid., 35.
[981] Bernard Shaw, *Practical Politics: Twentieth-Century Views on Politics and Economics*, ed. Lloyd J. Hubenka, University of Nebraska Press, 1976, 6.
[982] Shaw, 1905, 67.
[983] Griffith, 1993, 167.
[984] Shaw, 1898, xxvi.
[985] Shaw, 1905, 66.

said to be mystified in the traditional sense of the term."[986] That's why, when Sartorius responds to Trench by saying that "If, when you say you are as bad as I am, you mean that you are just as powerless to alter the state of society, then you are unfortunately quite right",[987] Shaw has reached "the most dramatic point ... [in which] the open and indecent rack-center turns on the decent young man of means and proves to him that he is equally guilty, that he also can only grind his corn by grinding the faces of the poor."[988]

Political Language of Orhan Asena

To describe Orhan Asena as a political writer is quite apt, for "he is counted in the 1950s generation of Turkish playwriting",[989] a period in which Turkey faced many ideological and political turbulences, including the transition period from the Ottoman Empire to Turkish Republic, the change of the regime in the country (from Islamic caliphate to Kemalist Republicanism), the major coup d'état during the ruling of president Adnan Menderes, and some other ideological tribulations.[990] In *Elli Yılın Türk Tiyatrosu*, Metin And categorizes the Republican period into three political phases: the first is the period of one-party rule encompassing 1923–1945, a revolutionary, idealistic, and vivacious era in which effort was made to create a democratic order;[991] the second is the 1945–1950 period during which the dominant political party gave up its power because of the transition to the multiparty era (the period during which the party in power legislated the State Theatre Law);[992] the third one is 1950–1960, during which time there were no improvements in respect to the theatre, until on 27th May 1960, as the result of a military coup, the Democrat Party collapsed,[993] and following

---

[986] Eagleton, 1991, 27.
[987] Shaw, 1905, 48.
[988] Chesterton, 1909, 132.
[989] Nutku, 1998, 14.
[990] We reach this conclusion through his biographical background: it is a fact that Asena was born in 1922, a year before the proclamation of Turkish Republic. He experienced both Kemalist way of life and the political ideologies and policies of Menderes government.
[991] And, 1973, 15.
[992] Ibid., 15.
[993] Ibid., 15–16.

the passing of the Constitution Act in 1961, playwriting blossomed once again.[994]

Being a playwright of 1950 onwards, Asena, in many of his plays, employs an ideological or political language well suited to the atmosphere and tone of the era. It is no wonder that Orhan Asena, in his political depictions, makes references to history and combines these historical details with the prevailing features of his own era, intermingling them with his own ideological point of view. As İlber Ortaylı notes in *Tiyatroda Tarihi Oyunlar Üzerinde Siyasal Bir Analiz Denemesi*, "[The] Republican period is rooted in a new historiography concept in terms of its ideological basis. That was a nationalist historiography seen in the 19th century Europe".[995] Asena, in *Hürrem Sultan'ı Sunarken*, expresses the significance of the historical plays, and maintains that not only Aeschylus, Sophocles, Euripides, but also Shakespeare, Racine, Corneille, Goethe, Schiller, and Hebbel all projected human beings within the limits of history by "putting the historical persons up against the historical persons".[996] However, surprisingly Asena himself depicted many historical figures such as Suleiman the Magnificent, Hürrem Sultan, Bayezid, Atçalı Kel Mehmet, Simavnalı Şeyh Bedrettin, and Salvador Allende.

Orhan Asena was among the playwrights whose interests were described by Ayşegül Yüksel: "In the early plays written in accordance with the Western model, such topics mirroring the enthusiasm of a society for a great revolution succeeded, criticizing the Ottoman period, and discussing the value changes in society gained great importance."[997] Being one of the best examples, and the first historical play, Asena's *Hürrem Sultan* projects the power politics of a sultan

---

[994] Ibid., 16.
[995] İlber Ortaylı, "Tiyatroda Tarihi Oyunlar Üzerinde Siyasal Bir Analiz Denemesi" in *Tiyatro Araştırmaları Dergisi*, Sayı: 7, 1976, 230.
[996] Orhan Asena, "Hürrem Sultan'ı Sunarken" in *Devlet Tiyatrosu Dergisi*, No: 5, Mart-Nisan-Mayıs 1995, Ankara, 26–27.
[997] Ayşegül Yüksel, "Cumhuriyet'in 70. Yılında Tiyatromuz" in *Tiyatro Araştırmaları Dergisi*, Sayı: 10, 1993, 24.

named Hürrem. Indeed, political language is used from the very beginning of the play when Hürrem exclaims that "Man has to kill to stay alive",[998] a comment which exhibits a Machiavellian point of view, as Strauss writes: "Machiavelli ... contends that a founder who is concerned with the common good, as distinguished from a tyrant, cannot be blamed if he commits murder in order to achieve his good end."[999] Though what Hürrem calls out is for the sake of the "good end", it is not for the sake of the "common good". Murray Edelman, in *Political Language and Political Reality*, stresses that:

> It is language about political events and developments that people experience; even events that are close by take their meaning from the language used to depict them. So political language *is* political reality; there is no other so far as the meaning of events to actor and spectators is concerned.[1000]

Though Asena thereby endorses the political realities that go well with the politics of writing, his language often contains the very accuracy and dynamism that he sponsored. Within *Hürrem Sultan*, as the play develops, we observe that Asena may be referring to the Aristotelian point of view that "women are half the free persons, and from children come those who participate in the constitution"[1001] when Hürrem Sultan, in order to elevate her son to the throne with an ambitious greed, yearns to be on her own. This is evidenced by her words: "I feel stronger when I'm alone".[1002] Abide Doğan, in her related article titled *Türk Tiyatrosunda Hürrem Sultan,* depicts Hürrem Sultan (Roxolana) as a woman "who—as the phrase goes—twists the mighty Sultan Suleiman the Magnificent around her finger; a woman who makes him do what she asks; and a woman who is an intriguer, trickster and

---

[998] Orhan Asena (a), *Hürrem Sultan*, Mitos-Boyut Yayınları, İstnabul, 2010, 9.
[999] Strauss, 1958, 44.
[1000] Murray Edelman, "Political Language and Political Reality" in *PS* Vol. 18, No. 1 (Winter 1985), 10.
[1001] Aristotle, 1995, 21.
[1002] Asena (a), 2010, 60.

magician".[1003] This idea is evidently addressed by Asena through the dialogues in the play. For example, when Kanuni asks, "Why does the state management become an enjoyable game for women when it becomes an unbearable burden for us?"[1004] Asena proposes the potential "power" of women over government policies. Such a kind of power politics is repeatedly seen in the dialogue, though sometimes Asena utilizes a paradoxical depiction of female characters. Unlike Hürrem Sultan, the other females are represented as fools that cannot do well when politics matters. For instance, Sayinur, Mustafa's wife, exclaims, "Sire! I'm a woman; it's beyond my ken ... I cannot think well".[1005] By these depictions, Asena reveals that Hürrem is someone who strongly opposed Ottoman traditionalism—a traditionalism which was a well-known and well-practised culture within the Ottoman dynasty. According to Abide Doğan, Asena tries to portray "Hürrem Sultan, devastated by the passion of her reign, with her all aspects (sultanate, motherhood, intrigue, trickery, jealousy etc.)",[1006] and in so doing he reflects the Shavian point of view that "unless Woman repudiates her womanliness, her duty to her husband, to her children, to society, to the law, and to everyone but herself, she cannot emancipate herself."[1007] Hürrem, defined by Asena as a character "like a female Iago"[1008] in *Hürrem Sultan'ı Sunarken*, represents the ideology of *valides* (mother) within the boundaries of the Ottoman Empire. Philip Emeritz, in his *Feminine Power in the Ottoman Harem*, says that "The power exercised by the *valides* in the Ottoman Empire is an excellent example of ... [the concept of Deniz Kandiyoti's 'patriarchal bargains'] as it reveals the extensive changes in Ottoman royal life and political authority during

---

[1003] Abide Doğan, "Türk Tiyatrosunda Hürrem Sultan" in *Hacettepe Üniversitesi Edebiyat Fakültesi Dergisi Osmanlı Devletinin Kuruluşunun 700.* Yılı Özel Sayısı, Ekim 1999, 58.
[1004] Asena (a), 2010, 51.
[1005] Ibid., 45–46.
[1006] Doğan, 1999, 61.
[1007] Shaw, 1913, 37.
[1008] Asena, 1995, 35.

this period."[1009] As Galina Yermolenko suggests in *Roxolana: The Greatest Empress of the East,* Hürrem or Roxolana, as a well-known *valide*, "reigned supreme not only in Suleiman's heart, but also in his court, as his chief political advisor,"[1010] a theme which is addressed in every dialogue between Hürrem and other figures. When Bayezid and Hürrem discusses on Mustafa's manners, Hürrem says that:

> the love towards the siblings is a beautiful thing. But it is a little expensive emotion for the crown owners like you. Never forget this! There are cottages in which the siblings do love each other, I see. Nevertheless, could you show me any palace in which a brother shall not make his brother choke?[1011]

This political stance is persistently illustrated by Asena through the sayings of Hürrem Sultan. In one of her conversations, she tells Kanuni that "What even can a female beast do other than attacking others for the sake of her offspring? I know Mustafa is a dear person. I know, at least at the moment he is innocent ... but in this bloody wheel, either he or we will be beheaded".[1012] In this way she succeeds in planting some suspicions into Kanuni's mind. The fact that Hürrem addresses Mustafa as a threat for the dynasty is not a lie, but it is nevertheless a kind of politics to take the rule into her own power. As Yermolenko stresses "That Roxolana was allowed to give birth to more than one son was a stark violation of the old royal harem principle",[1013] because Hürrem aimed to politicize the "descent from father to son'" and that "one concubine mother—one son," which was designed to prevent both the mother's influence over the sultan and the feuds of the blood brothers for the throne."[1014]

[1009] Phillip Emeritz, "Feminine Power in the Ottoman Harem" *Binghamton Journal of History* (Spring 2013), 1.
[1010] Galina Yermolenko, "Roxolana: "The Greatest Empress of the East" in *The Muslim World*, Vol 95, 2005, 231.
[1011] Asena (a), 2010, 12–13.
[1012] Ibid., 19.
[1013] Yermolenko, 2005, 233.
[1014] Ibid., 234.

On the other hand, considering the date of the production of the play, we might observe that the play touches on the power holders during a period in Turkey when troubles and relationships based on self-interests were to the fore. The play was written in 1958, a period in which Turkey was being ruled by Adnan Menderes. For that reason, the play can be considered to be a presentiment of the coup d'état of 27th May 1960. As is noted by Orhan Asena cited by Hülya Nutku:

> In Turkey, there was a conflict similar to that of between Suleiman the Magnificent and Mustapha, there was a war between the party in power and the opposition which would cost either of them beheaded. Such values as democracy, human rights, and free thought had all been laid aside. In short, we were in a depression.[1015]

After the elections in Turkey in 1950, the Democratic Party came to power under the rule of Adnan Menderes and Celal Bayar; however, the Democratic Party was said to "adopt a strictly majoritarian concept of democracy and interpreted its dominance as an expression of the popular will."[1016] Similarly, according to Asena, "Menderes myth, as a counter-revolution, forced Turkey to give up what he gained through his way of revolution",[1017] which was the main objection revealed by the Republican majority, and he continues, "This phase is a period in which the dictatorship of Menderes—which broke the hopes of progressive forces and tried to demolish Ataturk's revolution—reached its largest size".[1018]

The conflict between Kanuni and Mustafa represented within *Hürrem Sultan* was thus an analogy of the conflict between Menderes and Atatürk, by which Asena mooted the idea that "Times of crisis were many, but toppling the dynasty and installing another on the Ottoman

---

[1015] Nutku, quoted in, 1998, 46.
[1016] Tachau, 2000, 133.
[1017] Budak, quoted in, 2008, 67.
[1018] Ibid., 67.

throne occupied the political agenda to a surprisingly small degree throughout this period",[1019] and that bringing down one regime (Republicanism) and establishing another one (Islamic democracy) on the Turkish throne "occupied the political agenda to a surprisingly small degree throughout this period". Thus, through a depiction of a few well-known historical figures, Asena projected the interrelation between politics and historicism. As Cantor pertinently says "to draw the contrast sharply, in classical political philosophy, human beings make history; according to historicism, history makes human beings."[1020] As is addressed by Tachau, "On May 27, 1960 ... a military coup ... brought down the DP regime and resulted in the party's abolition, the arrest and trial of its leaders, three of whom were hanged on charges of unconstitutional behavior, and the writing of a new constitution",[1021] an event which is figuratively depicted within the sayings of Bayezid:

> History will write your story as follows: he was a great man, but an unfortunate man; he extended the boundaries of his country till the borders of Ural Mountains, and Vienna skirts, but he never left any beneficent prince behind. He was very fond of his state, so much so that he could sacrifice his son for the sake of it. Here is his greatest harm to the state![1022]

Asena's use of political language, projecting the conflicts between politicians onto a fictional or historical stage, epitomizes a Hobbesian point of view: "To this war of every man against every man, this also is consequent; that nothing can be unjust. The notions of right and wrong, justice and injustice have there no place".[1023] Kanuni says: "To be human and be fair! Oh, what do we fancy ourselves as?"[1024] Such a

---

[1019] Hakan T. Karateke, "Legitimizing The Ottoman Sultanate: A Framework for Historical Analysis" in *Legitimizing the Order: The Ottoman Rhetoric of State Power*, ed. Hakan T. Karateke and Maurus Leinkowski, Brill, Leiden and Boston, 2005, 14.
[1020] Cantor, 1995, 193.
[1021] Tachau, 2000, 134.
[1022] Asena (a), 2010, 63.
[1023] Hobbes, 1998, 85.
[1024] Asena (a), 2010, 56.

"war of every man against every man" is again and again mirrored within Asena's plays. Being a sequel of *Hürrem Sultan*, *Ya Devlet Başa Ya Kuzgun Leşe* was written in 1983; Orhan Asena notes that: "I wrote that play twenty-four years later.... In the play, I depicted a vicious circle of fear–crime–fear; in order to write the play, I was supposed to live before and after the 12th September."[1025] As Tachau affirms, after the elections in 1977, the Republican People's Party "garnered 41 percent of the popular vote, its best showing in competitive elections, and captured 47 percent of the parliamentary seats"[1026] in Turkey, but "there was also a proliferation of smaller parties":[1027] "the proto-fascist Nationalist Action Party (NAP) led by former Col. Alpaslan Turkes, a leading radical in the 1960 military junta, and the Islamist National Salvation Party (NSP) led by former professor Necmettin Erbakan".[1028] Tachau continues, "Turkey thus found itself plagued with both party fragmentation and ideological polarization, an explosive formula that spawned rising levels of physical violence between militants of the extreme right and left".[1029] This powder-keg situation gave rise to the explosion of 12th September, as is again explained by Tachau, "The result was not surprising: on September 12, 1980, the military once again intervened."[1030]

The political reflection of the language is at the very outset mirrored within the words of Dulkadiroğlu, a character in the play: "Sire! Those who base their life solely on expectation never think whether they will succeed or not!"[1031] The fact was that the evaporation of the political problems in Turkey was the main expectation of the politicians: Turkey was on a "political knife edge", as Bayezid says: "Anatolia is in a mess. The state is steadily losing blood. Deaths ... deaths ... deaths".[1032] The

---

[1025] Nutku, quoted in, 1998, 108–109.
[1026] Tachau, 2000, 136.
[1027] Ibid., 136.
[1028] Ibid., 136.
[1029] Ibid., 136.
[1030] Ibid., 138.
[1031] Orhan Asena (b), *Ya Devlet Başa Ya Kuzgun Leşe*, Mitos-Boyut Yayınları, İstnabul, 2010, 73.
[1032] Ibid., 75.

character's words serve to highlight the fact that, "Escalating violence, particularly assassinations of such political figures as members of parliament and an ex-prime minister, as well as prominent journalists and academics, engulfed society".[1033] Within these words of Bayezid "If he had not died, Anatolia would not have been in such a mess; a handful of people would not have attended a false person with their own peace. These people were those who had not found the thing they searched for".[1034] Here Menderes's death is metaphorically represented through the death of Mustafa by which Asena emphasizes the significance of the political ideologies which had enveloped Turkey.

On the other hand, *Ya Devlet Başa Ya Kuzgun Leşe* depicts a realist vision of the Ottoman Empire. During the time period in which Bayezid lived, his brother Selim II was a rival against him. "Selim was the third son of the famous Ottoman sultan Süleyman I (r. 1520–66); his mother was Süleyman's beloved concubine Hürrem Sultan (Roxolana)".[1035] As they express it: "The history of sultanic succession in the empire was marked by fierce competition for the throne among the Ottoman princes";[1036] similarly, such a kind of fierce competition was also between Bayezid and Selim. After some tensions between Selim and Bayezid, Suleiman the Magnificent accused Bayezid for crimes of which he was innocent, and planned to murder him, and in 1562 he was executed.[1037] In the play, Orhan Asena depicts Ottoman reality within a historiographic exposé to outline the accepted philosophy of his century concerning politics; he makes every effort in an era of deep politics to restore an implicit vision of Turkey. Lala Mustapha illustrates this vision through his statements: "The truth needs to be

---

[1033] Tachau, 2000, 138.
[1034] Asena (b), 2010, 96.
[1035] Gabor Agoston and Bruce Masters, *Encyclopedia of The Ottoman Empire*, Facts On File, Inc., New York, 2009, 513.
[1036] Ibid., 513.
[1037] Sadullah Gülten, "Kanuni'nin Maktül Bir Şehzadesi: Bayezid Bayezid" in *ODÜ Sosyal Bilimler Enstitüsü Sosyal Bilimler Aratırmaları Dergisi*, Cilt: 3 Sayı: 6, Aralık 2012, 198–203.

seen as truth. If the truth is not seen as it is, then the truth will inevitably be seen as untrue."[1038]

In each of his historical plays, Asena demonstrates politics of state management narratives, most of them original, and advises on how to differentiate between good and evil and how to intermingle the past with present. Asena almost certainly does this in order that the public can better appreciate the intricacy and unsteadiness of Turkey's politics. Through the lessons of history, the public can be made to see the growing hopelessness in Turkish politics, Turkey's discovery of Menderes's Islamic democracy, and others. It gives the impression that those occurrences have had some stern unconstructive costs in the Turkish Republic; as a result, historiography and realism help the public comprehend the intensity of depression, the change of regimes and social conflicts. In *Tohum ve Toprak,* written in 1964, Asena deals with the events in the three months comprising the inheritance of Ottoman Sultan Mahmud II as the result of a janissary rebellion, and the murder of Alemdar Mustafa Pasha who supported Mahmud to come to throne in 1809. Being another representation of "power politics", it exhibits the conflict between power holders and those who brought the power holders to power. As Gabore Agoston and Bruce Masters note:

> (Alemdar Mustafa Pasha is the) (b. 1765–d. 1808) ayan of Rusçuk, first grand vizier of Sultan Mahmud II (1808–1839). Thought to have been born in Rusçuk (present-day Ruse, Bulgaria) as the son of a soldier from the elite Ottoman Janissaries, Alemdar Mustafa Pasha began his official career in the Janissary corps. ... On July 28, 1808, at the head of an impressive military force, Alemdar Mustafa Pasha broke into the palace. He could not, however, save the sultan, who was killed by the men of the new sultan, Mustafa VI (r. 1807–08), whom the rebels put on the throne. Alemdar Mustafa Pasha deposed the

---

[1038] Asena (b), 2010, 74.

new sultan and enthroned Mustafa's reform-minded brother, Mahmud II (r. 1808–39).[1039]

To us, the realistic portrayal of Alemdar Mustapha Pasha does not only narrate the conflicts between the Ottoman sultans and janissaries, but it also mirrors the coup d'état on 27th May 1960 in Turkey. In that way, it can be put forward that Orhan Asena delves into history in order to reflect the socio-cultural and socio-political tribulations that affected both Ottoman and Turkish citizens significantly. Asena's realist historiography in *Tohum ve Toprak* revolves—politically and culturally—around a series of ideologies, stemming from the Republican Era to the coups of 1960, 1971 and 1980, attached to extensive images of the characteristics of the social, cultural, and economic status of the epochs under discussion and by the playwright's scrutiny of the relevant political ideologies. In one of his speeches, regarding *Tohum ve Toprak*, Asena says that "I confess that what urged me to pen such a theme was my feeling that the coup of 27 May and those who supported it were suffering loneliness. My starting point was the same. I had caught the projection of yesterday in today".[1040] Thus, the basic emphasis of the play is "the idea of revolution" (27th May is depicted as a revolution) by illustrating a previous event within the analysis of a socio-historical, socio-political, and socio-cultural agenda. According to Asena, this play depicts the common fate of those revolutionaries who would like to pioneer the society but are overthrown by great unseen powers; Alemdar Mustafa Pasha was such a revolutionary.[1041]

Alternatively, in *Tanrılar ve İnsanlar* (*Gilgamesh*) and *Korku,* Asena directly conveys his ideology by eulogizing Mustafa Kemal Atatürk's principles. Asena's highlighting is on the prominent aspects of Kemalist vision and Kemalist Turkism. Believing that *Gilgamesh* split his life

---

[1039] Agoston et al., 2009, 29–30.
[1040] Nutku, quoted in, 1998, 53.
[1041] Ibid., 53.

into "two definite lines just like BC and AD,"[1042] Asena saw 1950s Turkey (the play was written in 1954) as a period in which the impact of Atatürk's Kemalism and the newly-formed government collided. The clashes between social values and governmental policies produced conflict between the new and the old. This period, which comprises the years between 1950 and 1960, is the one in which Democrat Party came to power, taking over from Atatürk's successor İnönü.[1043] It was an epoch during which "DP's ideology and programme advocated more freedom for the people, a liberal economic policy with more support for private industry and less for the state sector, together with less restriction on the practice of the Muslim religion".[1044] However, "The officers, having been brought up to view themselves as the naturally appointed guardians of Atatürk reforms were especially sensitive to the claims of opposition parties that the DP was not sufficiently firm in defending Kemalist principles",[1045] and "Some were upset with the Democrats' concession in the matter of religion",[1046] which brought some anger against the DP government. Asena, being an eager supporter of Atatürk's reforms and principles, penned *Gilgamesh* not only to render a momentous epic, but to visualize the socio-political atmosphere of Turkish history.

In fact, Tzvi Abusch traces the history of the several major versions of The Epic of Gilgamesh,[1047] and concludes that:

> The Epic of Gilgamesh combines the power and tragedy of the Iliad with the wanderings and marvels of the Odyssey. It is a work of adventure, but it is no less a meditation on some fundamental issues of human existence. The Epic explores many

---

[1042] Ibid., 12.
[1043] Cihat Göktepe, "1960 'Revolution' in Turkey and the British Policy towards Turkey" in *The Turkish Yearbook*, vol. XXX, 140.
[1044] Ibid., 140.
[1045] Ibid., 143.
[1046] Ibid., 143.
[1047] Tzvi Abusch. "The Development and Meaning of the Epic of Gilgamesh: An Interpretive Essay" in *Journal of the American Oriental Society*, Vol. 121, No. 4 (Oct–Dec 2001), 614–622.

issues; it surely provides a Mesopotamian formulation of human predicaments and options. Most of all, the work grapples with issues of an existential nature. It talks about the powerful human drive to achieve, the value of friendship, the experience of loss, the inevitability of death.[1048]

Though the play thematically revolves around the Epic of Gilgamesh, Asena touches on the *Zeitgeist* of 1950s and through which he aims to depict what Tahsin Saraç notes:

> Of today, it is a façade of gods that have recently announced their weight on top of the piles. We can jolly well say it in one word as the old order. Think an actor who is aged, who now could not voice-over, and who is partly trampled from time to time; social values on which much discussion is held, conflicts and fights are held; any bigotries that divide people border to border, and that set them at odds; numerous bullying referenced on behalf of this or that dogma, traditions, customs, and various forms of government.... Here is the contemporary façade of gods.[1049]

The collisions between the newly formed government, the Menderes government, and the former one are progressively addressed in the dialogues in *Gilgamesh*. For example, in such words of Gilgamesh as, "My country will be in the dark, does it deem proper for me to stay in the light? The storms will ravage my country; does it deem proper for me to stand by the shore? The anger of Gods is threatening my country, does it deem proper for me to feel anxiety about my life?"[1050] Asena reveals his anxiety and worries about the DP government, whose new principles Asena believes are the main tribulations that create "despair, anxiety and the feeling of revolt in public".[1051] To many scholars, Asena links the characterization of Gilgamesh to Atatürk; for

---

[1048] İbid, 614.
[1049] Tahsin Saraç, "Asena'nın Oyunlarındaki Ezilmiş İnsancıklar" in *Türk Dili*, Year 20, No. 236 (May 1971), Ankara, 127–28.
[1050] Orhan Asena (c), *Tanrılar ve İnsanlar*, Mitos Boyut Yayınları, İstanbul, 2010, 189.
[1051] Nutku, 1998, 22.

instance, Prof. Rene Giraud, in his preface to the French translation of the play, states that "Obviously, Gilgamesh of generation of Orhan Asena is Ataturk",[1052] an idea which is propped up by Asena with the following words: "Just like Gilgamesh, it was Ataturk who had taken the imperialist powers imagined as modern gods, the sultan of authority and power, obsolete institutions, bodies, the Caliphate alliance on himself."[1053] Thus, Asena puts his finger on Atatürk's Republican ideology and his Kemalist perspectives, and projects them through "discourse analysis, which attends to the play of social power within language itself".[1054] Orhan Asena, with Utnapiştim's words "me eternal slave, you eternal rebel,"[1055] pejoratively goes deep into Aristotelian politics and reveals that "that which can use its intellect to look ahead is by nature ruler and by nature master, while that which has the bodily strength to labor is ruled, and is by nature a slave. Hence master and slave benefit from the same thing".[1056] This description is stressed within Engidu's statements: "In the forests I live, the right belongs to the strong",[1057] through which Asena foregrounds the distaste of "the old dissipated, rotten home environment"[1058] of Ottoman past and the present Menderes government. When Utnapiştim says that "All awakening is a little bitter,"[1059] Asena allegorically draws the attention to the reality of the military coup d'état of 27th May by which "The political influence of the Turkish armed forces has its roots in counter-majoritarian institutions that the military

---

[1052] Orhan Asena, *Les Dieux Et Les Hommes Ou Gilgamesh*, French Translator Rene Giraud-Fransızca'dan Türkçeye çeviren Tahsin Saraç, Ayyıldız Yayınları, Ankara, 1961.
[1053] Orhan Asena, *Deü Gsf Dünya Tiyatrolar Günü Kutlama Haftası*, Akm, İzmir, Mart 1998, quoted in Hülya Nutku, Cumhuriyet'in 75. Yılında 75. Yılın Tanığı Bir Yazar: Orhan Asena.
[1054] Eagleton, 1991, 195.
[1055] Asena (c), 2010, 189.
[1056] Aristotle, 1995, 252.
[1057] Asena (c), 2010, 186.
[1058] Berkes, 1998, 292.
[1059] Asena (c), 2010, 207.

established in a constitution drafted following a coup on May 27, 1960."[1060]

Asena's *Korku* is another play that gives a picture of the correspondence between power-hegemony and leader-public autonomy, which embodies a realistic historiography within the socio-cultural and socio-political description of Turkey. Hülya Nutku perceives that in *Korku*, Asena depicts a man "who is an outsider in his cause, and has lost his faith in his cause".[1061] *Korku* was written in 1956, two years after the publication of *Gilgamesh*. To Teresa Cicierska Chtapowa, these two years (1954–1956), "is the period during which Menderes dictatorship reached its widest dimensions, breaking all hope of progressive forces, and trying to annihilate Atatürk's principles."[1062]

Though the play revolves around the idea of revolution, in *Korku*, "the death of idealism" is powerfully accentuated just like what Shaw did in *Arms and the Man*; this perspective is announced in the words of the man: "Can you show a single successful revolution in history? No. Always the next one came and overpowered the former".[1063] It is very clear that Asena exhibits the aspiration for such a revolution with a realistic depiction, and thus attracts notice to the "significance of ideas" to revolutionize; however, he deals with a humane feeling in the simplest terms, the feeling of fear and death. In his preface to *Korku*, Asena expresses that "just like how the feeling of fear does not have a particular color, a certain shape and a certain country, and that it is as old as the world, the event I chose as my topic to my work cannot have a particular place and a specific time".[1064] Nevertheless, the play was reinterpreted within the circles of the War of Independence by State Theatre.[1065] But, the most significant thing to be addressed here is the

---

[1060] Ozan O Varol, "The Democratic Coup d'État" in *Harvard International Law Journal*, Vol. 53, Number 2 (2012), 323.
[1061] Nutku, 1998, 26.
[1062] Chtapowa, T. Cicierska, quoted in Hülya Nutku, "Orhan Asena'nın İlk Oyunlarında Devrim Düşüncesi" in *Folia Orientalia*, Polonya 1979, 27.
[1063] Orhan Asena (d), *Korku*. Mitos Boyut Yayınları, İstanbul, 2010, 193.
[1064] Ibid., 147.
[1065] Ibid., 147.

fact that the play was written in 1956, one year after the Events of September 6th–7th (also known as Istanbul Pogrom). As Alfred de Zayas explains, "The Istanbul pogrom (sometimes referred to as Septemvriana) was a government-instigated series of riots against the Greek minority of Istanbul in September 1955".[1066] The ideology of nationalism was the main reason behind the İstanbul pogrom and Asena metaphorically conveys the destructive effects of such an ideology:

THE WOMAN: I hate ideas, all kinds.

THE LIEUTENANT: Why? What for?

THE WOMAN: Because, they all want the blood, all blood-fed, and all develop with blood....[1067]

Thus, it is no wonder that this play symbolizes the War of Independence which foregrounds one of six principles of Atatürk: Nationalism. In one of his conversations with Muhsin Ertuğrul, Asena says that "The number one man of the War of Independence is Atatürk. I wrote the defeat in *Korku*, and that reminds Atatürk",[1068] by which Asena eulogizes Atatürk's Turkey, as is expressed by the Lieutenant in the play: "I wanted to save an idea; I wanted to save the most illustrious representative of an idea, I wanted to save a flag under which one day millions of people would gather in all its grandeur when it is unfurled".[1069]

Terry Eagleton, in *Ideology*, notes that "oppositional ideologies often seek to unify a diverse array of political forces, and are geared to effective action; they also strive to legitimate their beliefs in the eyes of the society as a whole."[1070] The push for "legitimating beliefs in the eyes

---

[1066] Alfred De Zayas, "The Istanbul Pogrom of 6–7 September 1955 in The Light of International Law" in *IAGS*, Volume 2 (2007), 137.
[1067] Asena (d), 2010, 161.
[1068] Nutku, 1998, 30.
[1069] Asena (d), 2010, 194.
[1070] Eagleton, 1991, 61.

of the society as a whole" is among the aims of Orhan Asena in *Şili Üçlemesi*. After his second enforced departure to Germany, which comprises the years between 1971–77, Asena wrote three major plays: *Şili'de Av, Ölü Kentin Nabzı,* and *Bir Başkana Ağıt*.[1071] Concentrating on the military coups and tragic depiction of events in Chile, Asena tries to give a picture of the "idealization of the need for a revolution" by which he supposedly mirrors the juxtapositions between Chile's new and old order through which Turkey's position is revealed. Considering the Chilean historiography, it is observed:

> After three previous unsuccessful electoral bids, Dr. Salvador Allende, a public health physician and leader of the Socialist Party, was elected President of Chile on September 4, 1970. Heading the Popular Unity electoral coalition of left-wing political parties, Allende initiated a series of reforms that included nationalizing the country's copper mines and extending the land reform program of his predecessor Eduardo Frei. The Chilean right wing and the Nixon administration immediately began a campaign to topple the Allende government. U.S. Secretary of State Henry Kissinger initiated an "invisible blockade" that helped wreak havoc on the Chilean economy. Internal opposition to the socialist measures of the Allende government coalesced under the leadership of the military, and on September 11, 1973, General Augusto Pinochet carried out a coup d'état. From the presidential palace, which was being bombarded by the Chilean air force, Allende made a last statement to the country before committing suicide, presumably to avoid the humiliation of being arrested by the military. In the aftermath of the coup d'état, thousands of Chileans were arrested and killed by the armed forces.[1072]

[1071] Nutku, 1998, 78.
[1072] "Salvador Allende's Final Speech, September 11, 1973" in *Chile and the Peaceful Road to Socialism* Document No. http://global.oup.com/us/companion.websites/9780195375701/pdf/SPD 13_Chile_Peaceful_Road.pdf. Accessed: 10. 07. 2015

Being an orthodox delineation of leader-public conflict, *Şili Üçlemesi* penetrates into Chile's political sphere. In one of his articles on the play, Asena expresses "I think Allende is one of the most tragic figures of the 20th century",[1073] by which he rationalizes his endeavour of writing such a play. Asena believes that Allende accomplished a great success by bringing democratic socialism to his country; that he made a lot of revolutions and brought a new order; that he never took up arms against every oppression or menace,[1074] all of which projects his "idealism", an idealism which comes *vis a vis* realism. Pedro, in *Şili'de Av*, characterizes such a point of view:

> if we are 25 years old; if we love our country with the enthusiasm which that age brings, and own its stones, earth, base and surface with the same enthusiasm; if we would like to bring Socialism and keep it alive without shedding blood; if we love a president who is in power because of our votes; if we devote ourselves to him, why do we die?[1075]

One of the actors of the play, Macit Koper, in one of his speeches, commented that it is vital to observe that the play ends with the fascist junta's murders. Allende and the revolutionaries are all murdered, which means that some miscalculations have surpassed Allende's revolutionary thoughts,[1076] something which points to Asena's description of Turkey's political sphere. Taking the dates of the production of three plays into consideration, we can see that in Turkey it coincides with "the military ultimatum of 12 March 1971" and "the 12 September 1980 Turkish coup d'état". As discussed by Erik Jan Zurcher, "By early 1971, Demirel's government, weakened by defections, seemed to have become paralyzed",[1077] which was the basic cause of the downfall. He continues, "This was the situation when, on

---

[1073] Asena, Orhan. "Şili'de Av'ın Yazarı Orhan Asena'dan Oyunu Üstüne" in *Tiyatro* 74 (January 1974), 27.
[1074] Ibid., 27.
[1075] Orhan Asena, *Şili'de Av,* Boyut Yayınları, İstanbul, 1992, 51.
[1076] Macit Koper, "Şili'de Av'ı Oyuncuları Anlatıyor" in *Tiyatro* 74 (January 1974), 38.
[1077] Zürcher, 2004, 258.

12 March 1971 the Chief of General Staff handed the prime minister a memorandum, which really amounted to an ultimatum by the armed forces".[1078] After this ultimatum, "It was made public on 2 January 1980, but ... at three o'clock in the morning of 12 September 1980 ... the Turkish army took power again".[1079] The ideological and political conflicts in Turkey produced much sorrow and Asena, by displaying the heroic fights of the revolutionaries, supported the "idealism of revolutions" by comparing Turkish politics and ideologies with Chilean Socialism. Thus, though being in Germany, Asena tackled the political tribulation in a way that brought it near to home. As Helmut says of Asena's approach: "Should a plague outbreak in Chile, tomorrow it is my hometown, the next day it is in Congo, Turkey, China and Japan.... If I were a German, and loved my country, when the plague outbreaks here, my duty would start here, or else it could be too late."[1080] Asena, with an Aristotelian point of view, takes in hand the very basic aphorism: "man is born with weapons to support practical wisdom and virtue, which are all too easy to use for the opposite purposes".[1081]

[1078] Ibid., 258.
[1079] Ibid., 269.
[1080] Asena, 1992, 55–56.
[1081] Aristotle, 1995, 253.

CHAPTER 5: SHAW VERSUS ASENA

> You have made for yourself something that you call a morality or a religion or what not. It doesn't fit the facts. Well, scrap it. Scrap it and get one that does fit. That is what is wrong with the world at present. It scraps its obsolete steam engines and dynamos; but it won't scrap its old prejudices and its old moralities and its old religions and its old political constitutions. What's the result? In machinery it does very well; but in morals and religion and politics it is working at a loss that brings it nearer bankruptcy every year.
>
> **G.B.S. Major Barbara**

In this book we have set out to explore the concept of politics and have identified the nature and form of political evolution in Bernard Shaw and Orhan Asena, the reasons and motivation for their evolutionary ideologies, the political approach in the style and language of their plays, and the role and impact of *Zeitgeist* on the political philosophies of the two playwrights. Our desire has also been to know whether differing cultures can result in different political agendas in literature, particularly in drama. The general theoretical literature on this subject and specifically in the context of Britain and Turkey is inconclusive on several of the vital questions we have raised within the second, third, and fourth chapters.

This study has sought to answer four of these questions: 1. Do Bernard Shaw and Orhan Asena mirror evolutionary politics in their writings? 2. Do history and Zeitgeist have some vital impacts on political approaches of Bernard Shaw and Orhan Asena? 3. How do political ideologies in Britain and in Turkey affect Shaw and Asena and their plays respectively? 4. How do they employ a political language within their plays?

The key findings are chapter specific and were abridged within the relevant chapters: in the second chapter, Politics and Ideology, we discovered that the modern depiction of politics and ideology has, for the most part, embraced the interpretations of such writers and philosophers as Plato, Aristotle, St. Thomas Aquinas, Machiavelli, John Calvin, Thomas Hobbes, John Locke, Jean Jacques Rousseau, Adam Smith, John Stuart Mill, and some others.[1082] Plato's theory of the ideal state, and the ideal regime; Aristotle's theory of ideals and phenomena; Thomas Aquinas's view of State, ethics, and religion; Machiavelli's view of virtue, ethics, and his ideologies on the Classical Republicanism; Calvin's approach to disciplined State order, and Laic/Secular ideologies on regimes, and the institution of religion; John Locke's standpoint of a trustful government and the right of protest against injustices, and his antagonism against monarchy; Rousseau's theory of liberalism and the protest against maladministration and moral corruption; Adam Smith's political views on economy and morality, and his theory of sympathy; John Stuart Mill's philosophies on Liberalism, freedom and equality are all the theoretical background of the history of politics, and political thoughts.[1083]

In the third chapter, Politics in Drama, we concluded, through a historic outline of both British and Turkish theatre in terms of politics and political satire, that the open-minded assessment of critical topics taking place right in the political heart of British and Turkish societies created a wide spectrum of self-examination with regard to earlier and modern political drama. In this respect, from the writings and assessments of prominent scholars and intellectuals, the origin of political drama and its evolutionary development till today have been re-evaluated and melted into one pot: British and Turkish political dramas. Thus, a historical outline of the well-known playwrights together with their significant masterpieces was considered.

In the fourth and fifth chapters, which made up the main body of this study, we evaluated the comparative and contrastive particulars of

---

[1082] See Brian Redhead, *Political Thought From Plato To NATO*, British Broadcasting Corporation, London, 1984, 9–183.
[1083] Ibid., 9–183.

Shaw and Asena. We concluded that, inevitably, Shaw and Asena, through their plays, reformulated political drama by means of their differing political and ideological philosophies. The central outline hints at the direct/indirect use of politics and ideology within their plays. It is however, noted from this study that Shaw and Asena do not employ obviously similar styles and languages to denote their political ideologies within their plays.

From a conclusive standpoint, "George Bernard Shaw grew up during the apex of the British Empire, the Victorian Age",[1084] a period in which he "engaged in diagnosis and treatment of the social and political ills that plagued England and Europe."[1085] As Margot Morgan stresses, Shaw "remained wedded to key tenets of bourgeois thinking—the faith in science, a belief in progress and a deep suspicion of mass politics."[1086] Though Shaw went through major political –*isms* including Socialism,[1087] Communism,[1088] Marxism,[1089] and Feminism,[1090] he was to write to Lady Marry Murray "Never have an Ism: never be an -ist" declaring in the same letter that the "object of Fabianism is to destroy Impossibilism".[1091] Alternatively, Asena grew up during the zenith of Turkish Republican Era, a period in which "after the proclamation of the Republic, while there were those who supported Mustafa Kemal, others were stuck to the Ottoman traditionalism and were strongly against revolutionary novelties".[1092]

[1084] Margot Morgan, *Politics and Theatre in Twentieth Century Europe*, Palgrave Macmillan, New York, 2013, 19.
[1085] Ibid., 20.
[1086] Ibid., 20.
[1087] Andrew Heywood, *Political Ideologies*, Plagrave Macmillan, New York, 2012, 112.
[1088] Samuel A. Weiss, ed., *Bernard Shaw's Letters to Siegfried Trebitsch*, Stanford University Press, Stanford, 1986, 330.
[1089] Devendra Kumar Singh, *The Idea of the Superman in the Plays of G. B. Shaw*, Atlantic Publishers, New Delhi, 1994, 73.
[1090] Sangeeta Jain, *Women in the Plays of George Bernard Shaw*, Discovery Publishing House, New Delhi, 2006, 20.
[1091] Paul Lewton, "George Bernard Shaw: Theory, Language and Drama in the Nineties" in *The Yearbook of English Studies*, Vol. 9, Theatrical Literature Special Number, 1979, 154.
[1092] Özlem Özmen, "Türkiye'de Politik Tiyatronun Gelişimi" in *Ankara Üniversitesi Dil Ve Tarih-Coğrafya Fakültesi Dergisi 55*, 1 (2015), 420.

Representing a bridge between Ottoman orthodoxy and Turkish modernism, Asena:

> left behind ... Ottoman tragedies depicting Suleyman the Magnificent and his queen Hürrem Sultan ... a play focusing on the assassination of Salvador Allende in Chile, ... a dramatization of the Gilgamesh epic ... horror stories of lies and fear ... a portrait of modernization of the Turkish theatre.[1093]

Though intermingling with differing philosophies, Asena, just like Shaw, experienced a variety of insinuations of such *–isms* as Turkish nationalism, republicanism, Kemalism, and some minor hints of socialism.

Despite the fact that Shaw's language contradicted Victorian fundamentalism, it was consistent with all his *–isms*. In the same way, Asena's diction eulogized his *-isms*, whilst he stressed the dichotomies of Ottoman orthodoxy. Shaw's insistence on the inclusion of socialism within his plays was because of his enthusiasm in theatre: "the theatre, my rightful kingdom"[1094] wrote Shaw in his letter to Daniel Macmillan. Asena, with a parallel approach to Shaw, in one of his interviews, stated "Theatre is a school; it does not teach, but educates. It educates by performance to gain knowledge of how a world man lives in; it educates by performance how to live in such a world."[1095]

Although the political ideologies of the two are different, both playwrights utilize ideological and political language that goes well with the dominant ideology of the regime in their countries. Both Shaw and Asena, for instance, project plays that depict war, power, autonomy, individual success, and political order in *Arms and the Man*, and *Hürrem Sultan,* respectively. Whilst Shaw uncovers the political corruption of war and mocks the idealism in war in *Arms and the Man*, Asena emphasizes the realization of power and the political

---

[1093] Talat Sait Halman, ed., *I, Anatolia and Other Plays*, Syracuse University Press, New York, 2008, 3.
[1094] Laurence, 1988, 675.
[1095] Orhan Asena, "Şili'de Av Yazarı Orhan Asena İle" in *Tiyatro* 74, Sayı 22 (Mart 1974), 28.

repercussion of idealism in *Hürrem Sultan*. As Lagretta Tallent Lenker writes:

> Having his unconventional hero profess the horrors of war yet execute exemplary feats in combat suggests Shaw's understanding of society's ambivalence towards war; having this hero assimilated into the family of his enemy through marriage demonstrates Shaw's notion that causes of battles are often shallow, unreasonable, and easily resolvable.[1096]

Such kind of "realism versus idealism" is repetitively anticipated within the political satires of both playwrights. While *Arms and the Man* reflects the political war of Macedonia and Bulgaria, *Hürrem Sultan* depicts the political war of the Ottoman dynasty. Talat Sait Halman notes "The vivid history of Ottoman Empire ... furnished material to ... some contemporary Turkish playwrights including Orhan Asena,"[1097] giving the impression that Asena depicted real politics within his plays. It is a fact that Asena, through such historical documentary plays as *Ya Devlet Başa Ya Kuzgun Leşe* and *Şili Üçlemesi*, grapples with the political turbulences of the period, the rulers and the ruling; Shaw, on the other hand, is "himself concerned almost to obsession with rulers and with ruling"[1098] specifically in *Major Barbara*. However, their stylistic approach is predominantly contrasting; Shaw employs an extremely hidden weapon under his linguistic tone in his vocabulary embellishing the plot structure of politics in disguise of religion (Salvation Army). Stephen M. Gill expresses this point of view as follows: "In *Major Barbara* (1905), he reveals that rich industrialists not only command politics but also religious groups."[1099] Asena, conversely, makes use of an uncomplicated language, generating an impossibility of dichotomies by which he puts into words direct messages for the

---

[1096] Lagretta Tallent Lenker, "Make War on War: A Shavian Conundrum" in *War and Words*, ed. Sara Munson Deaths et al., Lexington Books, 2004, 169.
[1097] Talat Sait Halman, *Rapture and Revolution*, ed. Jayne L. Warner, Syracuse University Press, New York, 2007, 131.
[1098] Matthew Yde, *Bernard Shaw and Totalitarianism*, Palgrave Macmillan, New York, 2013, 60.
[1099] Stephen M. Gill, *Political Convictions of G.B.S.*, Vesta, Canada, 1980, 27.

readers/audiences. The political language of Asena is as evidently exposed as the politics of the Ottoman reign within the play. Such a kind of "direct politics" is again observed within *Şili Üçlemesi*.

In *Pygmalion*, Shaw disrupts "received ideas about class, gender and virtue"[1100] through the simplistic mockery of poor language attuning to political standing of class discriminations with a realistic approach. It is no wonder that Shaw addresses political language in view of Orwell's famous quote: "political language has to consist largely of euphemism, question-begging and sheer cloudy vagueness";[1101] in contrast, Asena, in *Korku,* employs an ideological stance, utilizing language games through which he depicts the collapse of idealism; in *Korku*, in which the politics is probed by means of a close approximation of everyday speech addressing realist drama, "idealists whose zeal alienates them from contemporary Turkish reality are dealt with."[1102]

Power, autonomy, rule/ruling and political abuse is represented within *Mrs Warren's Profession, Widowers' Houses, Candida* and *Tanrılar ve İnsanlar (Gilgamesh),* and *Tohum ve Toprak* through the application of political language. In *Mrs Warren's Profession* Shaw addresses the political corruption of prostitution and re-creates the fashion of feminist politics by overestimating the gender equality issue through his opposition to Aristotelian "master-slave" politics. On the other hand, Asena, in *Tanrılar ve İnsanlar (Gilgamesh)*, rejects the Machiavellian political approach and eulogizes Kemalist vision and nationalist ideology by taking "Gilgamesh as a prototype of Atatürk and portraying him as the champion of freedom and a man of dauntless courage."[1103] With a similar power ideology, Asena tackles with "how Mahmud II owed his throne and life to Alemdar Mustapha Pasha but sacrificed him as ransom to the counter-revolutionaries to save his own

---

[1100] Debra Rae Cohen, "British Literature (After 1900)" in *Encyclopedia of Literature and Politics*, ed. Keith Booker, Greenwood Press, Westport and London, 2005, 100.
[1101] Orwell et al., eds., 1968, 136.
[1102] Metin And, "Turkish Drama" in *Encyclopedia of World Drama*, ed. Stanley Hochman, McGraw-Hill, USA, 1984, 61.
[1103] Nüvit Özdoğru, "Turkey: Modern Period" in *The Reader's Encyclopedia of World Drama*, ed. John Gassner and Edward Quinn, Dover Publications, New York, 1969, 875.

neck"[1104] in *Tohum ve Toprak*. However, he critically addresses the modern Turkish political era within the ideological implications of his tone. With a differing style and tone, Shaw has the characters talking in large chatty ways in *Widowers' Houses* and *Candida*, but the plot is perceptibly and impenitently political. As Shaw observes "In *Widowers' Houses* I have shewn middle class respectability and younger son gentility fattening on the poverty of the slum as flies fatten on filth".[1105] Though the play is set in the arena of Fabian socialism, being a propagandist play, it reflects the inconsistency between poverty and wealth referring to the political discriminations in class privileges within Britain. With a different approach, in *Candida*, Shaw pejoratively ridicules masculine self-sufficiency and tracks the political power of femininity.

The differences between these two playwrights are commonly due to the political ideologies by which they were affected and have something to do with the cultures, the *Zeitgeist*, the political atmosphere they belonged to. All these are an additional hint of the increased significance of this comparison as the content of the comparative drama curriculum widens. This study has identified the contrasts between the two playwrights projecting the political language and direct politics of their plays.

[1104] Ibid., 875.
[1105] George Bernard Shaw, *Plays Pleasant and Unpleasant I*, Brentano's, New York, 1905, xxvi.

Bernard Shaw vs. Orhan Asena	
Bernard Shaw	Orhan Asena
1. As a Victorian playwright, Shaw punitively lampoons the Victorian community, employing "techniques of farce to attack the moral dichotomies".[1106] A political intellectual, he affirms himself "the enemy of idealism".[1107] Fabianism was his starting ideology in political philosophy. 2. Within the political philosophies of Socialism, "Shaw, too, is a politician of the highest order—the order of the Holy Ghost. His party isn't Conservative, or Liberal, or even Labour (though he supports Labour fervently); his party is the wide teeming seas of all humanity".[1108] Shaw competes against Victorian fundamentalism and lauds the Fabian movement. 3. Shaw went through major political *isms* including Socialism,[1109] Communism,[1110] Marxism,[1111] and Feminism.[1112]	1. As a Republican playwright, Asena, in essence, eulogizes the Turkish community under the umbrella of the political creeds of Mustafa Kemal Atatürk. A political ideologue, he contrasts realism and holds idealist philosophies as his goal. 2. Though not personally publicized by him, Asena has some qualifications of a socialist thinker; he gives the impression of being a great enthusiast of Atatürk's Republican People's Party (Cumhuriyet Halk Partisi); from the literature review, we reach the conclusion that his party is the one that rejects the Ottoman orthodoxy; Asena, as a leading Turkist, "cultivated an unwavering enmity towards the dynastic "corruption" and perceived *Atatürk's Republican* Turkic culture as libertarian and free, in opposition to the submissive and rotten culture of the Ottoman dynastic polity and establishment" (italics mine).[1121] 3. Asena experienced a variety of

---

[1106] Stuart E. Baker, *Bernard Shaw's Remarkable Religion*, University Press of Florida, Gainesville, 2002, 12.
[1107] Ibid., 12.
[1108] John A. Bertolini, quoted in "The Shavian Tradition" in *George Bernard Shaw in Context*, ed. Brad Kent, Cambridge University Press, Cambridge, 2015, 351.
[1109] Andrew Heywood, Political Ideologies, Plagrave Macmillan, New York, 2012, 112.
[1110] Samuel A. Weiss, ed., *Bernard Shaw's Letters to Siegfried Trebitsch*, Stanford University Press, Stanford, 1986, 330.

4. Despite the fact that Shaw's language contradicted Victorian fundamentalism, it was consistent with all his *–isms*.	insinuations of such *–isms* as Turkish nationalism, republicanism, Kemalism, and some minor hints of socialism.
5. Shaw uncovers the political corruption of war and mocks its idealism in *Arms and the Man*, which reflects the political war of Macedonia and Bulgaria. Shaw employs an extremely hidden weapon under the linguistic tone of his vocabulary, embellishing the plot structure of politics in disguise of religion (Salvation Army).	4. Asena's diction eulogized his *-isms*, whilst he stressed the dichotomies of the Ottoman orthodoxy.
	5. Asena emphasizes the realization of power and the political repercussion of idealism in *Hürrem Sultan*, which depicts the political war of the Ottoman dynasty. Asena, conversely, makes use of an uncomplicated language generating impossibility of dichotomies by which he puts into words direct messages for the readers/audiences. The political language of Asena is as evidently exposed as the politics in Ottoman reign within the play.
6. In *Pygmalion*, Shaw disrupts "received ideas about class, gender and virtue"[1113] through the simplistic mockery of poor language to reveal political standing and class discrimination. It is no wonder that Shaw addresses political language in view of Orwell's famous quote: "political language has to consist largely of euphemism, question-begging and sheer cloudy vagueness".[1114]	
	6. Asena, in *Korku,* employs an ideological advance utilizing language games through which he depicts the collapse of idealism; in *Korku*, in which the politics is probed by means of a close approximation of everyday speech addressing realist drama, "idealists whose zeal alienates them from
7. In *Mrs Warren's Profession* Shaw addresses the political corruption of	

[1111] Devendra Kumar Singh, *The Idea of the Superman in the Plays of G. B. Shaw*, Atlantic Publishers, New Delhi, 1994, 73.
[1112] Sangeeta Jain, *Women in the Plays of George Bernard Shaw*, Discovery Publishing House, New Delhi, 2006, 20.
[1113] Debra Rae Cohen, "British Literature (After 1900)" in *Encyclopedia of Literature and Politics*, ed. Keith Booker, Greenwood Press, Westport and London, 2005, 100.
[1114] Orwell et al., eds., 1968, 136.

prostitution and re-creates the fashion of feminist politics by overestimating the woman issue through an opposition to Aristotelian "master-slave" politics. 8. With a differing style, Shaw addresses the characters in a mainly chatty way in *Widowers' Houses* and *Candida*, but the plot is perceptibly and impenitently political. As Shaw observes "In *Widowers' Houses* I have shewn middle class respectability and younger son gentility fattening on the poverty of the slum as flies fatten on filth".[1115] Though the play is set on Fabian socialism—as a propagandist play—it reflects the inconsistency between poverty and wealth referring to the political discriminations of British class privilege. With a different approach, in *Candida*, Shaw pejoratively ridicules masculine self-sufficiency and tracks the political power of femininity.	contemporary Turkish reality are dealt with."[1116] 7. Asena, in *Tanrılar ve İnsanlar (Gilgamesh)*, rejects Machiavellian political approach and eulogizes Kemalist vision by taking "Gilgamesh as a prototype of Atatürk and portraying him as the champion of freedom and a man of dauntless courage."[1117] 8. With a similar power ideology, Asena tackles with "how Mahmud II owed his throne and life to Alemdar Mustapha Pasha but sacrificed him as ransom to the counterrevolutionaries to save his own neck"[1118] in *Tohum ve Toprak*. However, he critically addresses modern Turkish political era within his ideological implications in his tone.

[1115] George Bernard Shaw, *Plays Pleasant and Unpleasant I*, Brentano's, New York, 1905, xxvi.
[1116] Metin And, "Turkish Drama" in *Encyclopedia of World Drama*, ed. Stanley Hochman, McGraw-Hill, USA, 1984, 61.
[1117] Nüvit Özdoğru, "Turkey: Modern Period" in *The Reader's Encyclopedia of World Drama*, ed. John Gassner and Edward Quinn, Dover Publications, New York, 1969, 875.
[1118] Ibid., 875.
[1121] Doğan Gürpınar, "Anatolia's Eternal Destiny Was Sealed: Seljuks Of Rum In The Turkish National(ist) Imagination From The Late Ottoman Empire To The Republican Era" in *European Journal of Turkish Studies*, 2012.

APPENDIX

SYNOPSIS OF ORHAN ASENA'S PLAYS

(1) Hürrem Sultan (Roxolana)

Kanuni (that is, "the lawgiver"—a reference to Ottoman Sultan Suleiman I) has returned victoriously from the Hungarian expedition, but whilst outside people celebrate these victories with great enthusiasm, inside the Sultan's favourite concubine (later his legal wife) Hürrem tells Grand Vizier Rüstem Pasha and her son Mihrimah that she is afraid of these sounds. Since the beginning of her life in the palace to that moment (she is twenty) she has learned that: "You must kill to stay alive". This statement is the turning point of the plot. If the Sultan's eldest son Mustapha, born to her rival concubine Mahidevran, inherits the throne, then her own sons Bayezid, Selim, Mihrimah and Cihangir will be beheaded to secure his position from rivals. Even her son-in-law Rüstem will not be able to prevent this, and so, threatening Rüstem, and gathering all her children to herself, Hürrem starts a war against Mustapha.

With the help of her children, she begins to implement her plan which involves making Mustapha fall out of favour with the Sultan the Magnificent. In an unyielding manner, she contrives some domestic disturbance in Anatolia. Kanuni is distressed because of the rumours about Mustapha, whilst Mustapha is dismayed because he is unable to explain his innocence to his father. Mustapha does not want Rüstem to come between him and his father, but Rüstem continues to fool Mustapha, finally causing him to be slaughtered.

The response is a great public outcry, with the people demanding that the offenders be punished, and therefore Rüstem to be beheaded. In this situation, Hürrem is forced to take drastic measures. She sets Rüstem on the rebels, but while the conflicts are ensuing outside, Bayezid appears. As soon as Bayezid learns the death of Mustapha, he sets out to call Hürrem to account. Cihangir, too, is upset at Mustafa's death. Kanuni listens to a captured rebel's speech. This person, the poet Yahya, was a close friend of Mustapha, and Kanuni does not have Yahya beheaded because the poet advocates Mustapha and says that Kanuni would be wrong to kill him. Instead, Kanuni would like to stay alone, and think over the matter. On the other hand, worried about Kanuni's situation, Hürrem tells Rüstem that she is scared. Rüstem has also the same feelings.

(2) *Ya Devlet Başa Ya Kuzgun Leşe*

The play starts with the murder of Prince Mustapha as a result of the conspiracies of Hürrem Sultan. Thus, Hürrem thinks the throne will be ruled by one of her children: Prince Selim or Prince Bayezid. However, she could not have predicted that the two princes would fall out with each other and begin to fight for the throne even before the death of Süleyman the Magnificent.

While Kanuni is on voyage, legal protection of the throne has been assigned to Bayezid. Meanwhile, Düzmece Mustapha (Pseudo-Mustapha) appears, claiming that he is Prince Mustapha, and that he escaped death at the last moment, and by receiving the support of the public he dares to take the throne. Bayezid recommends collaboration to Düzmece Mustapha and sends gifts for him. In this way he gains his confidence before capturing and executing him. However, being influenced by those around him, Kanuni thinks that Bayezid had a real alliance with Düzmece Mustapha, but is frightened to learn that Mehmed Pasha Sokolovic was on the way to Istanbul. Through the intervention of Hürrem Sultan, he is able to forgive Bayezid, but their trust remains broken.

As the conflict between the two princes continues, Bayezid's impulsive and confident character leads to an uprising against him. His tutor Lala Mustafa Pasha, on seeing that Selim is more likely to inherit the throne, plays a double game, causing Bayezid to take some decisions which lead him into difficulty.

In this unfortunate situation, Bayezid is perceived to be consistently provoking his brother; and once again he annoys Süleyman the Magnificent, and is sent to Amasya province. First, he does not want to go there. However, since the death of his only guard Hürrem has left alone and powerless, he goes, if only to protect himself from Selim. When Süleyman the Magnificent issues an edict announcing that soldiers are to be deployed, he walks over Selim with his army. Yet he is caught and put to death by Kanuni.

(3) *Tohum ve Toprak*

The Janissaries rebel against Selim the III. They aim to bring a statesman of their own choice after murdering Selim the III. Alemdar Mustafa Pasha, the proprietor of Rusçuk province, has put down this rebellion but did not prevent the massacre of Selim by the Janissaries. So, instead of Selim III, Sultan Mahmud II was brought to throne. The new sultan feels himself indebted to Alemdar Pasha both for his life and fidelity, and so remains torn between the power of a monarchy and his fidelity. In this way, Mahmud II, despite sitting at the top of the state authorities, is weaker than Alemdar Pasha, and it is Alemdar that implicitly calls the tune in matters of state administration.

Alemdar is an idealistic person who loves his state, and is not afraid to sacrifice his life for it. Although Alemdar is looking to help the state recover from the mess, his opponents seek to destroy him. Despite their machinations, Alemdar stands upright, rock-like. His stance even affects a young concubine who has been sent to kill him. But the more important thing affecting this concubine is actually the pure heart and clean heart of this tough and mighty Pasha. And more interestingly, this concubine also captures Alemdar Pasha's heart. One day, the Janissaries will rise much more strongly and everybody around him especially Sultan Mahmud—considering his power—will leave Alemdar Mustafa Pasha alone, except one.

(4) Tanrılar ve İnsanlar (Gilgamesh)

Gilgamesh, the king of Uruk, feels the fear of death and goes to Udnapiştim to find immortality after his friend Enkidu is killed by the beauty goddess Ishtar. But he renounces immortality when he learns that it is only possible at the expense of the disappearance of humanity. When Ishtar, to whom Gilgamesh is connected with an unrequited love, reciprocates to his love in the end, this act is punished with the destruction of the unity of Gilgamesh's face, because the Gods do not want this coupling.

(5) Şili Üçlemesi: Şili'de Av / Ölü Kentin Nabzı / Bir Başkana Ağıt Şili'de Av

This play describes the day, 11th September 1973, on which the armed forces made a military coup in Chile and seized the control of the government. The play revolves around Salvador Allende's overthrow and murder, and the developing events that took place that day, as a student-militia group enter the house of a priest and conceal themselves there.

In the play, on the one hand, Allende's honourable but sorrowful story is addressed; on the other hand, the discussion is about Allende's urge to keep alive the Socialist regime by means of legal procedures instead of military forces. The play highlights that this regime is not reached through the arming of the students and workers, but through politics.

(6) Ölü Kentin Nabzı

The play depicts an action against Pinochet's repressive regime in 1977; the withstanding of which began secretly to turn into a resistance movement.

(7) Bir Başkana Ağıt

This play depicts the tense hours Allende experienced in the Presidential Palace on the night of September 11th in which the coup d'état was staged. On that day in Chile over 35,000 people were killed. In the coup, President Allende was massacred by Pinochet's troops who took control of the Presidential Palace despite Allende's heroic resistance. Asena describes this contemporary tragedy in a realistic and documentary form, garnishing it with a poetic narrative. Witnessing one of the coups of our era, the play has a universal theme within its unique structure.

(8) Korku

Being Asena's second play, *Korku* tells how a man is dragged from heroism to death. It is Korku's lover who premeditates his killing, but this is no mere act of murder. The one who is killed is her beloved, and he wants her to do this action. In the play, a significant person who is a forerunner of freedom and revolution and a leader of the revolutionary movement has been disappointed by failure. At the same time, he is afraid of being caught. There remain two ways left to survive: to flee or to die with his honour. But he does not have the power to take his own life. This task falls to the woman he loves. The only thing that is important for the woman in the beginning of the play is her not being able to be with her beloved man. The woman has no relationship with such concepts as revolution or freedom.

Though she sees her beloved man changing from day to day, closed in on himself with ever increasing fear, the woman can do nothing. The woman is very sad, she believes that she has lost her beloved; there is now no hope of improvement in their relationship. The only thing to be done is to prepare him to face a heroic death. This would be done by the woman. Though the woman does not believe the cause, she believes that he must die like a hero, and so she fires two shots at the man. Yet Asena manages to set out these events in a way which makes it a surprising plot-twist for readers.

BIBLIOGRAPHY

Abusch, Tzvil. "The Development and Meaning of the Epic of Gilgamesh: An Interpretive Essay" in *Journal of the American Oriental Society*, Vol. 121, No. 4 (Oct–Dec 2001).

Adams, James Eli. *A History of Victorian Literature*, Wiley-Blackwell, West Sussex, 2009.

Ágoston, Gábor and Bruce Masters. *Encyclopedia of the Ottoman Empire*, Infobase Publishing, New York, 2009.

Ahmad, Feroz. *The Making of Modern Turkey*, Routledge, London and New York, 1993.

Akçam, Taner. *From Empire to Republic: Turkish Nationalism and the Armenian Genocide*, Zed Books, London and New York, 2004.

Akı, Niyazi. XIX. *Yüzyıl Türk Tiyatrosunda Devrin Hayat ve İnsanı*, Atatürk Üniversitesi Yayınları, Erzurum, 1974.

Alexander, Edward. *Matthew Artnold and John Stuart Mill*, Routledge, London and New York.

Allett, John. "Mrs Warren's Profession and The Politics Of Prostitution" in *Shaw And History*, ed. Gale K. Larson, The Pennysilvania State University Press, Pennysilvania, 1999.

Almond, Gabriel A. *Ventures in Political Science: Narratives and Reflections*, Lynne Rienner Publishers, London, 2002.

Althusser, Louis. *Ideology and Ideological State Apparatuses*, trans. Ben Brewser, Verso, London and New York, 2014

Althusser, Louis. *On The Reproduction Of Capitalism*, trans. G. M. Goshgarıan, Verso, London and New York, 2014.

And, Metin (a). *Türk Tiyatrosunun Evreleri*, Turhan Kitabevi, Ankara, 1983.

And, Metin (b). *Cumhuriyet Dönemi Türk Tiyatrosu*, Türkiye iş Bankası Kültür Yayınları, Ankara, 1983.

And, Metin. "Karagöz" in *Encyclopedia of World Drama*, ed. Stanley Hochman, McGraw-Hill, USA, 1984.

And, Metin. "The Communication Process in Turkish Traditional Performances" in *Tiyatro Araştırmaları Dergisi*, Sayı: 8, 1988.

And, Metin. *Elli Yılın Türk Tiyatrosu*, Türkiye iş Bankası Kültür Yayınları, İstanbul, 1973.

And, Metin. *Geleneksel Türk Tiyatrosu*, İnkılap Kitabevi, İstanbul, 1985.

And, Metin. *Meşrutiyet Döneminde Türk Tiyatrosu*, Türkiye İş Bankası Kültür Yayınları, Ankara, 1971.

And, Metin. *Tanzimat ve İstibdat Döneminde Türk Tiyatrosu*, İş Bankası Kültür Yayınları, Ankara, 1972.

And, Metin. "Turkish Drama" in *Encyclopedia of World Drama*, ed. Stanley Hochman, McGraw-Hill, USA, 1984.

Anglo, Sydney. "Niccolo Machiavelli: The Anatomy Of Political And Military Decadence" in *Political Thought From Plato to NATO*, British Broadcasting Corporation, London, 1984.

Aquinas, Thomas. *Commentary On Aristotle's Politics*, trans. Richard J. Regan, Hackett Publishing Company, Inc., Indianapolis and Cambridge, 2007.

Aristotle. *Nicomachean Ethics*, trans. and ed. Roger Crisp, Cambridge University Press, Cambridge, 2000.

Aristotle. *Politics*, trans. Benjamin Jowett, Clarendon Press, 1885.

Aristotle. *Politics*, trans. Trevor J. Saunders, Clarendon Press, Oxford, 1995.

Aristotle. *Politics*, trans. Trevor J. Saunders, Oxford University Press, New York, 2002.

Asena, Orhan (a). *Hürrem Sultan*, Mitos-Boyut Yayınları, İstanbul, 2010.

Asena, Orhan (b). *Ya Devlet Başa Ya Kuzgun Leşe*, Mitos-Boyut Yayınları, İstnabul, 2010.

Asena, Orhan (c). *Tanrılar ve İnsanlar*, Mitos Boyut Yayınları, İstanbul, 2010.

Asena, Orhan (d). *Korku*. Mitos Boyut Yayınları, İstanbul, 2010.

Asena, Orhan. *Les Dieux Et Les Hommes Ou Gilgamesh*, French Translator Rene Giraud-Fransızca'dan Türkçeye çeviren Tahsin Saraç, Ayyıldız Yayınları, Ankara, 1961.

Asena, Orhan. "Şili'de Av'ın Yazarı Orhan Asena'dan Oyunu Üstüne" in *Tiyatro* 74, January 1974.

Asena, Orhan. *Atatürk Bir Çıkıştır*, Varış Değil!, Ankara, 24.9.1991, http://www.turkishnews.com/Ataturk/siirleri/s6.htm Accessed: 01.04.2013.

Asena, Orhan. *Deü Gsf Dünya Tiyatrolar Günü Kutlama Haftası*, Akm, İzmir, Mart 1998; Quoted İn Hülya Nutku, Cumhuriyet'in 75. Yılında 75. Yılın Tanığı Bir Yazar: Orhan Asena.

Asena, Orhan. *Şili'de Av*. Boyut Yayınları, İstanbul, 1992.

Asena, Orhan. *Tanrılar ve İnsanlar*, Mitos Boyut Yayınları, İstanbul, 2010.

Asena, Orhan. "Hürrem Sultan'ı Sunarken" in *Devlet Tiyatrosu Dergisi*, No: 5, Mart-Nisan-Mayıs 1995, Ankara.

Ataöv, Türkkaya. "The Principles Of Kemalism" in *The Turkish Yearbook Of International Relations*, Milletlerarası Münasebetler Türk Yıllığı, Cilt: 20, 1980.

Azak, Umut. *Islam and Secularism in Turkey*, I. B. Tauris, New York, 2010.

Baker, Stuart E. *Bernard Shaw's Remarkable Religion*, University Press of Florida, Gainesville, 2002.

Balibar, Etienne. *Foreword to On The Reproduction Of Capitalism*, trans. G. M. Goshgarian, Verso, London and New York, 2014.

Banham, Martin. *The Cambridge Guide to Theatre*, Cambridge University Press, Cambridge, 1998.

Barker, Simon and Hilary Hinds, ed. *The Routledge Anthology of Renaissance Drama*, Routledge, New York, 2003.

Bealey, Frank et al. *The Blackwell Dictionary of Political Science*, Blackwell Publishing Ltd. 1999.

Bellah, Robert N. *The Robert Bellah Reader*, Duke University Press, Durham and London.

Bennet, Arnold. "Three Plays for Puritans" in *George Bernard Shaw*, ed. T. F. Evans, Routledge, London and New York, 1976.

Berkes, Niyazi. ed., *Turkish Nationalism and Western Civilization*, Columbia University Press, New York, 1959.

Berkes, Niyazi. *The Development of Secularism in Turkey*, Hurstand Company, London, 1998.

Bertolini, John A. "The Shavian Tradition" in *George Bernard Shaw in Context*, ed. Brad Kent, Cambridge University Press, Cambridge, 2015.

Berlin, Isaiah. *Against the Current: Essays in the History of Ideas*, ed. Henry Hardy, Princeton University Press, Princeton, 2013.

Bidet, Jacques. *Introduction to On The Reproduction Of Capitalism*, trans. G. M. Goshgarıan, Verso, London and New York, 2014.

Black, Antony. "St Thomas Aquinas: The State And Morality" in *Political Thought From Plato to NATO*, British Broadcasting Corporation, London, 1984.

Blocksome, Patricia. "The Birth, Death and Resurrection of Theatre: Religion's Cyclical Relationship with the Stage" in *Communicating Vocation*, ed. Rebecca Blocksome and Nagypál Szabolcs, Bgöi& Wscf-Cesr, Wien-Budapest, 2009.

Bloom, Allan and Harry V. Jaffa. *Shakespeare's Politics*, University of Chicago, Chicago and London, 1981.

Bloom, Harold. ed., *Elizabethan Drama*, Chelsea House Publishers, New York, 2004.

Bloom, Harold. *Dramatists and Dramas*, Chalsea House Publishers, Philadelphia, 2005, 161.

Bottomore, Tom. ed., *A Dictionary of Marxist Thought*, Blackwell Publishers, Oxford, 1991.

Boyd, Ernest A. *Appreciations and Depreciations*, Talbot Press, Dublin, 1918.

Braverman, Richard. "Capital Relations and The Way of the World" in *ELH* Vol. 52, No. 1 (Spring, 1985).

Brewer, Mary. "Empire and Class in the Theatre of John Arden and Margaretta D'Arcy" in *A Companion to Modern British and Irish Drama 1880–2005*, ed. Mary Luckhurst, Blackwell Publishing Ltd, Victoria, 2006.

Bromwich, David. "A Note On The Life And Thought Of John Stuart Mill" in *On Liberty*, ed. David Bromwich and George Kateb, Yale University Press, New Haven and London, 2003.

Budak, Oğuz. T*ürkiye'nin Sosyal/Kültürel Değişim Sürecinde Orhan Asena Tiyatrosu*, Ankara, 2008.

Bull, John. "Left in Front: David Edgar's Political Theatre" in *A Companion to Modern British and Irish Drama 1880–2005*, ed. Mary Luckhurst, Blackwell Publishing Ltd, Victoria, 2006.

Burton, Richard. *Bernard Shaw: The Man and The Mask*, Henry Holt and Company, New York, 1916.

Burwick, Frederick. *Romantic Drama*, Cambridge University Press, Cambridge, 2009.

Cagaptay, Soner. *Islam, Secularism, and Nationalism in Modern Turkey*, Routledge, London and New York, 2006.

Cañeque, Alejandro. "On Cushions and Chairs: The Ritual Contruction of Authority in New Spain" in *Acts and Texts*, ed. Laurite Postlewate and Wim Hüsken, Rodopi, Amsterdam and New York, 2007.

Cantor, Paul A. "Literature and Politics: Understanding the Regime" in *PS: Political Science & Politics* Volume 28 / Issue 02 / June 1995.

Chesterton, Gilbert K. *George Bernard Shaw*, The Plimpton Press, New York, 1909.

Chesterton, Gilbert K. *George Bernard Shaw*, John Lane, New York, 1909.

Chothia, Jean. "Sean O'Casey's Powerful Fireworks" in *A Companion to Modern British and Irish Drama 1880–2005*, ed. Mary Luckhurst, Blackwell Publishing Ltd, Victoria, 2006.

Chtapowa, Teresa Cicierska. *The Idea of Revolution in Orhan Asena's Early Plays*, quoted in Hülya Nutku, Folia Orientalia, Poland, 1979.

Cohen, Debra Rae. "British Literature (After 1900)" in *Encyclopedia of Literature and Politics*, ed. Keith Booker, Greenwood Press, Westport and London, 2005.

Cohn, Ruby. "The World of Harold Pinter" in *The Tulane Drama Review*, Vol. 6, No. 3 (Mar 1962).

Coleman, David. "Reviewed Work: Defining Acts: Drama and the Politics of Interpretation in Late Medieval England by Ruth Nisse" in *Mystics Quarterly*, Vol. 34, No. 1/2 (January–April 2008).

Coleman, Janet. "St Augustine: At The End Of The Roman Empire Christian Political Thought" in *Political Thought From Plato to NATO*, British Broadcasting Corporation, London, 1984.

Colletti, Lucio et al. *From Rousseau to Lenin*, Monthly Review Press, New York and London, 1972.

Coloura, Vanessa. "Cavaliar Ideals, Exile and Spectacle in The Rover and The Second Half of The Rover" in *Heroines and Heroes*, ed. Christopher Hart, Midrash Publications, West Midlands, 2008.

Coutinho, Carlos Nelson. *Gramsci's Political Thought*, Koninklijke Brill NV, Leiden, 2012.

Çağdaş, Hami. "Türk Tiyatrosunun Shakespeare'i Öldü" in *Hürriyet Daily News*, http://hurarsiv.hurriyet.com.tr/goster/ShowNew.aspx?id=-226855, 2001, Accessed: 12.10.2014.

Çınar, Alev. *Modernity, Islam, and Secularism in Turkey: Bodies, Places, and Time*, University of Minnesota Press, Minneapolis and London, 2005.

Dall, Jane. "The Stage and the State: Shakespeare's Portrayal of Women and Sovereign Issues in Macbeth and Hamlet" in *The Hanover Historical Review*, Volume 8,2000. http://history.hanover.edu/hhr/00/hhr00_2.html Accessed: 11.11.2014

De Sevilla, José Manuel González Fernández. "Political Strategies of Drama in Renaissance England" in *Proceedings of the First National conference of the Spanish Society for English Renaissance Studies*, ed. Javier Sánchez, Zaragoza: SEDERI, 1990. (SEDERI: Yearbook of the Spanish and Portuguese Society for English Renaissance Studies).

Deeney, John. "David Hare and Political Playwriting: Between the Third Way and the Permanent Way" in *A Companion to Modern British and Irish Drama 1880–2005*, ed. Mary Luckhurst, Blackwell Publishing Ltd, Victoria, 2006.

Diamond, Elin. "Caryl Churchill: Feeling Global" in *A Companion to Modern British and Irish Drama 1880–2005*, ed. Mary Luckhurst, Blackwell Publishing Ltd, Victoria, 2006.

DiCenzo, Maria. "John McGrath and Popular Political Theatre" in *A Companion to Modern British and Irish Drama 1880–2005*, ed. Mary Luckhurst, Blackwell Publishing Ltd, Victoria, 2006.

Dickens, Charles. *A Tale of Two Cities*, Fictionwise-e book.

Doğan, Abide. "Türk Tiyatrosunda Hürrem Sultan" in *Hacettepe Üniversitesi Edebiyat Fakültesi Dergisi Osmanlı Devletinin Kuruluşunun 700*. Yılı Özel Sayısı, Ekim 1999.

Dorney, Kate. *The Changing Language of Modern English Drama 1945–2005*, Palgrave Macmillan, Hampshire, 2009.

Dunkel, Wilbur Dwight. "George Bernard Shaw" in *The Sewanee Review* Vol. 50, No. 2 (Apr–Jun 1942).

Dunn, John (a). "John Locke: The Politics Of Trust" in *Political Thought From Plato to NATO*, British Broadcasting Corporation, London, 1984.

Dunn, John (b). "The Concept Of 'Trust' in The Politics Of John Locke" in *Philosophy in History*, Cambridge University Press, Cambridge, 1984.

Dunn, Susan. ed., *The Social Contract and The First and Second Discourses*, Yale University Press, New Haven and London, 2002.

Eagleton, Terry. *Ideology*, Verso Publishing, New York and London, 1991.

Ellis-Fermor, Una. "The Review of History of Late Nineteenth Century Drama" in *The Review of English Studies* Vol. 23, No. 90 (Apr 1947).

Emeritz, Phillip. "Feminine Power in the Ottoman Harem" *Binghamton Journal of History*, Spring 2013.

Énault, Louis. *Constantinople et la Turquie*, L. Hachette, Paris, 1855.

Engünin, İnci. "Orhan Asena'nın Oyunları" in *İstanbul Üniversitesi Türk Dili ve Edebiyatı Dergisi*, Cil 28, 1998.

Ervine, St. John. *G. Bernard Shaw: His Life, Work and Friends*, William Morrow & Co, 1972.

Esposito, John L. ed., *The Oxford Dictionary of Islam*, Oxford University Press, New York, 2003.

Faflak, Joel and Julia M. Wright. eds., *Victorian Recollections of Romanticism*, State University of New York Press, Albany, 2004.

Ferreıra-Ross, Jeanette D. "Jonson's Satire of Puritanism in The Alchemist" in *Sydney Studies in English*, 17.

Finch, R. *A Shaw Anthology*, Raplace Publications, USA and Great Britain, 2010, 115.

Finn, Stephen J. *Thomas Hobbes and the Politics of Natural Philosophy*, Continuum, London, 2004.

Fisk, Deborah Payne. ed., *The Cambridge Companion to English Restoration Theatre*, Cambridge University Press, Cambridge, 2000.

Foakes, R. A. *Hamlet Versus Lear*, Cambridge University Press, Cambridge, 1993.

Forster, Greg. *John Locke's Politics of Moral Consensus*, Cambridge University Press, Cambridge, 2005.

Fortich, Flórez. "Nietzsche's Übermensch: The Notion Of A Higher Aristocracy Of The Future" in *Civilizar* 10 (18):75–80, 2010.

Foucault, Michel. "Intellectuals and Power: A Conversation Between Michel Foucault and Gilles Deleuze" in *Language, Counter-Memory, Practice*, ed. Donald F. Bouchard, Cornell University Press, New York, 1977.

Gagnier, Regenia. "Wilde and The Victorians" in *The Cambridge Companion to Oscar Wilde*, ed. Peter Raby, Cambridge University Press, Cambridge, 1997.

Gainor, J. Ellen. *Shaw's Daughters: Dramatic and Narrative Constructions of Gender*, University of Michigan Press, Ann Arbor, 1991.

Ganz, Arthur. *George Bernard Shaw*, Macmillan, Hong Kong, 1983.

Gibbs, A. M. *A Bernard Shaw Chronology*, Palgrave, New York, 2001.

Gill, Stephen M. *Political Convictions of G.B.S.*, Vesta, Canada, 1980.

Gillespie, Gerald. ed., *Romantic Drama*, John Benjamins Publishing Co., Amsterdam and Philadelphia, 1994.

Gillespie, Michael Patrick. "The Victorian Impulse in Contemporary Audiences: The Regularization of the Importance of Being Earnest" in *Oscar Wilde*, ed. by Harold Bloom, Infobase Publishing, 2011.

Goldstein, Gary B. "Did Queen Elizabeth Use The Theatre For Social And Political Propaganda?" in *The Oxfordian*, Volume VII, 2004.

Gordimer, Nadine. *Living in Hope and History*, Bloomsbury Publishing, London, 1999.

Göktepe, Cihat. "1960 'Revolution' in Turkey and the British Policy towards Turkey" in *The Turkish Yearbook*, vol. XXX.

Gülten, Sadullah. "Kanuni'nin Maktül Bir Şehzadesi: Bayezid Bayezid" in *ODÜ Sosyal Bilimler Enstitüsü Sosyal Bilimler Aratırmaları Dergisi*, Cilt: 3 Sayı: 6, Aralık 2012.

Gürpınar, Doğan. "Anatolia's Eternal Destiny Was Sealed: Seljuks Of Rum In The Turkish National(ist) Imagination From The Late Ottoman Empire To The Republican Era" in *European Journal of Turkish Studies*, 2012.

Gray, John. "John Stuart Mill: The Crisis Of Liberalism" in *Political Thought From Plato To NATO*, British Broadcasting Corporation, London, 1984.

Griffith, Gareth. *Socialism and Superior Brains: The Political Thought of George Bernard Shaw*, Routledge, New York, 1993.

Grigsby, Ellen. *Analyzing Politics*, Wadsworth, Belmont, 2009.

Grotowski, Jerzy. *Towards a Poor Theatre*, ed. Eugenio Barba, Routledge, New York, 2002.

Hackett, J. *Shaw: George versus Bernard*, Sheed and Ward, New York, 1937.

Hadfield, Andrew. *Shakespeare and Renaissance Politics*, Arden Shakespeare, London, 2004

Hague, Rog, et al., *Comparative Government and Politics*, Palgrave Macmillan, New York, 2004.

Halman, Talat S. *A Milenium of Turkish Literature*, ed. Jayne L. Warner, Syracuse University Press, New York, 2011.

Halman, Talat Sait. ed., *I, Anatolia and Other Plays*, Syracuse University Press, New York, 2008.

Halman, Talat Sait. *Rapture and Revolution*, ed. Jayne L. Warner, Syracuse University Press, New York, 2007.

Hanioğlu, M. Şükrü. *A Brief History of the Late Ottoman Empire*, Princeton University Press, Princeton and London, 2008.

Hann, C. M. ed., *Socialism Ideals, Ideologies, and Local Practice*, Routledge, London and New York, 1993.

Harris, George S. "Military Coups and Turkish Democracy, 1960–1980" in *Turkish Studies* Vol. 12, No. 2, June 2011.

Heywood, A. *Political Theory*, Palgrave Macmillan, New York, 2004.

Heywood, Andrew. *Political Ideologies*, Plagrave Macmillan, New York, 2012.

Hill, Eugene D. "Senecan and Vergilian Perspectives in The Spanish Tragedy" in *Renaissance Historicism*, ed. Arthur F. Kinney and Dan S. Collins, The University of Massachusets Press, Massachusetts, 1987.

Hobbes, Thomas. *Leviathan,* ed. J. C. A. Gaskın, Oxford University Press, 1998.

Honohan, Iseult and Jeremy Jennings. eds., *Republicanism in Theory and Practice*, Routledge, London and New York, 2006.

Höpfl, Harro. "Jean Calvin: The Disciplined Commonwealth" in *Political Thought From Plato to NATO*, British Broadcasting Corporation, London, 1984.

Höpfl, Harro. *The Christian Polity of John Calvin*, Cambridge University Press, Cambridge, 1982.

http://people.hofstra.edu/alan_j_singer/CoursePacks/USImperialismDefeatsSalvadorAllendeandDemocracyinChile.pdf, Accessed: 09.09.2014.

http://web.calstatela.edu/faculty/jgarret/308/readings-4.pdf, Accessed: 04.04.2014.

Huneker, James. "A Word On the Dramatic Opinions and Essays of Bernard Shaw" in *Dramatic Opinions and Essays with an Apology Vol I (Bernard Shaw)*, Brentano's Rosings Digital Publications, New York, 1906; 2008.

Ideology. *Oxford Online Dictionary*, http://www.oxforddictionaries.com/definition/english/ideology Accessed: 10.01.2015

Innes, Christopher. *Modern British Drama*, Cambridge University Press, Cambridge, 1990.

Jack Schwartzman. "Henry George and George Bernard Shaw: Comparison and Contrast: The Two 19th Century Intellectual Leaders Stood for Ethical Democracy vs. Socialist Statism" in *The American Journal of Economics and Sociology* Vol. 49, No. 1, 1990.

Jackson, Russel. "The Importance of Being Earnest" in *The Cambridge Companion to Oscar Wilde*, ed. Peter Raby, Cambridge University Press, Cambridge, 1997.

Jackson, Russelli. "The Importance of Being Earnest" in *The Cambridge Companion to Oscar Wilde*, ed. Peter Raby, Cambridge University Press, Cambridge, 1997.

Jacobus, Lee A. *The Compact Bedford Introduction to Drama*, Bedford/St. Martin's, Boston and New York, 2005.

Jain, Sangeeta. *Women in the Plays of George Bernard Shaw*, Discovery Publishing House, New Delhi, 2006.

Jakopovich, Daniel. *The Concept of Class*, Cambridge Studies in Social Research SSRG Publications, Cambridge, 2014.

Jenkins, Anthony. *The Making of Victorian Drama*, Cambridge University Press, Melbourne, 1991.

Jesus, Charles De and John Heitner. "U.S. Imperialism Defeats Salvador Allende and Democracy in Chile" http://people.hofstra.edu/alan_j_singer/CoursePacks/USImperialismDefeatsSalvadorAllendeandDemocracyinChile.pdf, Accessed: 09.09.2014.

Jones, Norman. "The Politics of Renaissance England" in *A Companion to Renaissance Drama*, ed. Arthur F. Kinney, Blackwell Publishers, Massachusetts, 2002.

Jost, John T. et al. "Political Ideology: Its Structure, Functions, and Elective Affinities" in *The Annual Review of Psychology*, Issue 60, 2009.

Jowett, Benjamin. *The Works of Plato: Analysis of Plato and the Republic*, Cosimo Inc, New York, 2010.

Karasipahi, Sena. *Muslims in Modern Turkey*, I. B. Tauris, London and New York, 2009.

Karateke, Hakan T. "Legitimizing The Ottoman Sultanate: A Framework For Historical Analysis" in *Legitimizing The Order: The Ottoman Rhetoric of State Power*, ed. Hakan T. Karateke and Maurus Leinkowski, Brill, Leiden and Boston, 2005.

Kauffmann, Stanley. "George Bernard Shaw: Twentieth Century Victorian Authors" in *Performing Arts Journal*, Vol. 10. No. 2, 1986, 54–55.

Kehler, Grace. "Between Action and Inaction: The 'Performance' of the Prima Donna in Eliot's Closet Drama" in *Victorian Recollections of Romanticism*, ed. Joel Faflak and Julia M. Wright, State University of New York Press, Albany, 2004.

Kennedy, Dennis. ed., *The Oxford Companion to Theatre and Performance*, Oxford University Press, New York, 2010.

Kennedy, Emmet. "Ideology" from Destutt De Tracy to Marx" in *Journal of the History of Ideas*, Vol. 40, No. 3 (Jul–Sep 1979).

Khoury, Dina Rizk. "The Ottoman Centre Versus Provincial Power-Holders: An Analysis Of The Historiography" in *The Cambridge History of Turkey* (Vol 3), Cambridge University Press, Cambridge, 2006.

Kiberd, Declan. "Reinventing England" in *A Companion to Modern British and Irish Drama 1880–2005*, ed. Mary Luckhurst, Blackwell Publishing Ltd, Victoria, 2006.

Kinney, Arthur F. ed., *A Companion to Renaissance Drama*, Blackwell Publishers, Massachusetts, 2002.

Knowles, Ronald. "Bunburying with Bakhtin: A Carnivalesque Reading of The Importance of Being Earnest" in *Oscar Wilde*, ed. Harold Bloom, Infobase Publishing, 2011.

Koper, Macit. "Şili'de Av'ı Oyuncuları Anlatıyor" in *Tiyatro* 74, January 1974.

Krasner, David. *A History of Modern Drama Volume I*, Wiley-Blackwell, West Sussex, 2012.

Kritzer, Amelia Hower. *Political Theatre in Post-Thatcher Britain*, Palgrave Macmillan, 2008.

Laborde, Cécile and John Maynor. ed., *Republicanism and Political Theory*, Blackwell Publishing, Malden, 2008.

Laboulle, Louise J. "A Note on Bertolt Brecht's Adaptation of Marlowe's Edward II" in *The Modern Language Review*, Vol. 54, No. 2 (Apr 1959).

Lacey, Stephen. "When Was the Golden Age? Narratives of Loss and Decline: John Osborne, Arnold Wesker and Rodney Ackland" in *A Companion to Modern British and Irish Drama 1880–2005*, ed. Mary Luckhurst, Blackwell Publishing Ltd, Victoria, 2006.

Lang, Anthony F. Jr. ed., *Political Theory and International Affairs*, Praeger, Westport, 2004.

Laswell, Harold D. *Politics: Who Gets What, When, How*, Whittlesey House, New York, 1936.

Laurence, Dan H. *Bernard Shaw: Collected Letters 1926–1950*, Max Reinhardt, London, 1988.

Dan H. Laurence. ed., *Bernard Shaw Theatrics*, University of Toronto Press, Toronto, 1995.

Lears, T. J. Jakson. "The Concept of Cultural Hegemony: Problems and Possibilities" in *The American Historical Review*, Vol. 90, Issue 3 (June 1985).

Leggatt, Alexander. *Shakespeare's Political Drama*, Routledge, London and New York, 1988.

Lenker, Lagretta Tallent. "Make War on War: A Shavian Conundrum" in *War and Words*, ed. Sara Munson Deaths et al., Lexington Books, 2004.

Lewton, Paul. "George Bernard Shaw: Theory, Language, and Drama in the Nineties" in *The Yearbook of English Studies*, Vol. 9, Theatrical Literature Special Number (1979).

Lichtheim, George. "The Concept of Ideology" in *History and Theory*, Vol. 4, No. 2 (1965).

Lock, John. *Two Treatises of Government and A Letter Concerning Toleration*, ed. Ian Shapiro, Yale University Press, New Haven and London, 2003.

Lucaks, Georg. *History and Class Consciousness: Studies in Marxist Dialectics*, trans. Rodney Livingstone, The MIT Press, Cambridge, 1968.

Luckhurst, Mary. "Torture in the Plays of Pinter" in *A Companion to Modern British and Irish Drama 1880–2005*, ed. Mary Luckhurst, Blackwell Publishing Ltd, Victoria, 2006.

Machiavelli, Niccolo. *The Prince*, trans. Harvey C. Mansfield, The University Of Chicago Press, Chicago and London, 1998.

Mack, Eric et al. *John Lock*, Continuum International Publishing Group, London, 2009.

Maclean, Gerald. ed., *Culture And Society in The Stuart Restoration*, Cambridge University Press, Cambridge, 1995.

Mannheim, Karl. *Ideology and Utopia*, Routledge, New York, 1936.

Marsden, Jean I. "Restoration Drama" in *The Oxford Encyclopedia of British Literature*, ed. David Scott Kastan, Oxford University Press, Oxford and New York, 2006.

Martin, L. H. et al. *Technologies of the Self: A Seminar with Michel Foucault*, Tavistock, London, 1988.

Martin, Randy. *Performance As Political Act: The Embodied Self*, Bergin & Garvey Publishers, 1990.

Marx, Karl. *A Contribution to the Critique of Political Economy*, Charles H. Kerr Comp., Chicago, 1904.

Marx, Karl and Frederick Engels. *German Ideology*, Premetheus Books, New York, 1998.

Mazer, Cary M. "Granville Barker and the Court Dramatists" in *A Companion to Modern British and Irish Drama 1880–2005*, ed. Mary Luckhurst, Blackwell Publishing Ltd, Victoria, 2006.

Mcdowell, Frederick W. "Bernard Shaw: Socialist And Dramatist" in *Shaw* Vol. 16, Unpublished Shaw (1996).

Mcneill, John T. ed., *The Institutes of Christian Religion*, Westminster John Knox Press, Louisville and London, 1960.

Mill, John Stuart. *On Liberty*, ed. David Bromwich and George Kateb, Yale University Press, New Haven And London, 2003.

Morgan, Margot. *Politics and Theatre in Twentieth Century Europe*, Palgrave Macmillan, New York, 2013.

Morris, William. *Communism*, https://www.marxists.org/archive/morris/works/1893/commune.htm Accessed: 08. 05. 2015.

Mouritsen, Per. "Four Models Of Republican Liberty And Self-Government" in *Republicanism in Theory and Practice*, ed. Iseult Honohan and Jeremy Jennings, Routledge, London and New York, 2006.

Moyra Grant. *Key Ideas in Politics*, Nelson Thornes Ltd, Cheltenham, 2003, 140.

Muir, Lynette R. *The Biblical Drama of Medieval Europe*, Cambridge University Press, Cambridge, 1995.

Murray, Edelman. "Political Language and Political Reality" in *Political Science & Politics* Vol. 18, No. 1 (Winter 1985).

Mystery. *Online Ethymology Dictionary*, http://www.etymonline.com/index.php?term=mystery, Accessed: 04.04.2014

Needler, Martin. *Identity, Interest and Ideology*, Praeger Publishers, Westport, 1996.

Nicholson, Peter. "Aristotle: Ideals and Realities" in *Political Thought From Plato to NATO*, British Broadcasting Corporation, London, 1984.

Nicollin, Allardyce. *History of Late Nineteenth Century Drama*, Cambridge University Press, Cambridge, 1946.

Nutku, Hülya. "Cumhuritet Tarihimizin Yakın Tanığı Bir Yazar: Orhan Asena" in *Bütün Dünya*, Başkent Üniversitesi Kültür Yayını, 2000.

Nutku, Hülya. "Orhan Asena'nın Oyun Yazarlığının Gelişimi ve Oyunları" in *Orhan Asena: Toplu Oyunları 1*, Boyut Yayınları, İstanbul, 1992.

Nutku, Hülya. *Cumhuriyet'in 75. Yılında 75 Yılın Tanığı Bir Yazar: Orhan Asena*, Kültür Bakanlığı Yayınları, Ankara, 1998.

Nutku, Özdemir. *Dünya Tiyatrosu Tarihi*, Cilt 1, Remzi Kitabevi, İstanbul, 1993.

Nyoni, Mika. "The Culture of Othering: An Interrogation of Shakespeare's Handling of Race and Ethnicity in the Merchant of Venice and Othello" in *Greener Journal of Art and Humanities* Vol. 1 (1), December 2011.

Ohmann, Richard M. *Shaw: The Style and The Man*, Wesleyan University Press, Middeltown/Connecticut, 1962.

Omohundro, Clinton. "Politics And Literature" in *Amalgam*, Issue 1, 2006.

Ortaylı, İlber. "Tiyatroda Tarihi Oyunlar Üzerinde Siyasal Bir Analiz Denemesi" in *Tiyatro Araştırmaları Dergisi*, Sayı: 7, 1976.

Orwell, George. *Why I Write?*, 1946.

Orwell, Sonia and Ian Angus. eds., *The Collected Essays, Journalism And Letters Of George Orwell*, Vol IV, Secker And Warburg, London, 1968.

Ozankaya, Özer. *Türkiye'de Laiklik*, Cem Yayınevi, İstanbul, 1990.

Özbudun, Sibel. *Ayinden Törene*, Anahtar Yayınları, İstanbul, 1997.

Özdoğru, Nüvit. "Turkey: Modern Period" in *The Reader's Encyclopedia of World Drama*, ed. John Gassner and Edward Quinn, Dover Publications, New York, 1969.

Özmen, Özlem. "Türkiye'de Politik Tiyatronun Gelişimi" in *Ankara Üniversitesi Dil Ve Tarih-Coğrafya Fakültesi Dergisi 55*, 1 (2015).

Öztürk, Serdar. "Karagoz Co-Opted: Turkish Shadow Theatre of the Early Republic (1923–1945)" in *Asian Theatre Journal*, Volume 23, Number 2, Fall 2006.

Pathak, D. N. *George Bernard Shaw: His Religion and Values*, Mittal Publications, Delhi, 1985.

Patterson, Annabel. "Political Thought and the Theatre, 1580–1630" in *A Companion to Renaissance Drama*, ed. Arthur F. Kinney, Blackwell Publishers, Massachusetts, 2002.

Patterson, Michael. "Edward Bond: Maker of Myths" in *A Companion to Modern British and Irish Drama 1880–2005*, ed. Mary Luckhurst, Blackwell Publishing Ltd, Victoria, 2006.

Pattie, David. "Theatre Since 1968" in *A Companion to Modern British and Irish Drama 1880–2005*, ed. Mary Luckhurst, Blackwell Publishing Ltd, Victoria, 2006.

Peters, Sally. *Bernard Shaw: The Ascent of the Superman,* Yale University Press, 1998.

Phelps, William Lyon. *Essays on Modern Dramatists*, The Macmillan Company, New York, 1921.

Plato. *The Republic*, trans. Benjamin Jowett, Cosimo Inc, New York, 2010, 212.

Plato. Politics, Online Merriam-Webster Dictionary, http://www.merriam-webster.com/dictionary/politics, Accessed: 09.02.2015.

Plato. *Politics*, Online Oxford Dictionary, http://www.oxforddictionaries.com/definition/english/politics, Accessed: 09.02.2015.

Postlewate, Laurite and Wim Hüsken. eds., *Acts and Texts*, Rodopi, Amsterdam and New York, 2007.

Raby, Peter. ed., *The Cambridge Companion to Oscar Wilde*, Cambridge University Press, Cambridge, 1997.

Raphael, D. D. et al. eds., *The Theory of Moral Sentiments*, Liberty Fund, Inc., Indianapolis, 1984.

Redhead, Brian. *Political Thought From Plato to NATO*, British Broadcasting Corporation, London, 1984.

Rehmann, Jan. *Theories of Ideology*, Brill, Leiden and Boston, 2013.

Resnick, Setphen A. et al. eds., *New Departures in Marxian Theory*, Routledge, New York, 2006.

Reynolds, Jean. *Pygmalion's Wordplay: The Postmodern Shaw*, University Press of Florida, Gainesville, 1999.

Ricento, Thomas. ed., *Ideology, Politics And Language Policies*, John Benjamins Publishing Company, Amsterdam and Philadelphia, 2000.

Robertson, David. *The Routledge Dictionary of Politics*, Routledge, London and New York, 2004.

Robertson, John. "Adam Smith: the Enlightenment and the philosophy of society" in *Political Thought From Plato to NATO*, British Broadcasting Corporation, London, 1984.

Rodgers, Daniel T. *Contested Truths*, Harvard University Press, Canada, 1987.

Rousseau, Jean Jacques. *Emile, or On Education*, trans. Allan Bloom, Basic Books, USA, 1979.

Rousseau, Jean Jacques. *The Social Contract and The First and Second Discourses*, ed. Susan Dunn, Yale University Press, New Haven and London, 2002.

Rowe, Christopher. "Plato: The Search For An Ideal Form Of State" in *Political Thought From Plato to NATO*, British Broadcasting Corporation, London, 1984.

Roy, R. N. *George Bernard Shaw's Historical Plays*, Macmillan, London, 1976.

Rush, Kimberly Reynolds. *"Princes Upon Stages" The Theatricalization Of Monarchy In The Reign Of Elizabeth I, 1558–1569*, Unpublished PhD Dissertation, Louisiana State University, May 2015.

Ryan, Alan. "The Moderns: Liberalism Revived" in *Political Thought From Plato To NATO*, British Broadcasting Corporation, London, 1984.

Sakallioglu, Umit Cizre. "Parameters and Strategies of Islam-State Interaction in Republican Turkey" in *International Journal of Middle East Studies*, Vol. 28, No. 2 (May, 1996).

Santucci, Antonio A. et al. *Antonio Gramsci*, Monthly Review Press, New York, 2010.

Scruton, Roger. *The Palgrave Macmillan Dictionary of Political Thought*, Palgrave Macmillan, New York, 2007.

Shafer, Gregory. "Political Language, Democracy, and the Language Arts Class" in *English Journal* 103, 2 (2013).

Shapiro, Ian. ed., *Two Treatises of Government and A Letter Concerning Toleration*, Yale University Press, New Haven and London, 2003.

Shaw, Bernard. *Practical Politics: Twentieth-Century Views on Politics and Economics*, ed. Lloyd J. Hubenka, University of Nebraska Press, 1976.

Shaw, G. Bernard. *Fabian Essays in Socialism*, ed. H. G. Wilshire, The Homboldt Publishing Co. New York, 1891.

Shaw, George Bernard. *Arms and the Man*, Grant Richards, London, 1898.

Shaw, George Bernard. *Back to Methuselah*, 1st World Library, Fairfield, 2007.

Shaw, George Bernard. *Candida*, Grant Richards, London, 1898.

Shaw, George Bernard. *Collected Letters*, ed. Dan H. Laurence, Max Reinhardt, London, 1988.

Shaw, George Bernard. *Major Barbara*, Dover publications Inc., Mineola/New York, 2002.

Shaw, George Bernard. *Mrs Warren's Profession*, Brentano's Publishers, New York, 1905.

Shaw, George Bernard. *Plays Pleasant and Unpleasant I*, Brentano's, New York, 1905.

Shaw, George Bernard. *Plays Pleasant and Unpleasant II*, Grant Richards, London, 1898.

Shaw, George Bernard. *Preface to John Bull's Other Island and Major Barbara*, Brentano's, New York, 1907.

Shaw, George Bernard. *Preface to Major Barbara*. E-book, The University of Adelaide, 2014.

Shaw, George Bernard. *Preface to Man and Superman*. E-book, The University of Adelaide, 2014.

Shaw, George Bernard. *Pygmalion and Major Barbara*, Bantam Dell, New York, 1992.

Shaw, George Bernard. *Pygmalion*, The Electronic Classics Series, Hazleton, 2013.

Shaw, George Bernard. *The Fabian Society: Its Early History*, The Fabian Society, London, 1906.

Shaw, George Bernard. *The Intelligent Woman's Guide to Socialism*, Capitalism, Sovietism and Fascism, Alma Classics Ltd, Surrey, 2012.

Shaw, George Bernard. *The Quintessence of Ibsenism*, The University Press, Cambridge, 1913.

Shaw, George Bernard. *Widowers' Houses*, Brentano's Publishers, New York, 1905.

Shaw, Stanford J. and Ezel Kural Shaw. *History of The Ottoman Empire and Modern Turkey*, Vol. II, Cambridge University Press, Cambridge, 1977.

Silagi, Michael and Susan N. Faulkner. "Henry George and Europe: As Dissident Economist and Path-Breaking Philosopher, He Was a Catalyst for British Social Reform" in *American Journal of Economics and Sociology*, Vol. 48, No. 1 (Jan 1989).

Singh, Devendra Kumar. *The Idea of the Superman in the Plays of G. B. Shaw*, Atlantic Publishers, New Delhi, 1994.

Slosson, Edwin E. *Six Major Prophets*, Little Brown and Company, Boston, 1917.

Smit, Dirk J. *Essays on Being Reformed*, ed. Robert Vosloo, Sun Media, Stellenbosch, 2009.

Smith, Adam. *The Theory of Moral Sentiments*, ed. D. D. Raphael et al., Liberty Fund, Inc., Indianapolis, 1984.

Sokullu, Sevinç. "Geleneksel Türk Tiyatrosunun Ulusal Tiyatromuza Kaynaklığı Üzerinde Yeniden Durmak" in *Tiyatro Araştırmaları Dergisi*, Sayı: 28, 2009.

Star, Alexander. "Orhan Pamuk: 'I Was Not A Political Person' (An Interview)", <http://www.nytimes.com/2004/08/15/books/review/ STAR15.html> Accessed: 12. 02. 2015

Strauss, Leo. *Thoughts On Machiavelli*, The Free Press, Qzencoe, Illinois, 1958.

Styan, J. L. *Restoration Comedy in Performance*, Cambridge University Press, Cambridge, 1986.

Suleiman, Azhar. *George Bernard Shaw*, Mena Printing, Baghdad, 2010.

Suvin, Darko. "Modes of Political Drama" in *The Massachusetts Review*, Vol. 13, No. 3 (Summer, 1972).

Szalai, Erzsébet. *Socialism: An Analysis Of Its Past And Future*, Central European University Press, Budapest and New York, 2005.

Şener, Sevda. "Memet Baydur Tiyatrosu" in *Tiyatro Araştırmaları Dergisi Sayı*: 31, 2011.

Şener, Sevda. "Moliere ve Türk Komedyası" in *Tiyatro Araştırmaları Dergisi, Sayı*: 5, 1974.

Şener, Sevda. *Gelişim Sürecinde Türk Tiyatrosu*, Mitos-Boyut Yayınları, İstanbul, 2011.

Şener, Sevda. *Gelişim Sürecinde Türk Tiyatrosu*, Mitos-Boyut Yayınları, İstanbul, 2011.

Tachau, Frank. "Turkish Political Parties and Elections: Half a Century of Multiparty Democracy" in *Turkish Studies*, Vol.1, No.1 (Spring 2000).

Tahsin, Saraç. "Asena'nın Oyunlarındaki Ezilmiş İnsancıklar" in *Türk Dili*, year 20, nu 236, May 1971, Ankara.

Tanpınar, Ahmet Hamdi. *On Dokuzuncu Asır Türk Edebiyatı Tarihi*, ed. Abdullah Uçman, Dergah Yayınları, İstanbul, 2013.

Tayhani, İhsan. "Türkiye Cumhuriyeti'nin Temeli: Laiklik" in *Ankara Üniversitesi Türk İnkılâp Tarihi Enstitüsü Atatürk Yolu Dergisi*, Vol. 43, 2009.

Töre, Enver. "Türk Tiyatrosunun Kaynakları" in *Turkish Studies International Periodical For the Languages, Literature and History of Turkish or Turkic*, Volume 4, I–II, Winter 2009.

Tuck, Richard. "Thomas Hobbes: The Sceptical State" in *Political Thought From Plato to NATO*, British Broadcasting Corporation, London, 1984.

Tunçel, Ayşe Ulusoy. "Tiyatro Eserlerinde Oyun Kişisi Olarak"Atatürk" in *Journal Of Turkish World Studies*, XIII/1 (Yaz 2013).

Uluskan, Seda Bayındır. *Atatürk'ün Sosyal ve Kültürel Politikaları*, Korza Basım, Ankara, 2010.

Ümit, Nazlı Miraç. "Çadırlardan Saraylara Türk Tiyatrosunun Sahneleri" in *Art-Sanat Journal*, 2014/1.

Ünlü, Aslıhan. *Türk Tiyatrosunun Antropolojisi*, Aşina Kitaplar, Ankara, 2006.

Van Dijk, Teun A. *Politics, Ideology, and Discourse*, Elsevier Ltd, Spain, 2006.

Varol, Ozan O. "The Democratic Coup d'Etat" in *Harvard International Law Journal*, Vol. 53, Number 2, 2012.

Walkling, Andrew R. "Politics and the Restoration Masque: the Case of Dido and Aeneas" in *Culture And Society in The Stuart Restoration*, ed. Gerald Maclean, Cambridge University Press, Cambridge, 1995.

Webb, Sidney et al. *Socialism and Individualism*, John Lane Company, New York, 1911.

Weiss, Samuel A. ed., *Bernard Shaw's Letters to Siegfried Trebitsch*, Stanford University Press, Stanford, 1986.

Winch, Donald. *Adam Smith's Politics*, Cambridge University Press, Cambridge, 1978.

Wokler, Robert. "Jean: Jacques Rousseau: Moral Decadence And The Pursuit Of Liberty" in *Political Thought From Plato to NATO*, British Broadcasting Corporation, London, 1984.

Woldring, Henk E. S. "On the Purpose of the State: Continuity and Change in Political Theories" in *The Failure of Modernism: The Cartesian Legacy and Contemporary Pluralism*, ed. Brendan Sweetman, American Maritain Association, 1999, 155–70.

Wood, John Cunningham. ed., *John Stuart Mill*, Routledge, London and New York, 1991.

Worrall, David. *Theatric Revolution*, Oxford University Press Inc., New York, 2006.

Wydra, Harold. *Communism and the Emergence of Democracy*, Cambridge University Press, New York, 2006.

Yavuz, M. Hakan. *Secularism and Muslim Democracy in Turkey*, Cambridge University Press, New York, 2009.

Yde, Matthew. *Bernard Shaw and Totalitarianism*, The Palgrave Macmillan, New York, 2013.

Yermolenko, Galina. "Roxolana: 'The Greatest Empresse of the East' in *The Muslim World*, Vol 95, 2005.

Yüksel, Ayşegül. "Cumhuriyet'in 70. Yılında Tiyatromuz" in *Tiyatro Araştırmaları Dergisi, Sayı*: 10, 1993.

Yüksel, Ayşegül. *Haldun Taner Tiyatrosu*, Bilgi yayınevi, İstanbul, 1986.

Zayas, Alfred De. "The Istanbul Pogrom Of 6–7 September 1955 in The Light Of International Law" in *IAGS*, Volume 2, 2007.

Zizek, Slavoj. *The Sublime Object Of Ideology*, Verso, London and New York, 1989.

Zürcher, Erik J. *Turkey: A Modern History*, I. B. Tauris, New York, 2007.

Zürcher, Erik J. *The Young Turk Legacy and Nation Building*, I. B. Tauris, New York, 2010.

"Salvador Allende's Final Speech, September 11, 1973" in *Chile and the Peaceful Road to Socialism Document* No. http://global.oup.com/us/companionwebsites/9780195375701/pdf/SPD13_Chile_Peaceful_Road.pdf. Accessed: 10. 07. 2015

www.ingramcontent.com/pod-product-compliance
Lightning Source LLC
Chambersburg PA
CBHW071229170426
43191CB00032B/1198